Van Gogh's Bedrooms

Edited by
Gloria Groom

With essays by
Gloria Groom
David J. Getsy
Louis van Tilborgh
and Inge Fiedler,
Ella Hendriks,
Teio Meedendorp,
Michel Menu,
and Johanna Salvant
and with contributions by
Allison Perelman

The Art Institute
of Chicago

Distributed by
Yale University Press
New Haven and London

VAN GOGH'S BEDROOMS

Van Gogh's Bedrooms was published in conjunction with an exhibition of the same title organized by and presented at the Art Institute of Chicago, February 14 to May 10, 2016.

Lead support has been provided by the Estate of Jacquet McConville.

Major support has been generously provided by Caryn and King Harris, The Harris Family Foundation; the Gilchrist Foundation; The Morris and Dolores Kohl Kaplan Fund; and Evonne and John Yonover.

Additional funding has been contributed by Constance and David Coolidge, the Mason Foundation, Charlene and Mark Novak, and the Comer Family Foundation.

Annual support for Art Institute exhibitions is provided by the Exhibitions Trust: Kenneth Griffin, Robert M. and Diane v.S. Levy, Thomas and Margot Pritzker, Betsy Bergman Rosenfield and Andrew M. Rosenfield, the Earl and Brenda Shapiro Foundation, and the Woman's Board.

The exhibition is supported by an indemnity from the Federal Council on the Arts and the Humanities.

Lead Corporate Sponsors

CHASE J.P.Morgan

Conservation Sponsor

First edition
Printed in Canada

ISBN: 978-0-300-21486-4 (hardcover)
ISBN: 978-0-86559-280-3 (softcover)

Library of Congress Cataloging-in-Publication Data

Names: Groom, Gloria Lynn. editor. | Art Institute of Chicago, organizer, host institution.

Title: Van Gogh's Bedrooms/edited by Gloria Groom; with essays by Gloria Groom, David J. Getsy, Louis van Tilborgh, and Inge Fiedler, Ella Hendriks,Teio Meedendorp, Michel Menu, and Johanna Salvant and with contributions by Allison Perelman.

Description: Chicago: Art Institute of Chicago, 2016. | "Van Gogh's Bedrooms was published in conjunction with an exhibition of the same title organized by and presented at the Art Institute of Chicago, February 14 to May 10, 2016." | Includes bibliographical references and index.

Identifiers: LCCN 2015051280 | ISBN 9780300214864 (hardback)

Subjects: LCSH: Gogh, Vincent van, 1853–1890. Bedroom (Van Gogh Museum, Amsterdam)—Exhibitions. | Gogh, Vincent van, 1853–1890. Bedroom (Art Institute of Chicago)—Exhibitions. | Gogh, Vincent van, 1853–1890. Van Gogh's bedroom in Arles (Musée d'Orsay)—Exhibitions.| Home in art—Exhibitions. | BISAC: ART/Individual Artists/Monographs. | ART/ History/Modern (late 19th Century to 1945). | ART/Collections, Catalogs, Exhibitions/General.

Classification: LCC ND653.G7 A62 2016 | DDC 759.9492—dc23

LC record available at http://lccn.loc.gov/2015051280

Published by
The Art Institute of Chicago
111 South Michigan Avenue
Chicago, Illinois 60603-6404
www.artic.edu

Distributed by
Yale University Press
302 Temple Street
P.O. Box 209040
New Haven, Connecticut 06520-9040
www.yalebooks.com/art

Produced by the Department of Publishing, the Art Institute of Chicago, Sarah E. Guernsey, Executive Director

Edited by Margherita Andreotti and Maia M. Rigas

Production by Joseph Mohan and Lauren Makholm

Photography research by Katie Levi

Indexing by Kate Mertes

Proofreading by Trevor Perri

Translations from the Dutch by Michael Hoyle

Unless otherwise noted, photography of works of art is by Christopher Gallagher, Aidan Fitzpatrick, Bob Hashimoto, and Robert Lifson, with postproduction by Jonathan Mathias, Department of Imaging, the Art Institute of Chicago.

Design and typesetting by Studio Blue, Chicago

Separations by Professional Graphics, Inc., Rockford, Illinois

Printing and binding by Friesens Corp., Altona, Manitoba, Canada

This book was made using paper and materials certified by the Forest Stewardship Council, which ensures responsible forest management.

Front
Top: Vincent van Gogh. *The Bedroom*, 1888 (detail). Van Gogh Museum, Amsterdam (Vincent van Gogh Foundation) (plate 20).
Middle: Vincent van Gogh. *The Bedroom*, 1889 (detail). The Art Institute of Chicago, Helen Birch Bartlett Memorial Collection, 1926.417 (plate 21).
Bottom: Vincent van Gogh. *The Bedroom*, 1889 (detail). Musée d'Orsay, Paris, sold to national museums under the Treaty of Peace with Japan, 1959 (plate 22).
Back
Vincent van Gogh. *Letter to Theo van Gogh with the Sketch "The Bedroom,"* Oct. 16, 1888. Van Gogh Museum, Amsterdam (Vincent van Gogh Foundation) (plate 19).

Contents

Lead support has been provided by the Estate of Jacquet McConville.

Major support has been generously provided by Caryn and King Harris, The Harris Family Foundation; the Gilchrist Foundation; The Morris and Dolores Kohl Kaplan Fund; and Evonne and John Yonover.

Additional funding has been contributed by Constance and David Coolidge, the Mason Foundation, Charlene and Mark Novak, and the Comer Family Foundation.

The exhibition is supported by an indemnity from the Federal Council on the Arts and the Humanities.

Annual support for Art Institute exhibitions is provided by the Exhibitions Trust: Kenneth Griffin, Robert M. and Diane v. S. Levy, Thomas and Margot Pritzker, Betsy Bergman Rosenfield and Andrew M. Rosenfield, the Earl and Brenda Shapiro Foundation, and the Woman's Board.

Lead Corporate Sponsors

CHASE

J.P.Morgan

Conservation Sponsor

AkzoNobel

Foreword

During his thirty-seven years of life, Vincent van Gogh lived in thirty-seven different homes. He stayed in some of these for years, in others just weeks; in most cases he was a boarder or guest dependent on the hospitality of family or friends. In 1888 the artist moved into the only place he considered his own: his beloved "Yellow House" in Arles, France. His second-floor bedroom became a sanctuary, and it inspired him to record it in paint. Van Gogh so prized *The Bedroom*, which he deemed one of his best canvases, that he created two similar but distinct versions of it almost a year later, after being forced to leave his Yellow House following a nervous breakdown. In this reunion at the Art Institute of Chicago, the public has the extraordinary opportunity to see these three paintings hanging together as they did in Van Gogh's asylum studio.

Presented only in Chicago, *Van Gogh's Bedrooms* is a momentous occasion that, along with this accompanying catalogue, sheds new light on these iconic compositions and the circumstances of their making. The exhibition is groundbreaking also because it is the first to consider the theme of home in the artist's work, demonstrating that his relentless search for refuge permeated not only his thoughts and letters but also the paintings, pastels, and sketches in which he depicted his parents' parsonage in Nuenen, his brother's Paris apartment, the Yellow House, the asylum in Saint-Rémy-de-Provence, and his final home in Auvers-sur-Oise. These images reflect the impact of each environment on Van Gogh's aesthetic as he tried to shape his world to fit his artistic ideal. Seen in this context, his *Bedroom* compositions can be fully appreciated as his personal and artistic pinnacle.

Having been at the forefront of collecting and exhibiting modern art since its founding, the Art Institute of Chicago was the first museum to own one of the *Bedroom* canvases, acquiring the second version in 1926. It had been sold by the artist's family at the turn of the century and belonged to a series of Paris dealers until 1926, when it was purchased by Art Institute trustee Frederic Clay Bartlett. He and his second wife, Helen Birch Bartlett, were pioneering collectors responsible for giving the museum some of its most important modern paintings, including Georges Seurat's *A Sunday on La Grande Jatte—1884* (1884–86). Remarkably, when Bartlett donated the second *Bedroom* to the Art Institute, he was evoking one of Van Gogh's foremost artistic inspirations—the artist had described that work as having "a simplicity à la *Seurat.*" The Bartletts purchased paintings by important modern masters such as Paul Cézanne, Paul Gauguin, Pablo Picasso, and, above all, Van Gogh, who was the most represented artist in their collection with *The Bedroom*; *Terrace and Observation Deck at the Moulin de Blute-Fin, Montmartre*; and *Madame Roulin Rocking the Cradle* (*La berceuse*), all featured in this exhibition and catalogue. The twenty-five paintings that form the Bartlett gift cemented the Art Institute as an early international leader in the realm of modern art, a reputation it maintains to this day.

The two other *Bedroom* paintings eventually found homes in public collections as well. The third and final version was acquired by the Musée du Louvre, Paris, in 1959 (transferred to the newly opened Musée d'Orsay, Paris, in 1986). The first version, painted in Arles, was the last to enter a museum. Given to his brother Theo, it remained with the Van Gogh family and joined the permanent collection of the Van Gogh Museum, Amsterdam, in 1973. The *Bedroom* paintings are among the most popular and revered works in all three institutions.

Two decades of intense collaboration between our museums have paved the way for this extraordinary reunion of the *Bedroom* works. Prior to this partnership, questions as fundamental as the chronology of their making were still unresolved. Cooperation between the Art Institute and the Van Gogh Museum began in preparation for *Van Gogh and Gauguin: The Studio of the South*, presented in Chicago and Amsterdam in 2001–02. That landmark exhibition offered unprecedented insight into Van Gogh's time in Arles—the seminal period in his life and career that continues to be the subject of numerous studies. Building on this wealth of research and benefiting from recent advances in conservation science and technology, the teams from the Art Institute and Van Gogh Museum were joined by staff from the Musée d'Orsay. Together, they carried out extensive, coordinated analysis and imaging of all three *Bedroom* works, the results of which are explained in the conservation essay featured in this catalogue, authored by Inge Fiedler, Ella Hendriks, Teio Meedendorp, Michel Menu, and Johanna Salvant. This groundbreaking collaboration has finally solved century-old mysteries about the three paintings, and we are delighted to present the exciting results not only in this publication but also through in-depth analysis and interactive components in the exhibition itself.

Van Gogh's Bedrooms has also occasioned no less innovative art historical inquiry, the fruits of which appear here in important contributions by Gloria Groom, David J. Getsy, Louis van Tilborgh, and Allison Perelman. The Art Institute owes special thanks to Gloria Groom, Chair of European Painting and Sculpture and David and Mary Winton Green Curator, who conceived the exhibition and has been its steadfast leader from the beginning.

In addition to the collaborators, lenders, and authors who have made this project possible, we would also like to express our profound thanks to the exhibition sponsors. The Lead Corporate Sponsors, JPMorgan Chase and PowerShares QQQ, as well as the Conservation Sponsor, AkzoNobel, provided invaluable support of this massive undertaking. We are particularly indebted to the Estate of Jacquet McConville, which has provided lead support for this exhibition. We are also grateful for the major support generously provided by Caryn and King Harris, The Harris Family Foundation; the Gilchrist Foundation; The Morris and Dolores Kohl Kaplan Fund; and Evonne and John Yonover. Thanks also for the additional funding contributed by Constance and David Coolidge, the Mason Foundation, Charlene and Mark Novak, and the Comer Family Foundation. Additional thanks go to the members of the Exhibitions Trust: Kenneth Griffin, Robert M. and Diane v.S. Levy, Thomas and Margot Pritzker, Betsy Bergman Rosenfield and Andrew M. Rosenfield, the Earl and Brenda Shapiro Foundation, and the Woman's Board. Their annual support makes projects like *Van Gogh's Bedrooms* possible at the Art Institute. Finally, we thank the Federal Council on the Arts and the Humanities, whose indemnity assisted substantially with the insurance costs of the exhibition.

Douglas Druick
President and Eloise W. Martin Director
The Art Institute of Chicago

Acknowledgments

The goal to bring together all three versions of Vincent van Gogh's painting *The Bedroom* would not have been possible without the generous early commitment of the Van Gogh Museum, Amsterdam, and the Musée d'Orsay, Paris. We are grateful to Axel Rüger, Director of the Van Gogh Museum, and Guy Cogeval, President of the Musée d'Orsay and the Musée de l'Orangerie, whose participation has allowed us to realize this goal. From this initial accord and over the subsequent four years, the Art Institute of Chicago organized an exhibition that not only reunites the three canvases but also marshals the extensive documentary, scientific, and physical evidence related to them. From across Europe and the United States, colleagues in museums, universities, libraries, conservation labs, auction houses, and elsewhere have collaborated in shedding new light on the making and meanings of paintings that Van Gogh held in particularly high esteem. We also extend profound gratitude to the lenders listed here and to those who wish to remain anonymous for sharing works that are absolutely essential to this tightly focused yet fulsome exploration of the *Bedroom* paintings and their significance to the artist's life and work.

As our project progressed, we benefited from the rich field of Van Gogh scholarship. Among the many monographs and exhibition catalogues produced over the past decade, none has been more central to our focus than the Van Gogh Museum's new edition of the artist's complete correspondence, offered both in book form and free of charge online. We would like to thank the team at the Van Gogh Museum, especially Leo Jansen, Hans Luijten, and Nienke Bakker, for their work on that fifteen-year-long endeavor to publish all 902 surviving letters written and received by Van Gogh, which have been transcribed, translated, and richly annotated and illustrated.

This catalogue and exhibition are truly in dialogue, and we are grateful that the authors wrote so sensitively on the materiality of Van Gogh's paintings and its relationship to their meanings. First, we thank Louis van Tilborgh, Senior Researcher at the Van Gogh Museum and Professor in Art History, Universiteit van Amsterdam. A specialist on Van Gogh and the author of the primary essay in the catalogue, Van Tilborgh offers a thoughtful overview of the significance of *The Bedroom* to Van Gogh's personal and artistic aesthetic. We are also grateful to David J. Getsy, Goldabelle McComb Finn Distinguished Professor of Art History and Chair, Department of Art History, Theory, and Criticism, at the School of the Art Institute of Chicago, for his insightful analysis of one of the Art Institute's lesser-known paintings, *The Poet's Garden*, and its role in Van Gogh's ambitious decorative scheme for the Yellow House. Finally, we are extremely indebted to Allison Perelman, Research Associate at the Art Institute, who authored the illustrated chronology; her rich engagement with the contextual background has greatly benefited the project.

The groundbreaking research into the relationship of materials, color, technique, and process among the three versions of *The Bedroom* was the result of a major collaboration undertaken by the Conservation Departments at the Art Institute, the Van Gogh Museum, and the Musée d'Orsay with the Centre de Recherche et de Restauration des Musées de France, Paris. For this important chapter in the catalogue and for their guidance in helping us to visualize their research within the exhibition itself, we owe our deepest thanks to our colleagues Ella Hendriks, Senior Paintings Conservator, and Teio Meedendorp, Senior Researcher, both at the Van Gogh Museum; Michel Menu, Chef du Département de Recherche, Centre de Recherche et de Restauration des Musées de France; and Johanna Salvant, Postdoctoral Fellow, Northwestern University, Evanston, Illinois. At the Art Institute we recognize the organizational and authorial contributions of Inge Fiedler, Associate Research Microscopist.

The exhibition's close emphasis on the *Bedroom*s and related artworks has been achieved thanks to a number of individuals who located objects or facilitated loans from private collections. Special thanks go to Lana Baumeister, Chicago; Joseph A. Berton, Oak Park, Illinois; Maite van Dijk, Van Gogh Museum; Christopher Eykyn, Susan Wallach, and Rachel Schaefer at Eykyn Maclean, LP, New York; Barbra Goering, Miami Corporation, Chicago; Helyn Goldenberg, Sotheby's, Chicago; Sharon Kim, Christie's, New York; Glen Miller and Erin Flanagan, VGRP Holdings, LLC, Chicago; Dr. Charles de Mooij, Fiona Zachariasse, and Sara Verboven, het Noordbrabants Museum, 's-Hertogenbosch; Tobias Mueller Ammann and Maya Pfeifer, Galerie Bruno Bischofberger, Switzerland; David Norman, Sotheby's, New York; Lionel Pissarro, Paris; Thomas Seydoux of Connery, Pissarro, Seydoux, Paris; and independent curators Connie Homberg and Sjraar van Heugten, from France and the Netherlands, respectively.

We are particularly grateful to the following colleagues from lending institutions whose enthusiasm and support were essential to the success of our loan requests: Fleur Roos Rosa de Carvalho and Marije Vellekoop, Van Gogh Museum; the Van Gogh family and the Vincent van Gogh Foundation, Amsterdam; Isabelle Cahn and Claire Bernardi, Musée d'Orsay; Katy Rothkopf, Baltimore Museum of Art; Mary Jane Keitel, Ben Marks, and Dave Willard, the Field Museum of Natural History, Chicago; Cindy Burlingham, Hammer Museum, Los Angeles; Lisette Pelsers and Liz Kreijn,

Kröller-Müller Museum, Otterlo; Nadine Orenstein and Marjorie Shelly, The Metropolitan Museum of Art, New York; Tobia Bezzola, Ute Eskildsen, and Sandra Gianfreda, Museum Folkwang, Essen; Chris Riopelle, National Gallery, London; Mary G. Morton and Kimberly Jones, National Gallery of Art, Washington, D.C.; Paul Gehl and Lesa Dowd, the Newberry Library, Chicago; Dorothy Kosinski and Eliza Rathbone, the Phillips Collection, Washington, D.C.; Brian Kennedy and Laurence W. Nichols, the Toledo Museum of Art; and Brenda L. Johnson, Daniel Meyer, and Patti Gibbons, the University of Chicago Library.

In addition to the generous lenders to the exhibition, we especially thank the sponsors who have supported many aspects of *Van Gogh's Bedrooms*. Lead support of the exhibition has been provided by the Estate of Jacquet McConville. Major support has been generously provided by Caryn and King Harris, The Harris Family Foundation; the Gilchrist Foundation; The Morris and Dolores Kohl Kaplan Fund; and Evonne and John Yonover. Additional funding has been contributed by Constance and David Coolidge, the Mason Foundation, Charlene and Mark Novak, and the Comer Family Foundation. Annual support for Art Institute exhibitions is provided by the Exhibitions Trust: Kenneth Griffin, Robert M. and Diane v.S. Levy, Thomas and Margot Pritzker, Betsy Bergman Rosenfield and Andrew M. Rosenfield, the Earl and Brenda Shapiro Foundation, and the Woman's Board. Lead Corporate Sponsors JPMorgan Chase and PowerShares QQQ, as well as Conservation Sponsor AkzoNobel, have offered further invaluable support to the exhibition. Likewise, we are indebted to the Federal Council on the Arts and the Humanities, whose indemnity has assisted with the insurance costs of the exhibition. We particularly thank Patricia Loiko, Indemnity Administrator, who assisted us greatly in the application process.

We also acknowledge the contributions of the following individuals: Mary Winton Green, whose fund for research on the nineteenth century made possible additional travel to see works of art; Eugênia Gorini Esmeraldo; Marc Gaynes; and Gerard Kerr. Steven Naifeh—whose own work, *Van Gogh: A Life*, was co-written with his partner, the late Gregory White Smith—greatly enriched our thinking about the emotional and physical circumstances that gave rise to the three *Bedroom* paintings.

In addition to the conservators and color scientists who authored the catalogue essay, an international cadre of scientists and conservators shared expertise, greatly benefiting the project. For their essential cooperation and support, we extend our thanks to the following colleagues: at the Art Institute, Zuccari, Grainger Executive Director of Conservation and Senior Painting Conservator, and his team, including Kelly Keegan, Assistant Paintings Conservator; Kristin Hoermann Lister, Conservator of Paintings; Kimberley Muir, Assistant Research Conservator; Federica Pozzi, former Andrew W. Mellon Conservation Science Fellow; Suzanne R. Schnepp, Senior Conservator of Objects; Kenneth Sutherland, Conservation Scientist; and Faye Wrubel, Conservator of Paintings. In particular, we are indebted to the contributions of Francesca Casadio, Andrew W. Mellon Senior Conservation Scientist. We would also like to thank Benjamin Myers and Vinayak Dravid at Northwestern University's EPIC facility (NUANCE Center); Joris Dik, Technische Universiteit Delft; Koen Janssens, Universiteit Antwerpen; Ken Romalino and formerly Michael Haschke, Bruker AXS Inc., Madison, Wisconsin; and Nederlandse Organisatie voor Wetenschappelijk Onderzoek, The Hague. We are particularly indebted to Roy S. Berns and Brittany Cox, Munsell Color Science Laboratory, Rochester Institute of Technology, for the digital recolorized visualization of the original colors of the Art Institute's *Bedroom*; to John Delaney and Kathryn A. Dooley, National Gallery of Art, Washington, D.C., for the hyperspectral imaging and fiber-optical reflectance spectroscopy; and to C. Richard Johnson, Jr., Cornell University; Don H. Johnson, Rice University; and Robert Erdmann, Rijksmuseum and Universiteit van Amsterdam, for providing the automated thread count analysis for all three *Bedroom* canvases.

The Van Gogh Museum team acknowledges the invaluable research support provided by the following colleagues: Muriel Geldof; Luc Megens; and Maarten van Bommel, now Professor of Conservation Science, Universiteit van Amsterdam, Rijksdienst voor het Cultureel Erfgoed, Amersfoort; Geert Van der Snickt, Universiteit Antwerpen; and Maurice Tromp, Van Gogh Museum. The Paris team would like to express as well their gratitude to the following colleagues at the Centre de Recherche et de Restauration des Musées de France: Elisabeth Ravaud, Myriam Eveno, Elsa Lambert, Ruven Pillay, Eric Laval, Laurence de Viguerie, Sandrine Pagès-Camagna, Witold Nowik, and formerly Jacques Castaing; and at the Musée d'Orsay: Anne Roquebert and former curator Laurence Madeline.

For guiding us in the challenge of integrating letters by Van Gogh and scientific explorations of the three paintings into exciting and easily accessible, immersive environments, we are profoundly grateful to the creativity of the team at Bluecadet, Philadelphia: Troy Lachance, Russell Edling, Dan King, Aaron Richardson, and Liz Russell. In Chicago the exhibition design was thoughtfully and collaboratively carried out by John Vinci, Dan Roush, and Alex Saavedra, Vinci-Hamp Architects, Inc. We extend our sincere thanks to them for an architecture that successfully blends the curatorial, scientific, and digital elements of the exhibition story into one immensely satisfying space.

At the Art Institute, the project has been remarkably embraced and supported by many, beginning with Douglas Druick, President and Eloise W. Martin Director, with whom I started this project and who has been so supportive of our goal to enrich our art historical narrative with exciting new media. Equally important and essential was the support of David Thurm, Chief Operating Officer; Martha Tedeschi, Deputy Director for Art and Research; and Dorothy Schroeder, former Vice President for Exhibitions and Museum Administration. Projects like this would not be possible without the dedication of our colleagues in the Departments of Registration and Museum Exhibitions, who help to navigate the muddy waters of shipments and schedules. Thus, we are grateful to Jennifer Draffen, Executive Director for Exhibitions and Registration; Jennifer Paoletti, Director of Exhibitions; Megan Rader, Manager for Exhibitions; Darrell Green, Senior Registrar, Loans and Exhibitions; and Associate Registrars Susanna Hedblom and Joyce Penn. Special thanks are also due to Jeanne Ladd, Vice President of Museum Finance; Andrew Simnick, Head of Strategy and Implementation; and Maureen Ryan and Kate Tierney Powell in the President and Director's Office. We also acknowledge the support and expertise of Maria Simon, Associate General Counsel, and Troy Klyber, Intellectual Property Manager, who kept us clear on the many complicated facets of the exhibition loans and presentation.

In the Department of European Painting and Sculpture, we thank Sylvain Bellenger—former Searle Chair and Curator of the department and now Director of the Museo di Capodimonte, Naples—for his encouragement and support. We are grateful to Megan Kosinski, Departmental Exhibitions Manager, who came to the Art Institute after this project was well under way. Her meticulous attention to detail and proactive approach helped us stay on schedule and navigate the complex loan agreements that have brought such exquisite works to our walls. For her collegiality and support we wish to thank Stephanie D'Alessandro, formerly in the department and now the Gary C. and Frances Comer Curator of International Modern Art in the Department of Modern and Contemporary Art. We gratefully acknowledge the assistance of department colleagues: Geri Banik, Secretary; Robert Burnier, Departmental Specialist; Aza Quinn-Brauner, Department Technician; Devon Pyle-Vowles, Collection Manager; Stephanie Strother, Secretary and Coordinator of the Old Masters Society; Kat Baetjer, former Exhibitions Assistant; and departmental interns Stacy Kammert, now Secretary and Assistant to the Chair of American Art; Charline Fournier-Petit; Kimberly Chin; and Susanna Rudofsky.

In the Department of Prints and Drawings, we thank our colleagues for their help in choosing works on paper by Van Gogh and other artists who inspired him: Suzanne Folds McCullagh, Anne Vogt Fuller and Marion Titus Searle Chair and Curator; Nancy Ireson, former Rothman Family Associate Curator; Toni Owen, Senior Conservator of Prints and Drawings; Harriet Stratis, Senior Research Conservator; Suzanne Karr Schmidt, Assistant Curator; and Emily Vokt Ziemba, Collection and Exhibition Manager. We also acknowledge the attention given to the presentation of these works by Chris Conniff-O'Shea, Assistant Conservator for Preparation and Framing; Kristi Dahm, Associate Conservator; and Mardy Sears, Conservation Technician. In the Department of Asian Art, we are grateful to the collegial interest and generosity of Janice Katz, Roger L. Weston Associate Curator of Japanese Art; Annette Gaspers, Departmental Specialist; and Rachel Freeman, Assistant Paper Conservator.

Supporting our research from the beginning was Jack Perry Brown, former Director of the Ryerson and Burnham Libraries, and we thank him, along with Mary Woolever, former Acting Director, and their successor, Douglas Litts, for their continued support and interest. We are particularly indebted to Bart Ryckbosch, Glasser and Rosenthal Family Archivist, and Autumn Mather, Head of Reader Services, for their guidance, as well as to Christine Fabian, Library Collections Conservator, for her help in realizing the display of books within the exhibition.

Supporting our ideas for an exhibition on Van Gogh's *Bedroom*s since joining the Art Institute last year was Michael Neault, Director of Digital Experience and Access, whose team—including Kelly McHugh and Will Robertson—has been extremely helpful in aligning our desire for an interactive experience with Bluecadet and Pilcrow Studios, Chicago. Together with Erin Hogan, former Head of Interpretation and Communication, and the specialists in Media Production and Services, Raymond Carlson, Jr., Bill Foster, and Tom Riley, they have gently helped us to navigate this relatively new and very exciting terrain. Aiding this aspect of the project (as well as the Acoustiguide and other educational outreach components) were our colleagues in Museum Education: Judith Kirshner, Deputy Director, Education, and Woman's Board Endowed Chair; Annie Morse, Assistant Director of Museum Education; Fawn Ring, Director of Lectures and Performance Programs; and Mary Erbach, Assistant Director of Experimental Exhibitions.

The exhibition catalogue would not have been possible without the energy, creativity, and unfailing dedication of the Department of Publishing. We are grateful to Sarah E. Guernsey, Executive Director, and to those members of her team who demonstrated remarkable patience and flexibility as the original concept necessarily morphed due to multiauthored texts, new research, and sometimes last-minute changes. We thank those who were in the trenches with us: Gregory Nosan, Editorial Director; Maia M. Rigas, Editor; Joseph Mohan, Associate Director of Production; Katie Levi, Photography Editor; Lauren Makholm, Production Coordinator; and Wilson McBee, Assistant Editor. Instrumental in photographing a number of works for the catalogue were the following members of the Department of Imaging: Louis Meluso, Director of Imaging Technology; Christopher Gallagher, Director of Photography; P. D. Young, Production Coordinator; Aidan Fitzpatrick, Bob Hashimoto, and Robert Lifson, photographers; and Jonathan Mathias, postproduction. For the strikingly bold and yet poetic design, we thank also the design team of Studio Blue, Chicago: Cheryl Towler Weese, Silja Hillmann, and Tuan Pham. Not only were they receptive to our evolving ideas, but they also guided us through the challenge of presenting the three *Bedroom* paintings in a way that would make them the center of the catalogue and yet always accessible to the reader. We also owe a great deal to color specialists Pat Goley and his team at Prographics, Rockford, Illinois. We are also happy to acknowledge the careful attention of freelance editor Margherita Andreotti and her intellectually stimulating feedback. We also thank proofreader Trevor Perri and indexer Kate Mertes. We extend sincere thanks to the lenders and their respective curators, collection managers, registrars, imaging specialists, and assistants who accommodated our requests for high-resolution photography. We are also thankful for our publishing partners at Yale University Press.

For the design and construction of the exhibition, we thank Sara Urizar, Executive Director of Design and Construction; Yau-mu Huang, Senior Exhibition Designer; and Joe Vatinno, Director of Museum Facilities, who helped us every step of the way to realize our vision despite the many complications involving deadlines and budgets. Our thanks also go to the Department of Graphic Design, including Jeff Wonderland, Director of Graphic Design; Salvador Cruz, Graphic Designer; and Erin Clark, Project Manager, for their creative input and captivating designs seen throughout the exhibition. We are also thankful to our colleagues in Development for their boundless enthusiasm and support: Eve Coffee Jeffers, Vice President for Development; George Martin, Director of Corporate Gifts and Sponsorships; Nina Yung, Director of Sustaining Fellows; Jennifer Moran, Director of Major Gifts; Jennifer Oatess, Director of Foundation and Government Grants; James Allan, Director of Planned Giving and Special Gifts; and Stephanie L. Henderson, Director of Special Events and Auxiliary Events. Special thanks go to those who helped market and develop the exhibition for which this catalogue serves as the permanent record. We are particularly grateful to Cliff Schwander and his team at Leo Burnett, Chicago, as well as the Art Institute's marketing team led by Gordon Montgomery, Vice President for Marketing, along with Tracey Button, Director of Marketing; Nora Gainer, Director of Tourism Marketing; Nadine Schneller, Marketing Coordinator; Oksana Schak, Tourism Marketing Manager; and Katie Rahn, Associate Director of Marketing. Special support for our project came from Elizabeth Grainer, Vice President for Auxiliary Operations; Sue Meyer, Director of Merchandising and Direct Mail, and her team in the Museum Shop: Marianne Rathslag, Director, Visitor Services and Museum Shop; Stanley Conlon, Director On Site Sales; Ann Sugg, Merchandise Buyer, Product Developer; Jennifer Evanoff, Merchandise Buyer, Product Developer; and Donna Unger, Merchandise Buyer, Product Developer.

Finally, I would like to add my personal thanks to the Old Masters Society, which has been so enthusiastically supportive of and engaged with the project from its inception, and to the friendship and support of Douglas Druick and Peter Zegers, whose scholarship for the publication and exhibition *Van Gogh and Gauguin: The Studio of the South* (2001–02) inspired us to dig more deeply into one of Van Gogh's favorite artworks.

Gloria Groom
Chair of European Painting and Sculpture
and David and Mary Winton Green Curator
The Art Institute of Chicago

12
Great Britain
The Nethe
4
11
2
1
3
10 5
9
21
13
17
6
14 16
15
Belgiu
24
7
France
23
22

Vincent van Gogh's restless life:
37 residences, 24 cities, 4 countries, 37 years

1 Groot-Zundert, the Netherlands: 1853–64, 1868–69

2 Zevenbergen, the Netherlands: 1864–66

3 Tilburg, the Netherlands: 1866–68

4 The Hague, the Netherlands: 1869–73, 1881–83

5 London, England: 1873, 1874, 1875

6 Brixton, England: 1873–74

7 Paris, France: 1874, 1875–76, 1886–88

8 Etten, the Netherlands: 1876

9 Ramsgate, England: 1876

10 Isleworth, England: 1876–77

11 Dordrecht, the Netherlands: 1877

12 Amsterdam, the Netherlands: 1877–78

13 Laken, Belgium: 1878

14 Pâturages, Borinage, Belgium: 1878

15 Wasmes, Borinage, Belgium: 1878–79

16 Cuesmes, Borinage, Belgium: 1879–80

17 Brussels, Belgium: 1880–81

18 Hoogeveen, Drenthe, the Netherlands: 1883

19 Nieuw-Amsterdam/Veenoord, Drenthe, the Netherlands: 1883

20 Nuenen, the Netherlands: 1883–85

21 Antwerp, Belgium: 1885–86

22 Arles, France: 1888–89

23 Saint-Rémy-de-Provence, France: 1889–90

24 Auvers-sur-Oise, France: 1890

VAN GOGH'S SEARCH FOR A HOME

—

CHRONOLOGY

"Painting is a *home*" —Van Gogh's Bedrooms before Arles

Vincent van Gogh's life as a youth and adult was marked by the constant search for a home and a place to belong. Prior to moving to Arles in February 1888 at the age of thirty-four, he had lived in over thirty residences in twenty-one cities across four countries, yet he confessed, when he was not yet twenty, that he found moving "terrible" (Aug. 7, 1873, in Jansen, Luijten, and Bakker, *Vincent van Gogh: The Letters* [hereafter *Letters*], 12). Perhaps to cope with past failures and lost homes, Van Gogh often regarded a new residence as an opportunity to reinvent himself and forge a fresh identity.

When Van Gogh began a new endeavor, his enthusiasm was reflected in his bedroom's decoration, which evolved to better suit each new identity. Although his bedroom in Arles was the only one the artist ever recorded in paint, in his letters he left accounts of many of his bedrooms—their architecture, their furniture, and, most of all, the beloved prints he hung on their walls. When his dreams went unrealized, his professional and personal failures precipitated periods of despair, during which he would deprive himself of the comfort and refuge of a bedroom. Beginning in his early twenties, he practiced strict discipline and self-punishment whenever he considered himself a failure or unworthy. He would take arduously long walks, deny himself food and soap, and forgo a comfortable night's sleep as acts of penance.

In 1880 Van Gogh decided that art was his true calling. Describing his decision to his brother Theo, he used the language not of professional choice but of belonging: "I often feel homesick for the country of paintings" (June 22 and 24, 1880, *Letters*, 155). Having become financially dependent on his brother, in 1883 he had to move back in with his parents in Nuenen, where his father served as a pastor. Here, the artist summed up the feeling he experienced in the act of painting with the phrase, "Painting is a *home*" (on or about June 22, 1885, *Letters*, 509). He increasingly focused his art on the theme of home and haven, which would resonate throughout his career. This theme manifested itself explicitly in Van Gogh's paintings of the interiors and exteriors of peasant houses and in his two depictions of the Nuenen parsonage; it also can be recognized more indirectly in his series of birds' nests.

Van Gogh expressed his experience of failure in terms of homelessness: "I am not an adventurer by choice but by fate and feeling nowhere so much myself a stranger as in my family and country" (Sept. or Oct. 1886, *Letters*, 569). In 1886 he left the Netherlands for France—where he would spend the remainder of his life—and moved in with Theo in Paris. There, he discovered the brilliant palette of the Impressionists and befriended the next generation of avant-garde artists. Van Gogh continued his interest in humble subject matter, but he abandoned the muted palette of browns and grays in favor of the vibrant colors that became his trademark. Although he was becoming increasingly assured as an artist, the bohemian life in Paris was taking a heavy physical and mental toll on him. Thus, in 1888 Van Gogh left Paris for the South of France.

Mar. 30, 1853
Groot-Zundert, the Netherlands

Vincent van Gogh is born in his parents' parsonage.

The Markt in Zundert with the Van Gogh parsonage at center. Van Gogh Museum, Amsterdam, Archives.

May 1, 1857
Groot-Zundert

Theo is born. The two brothers grow up sharing an attic bedroom.

Van Gogh's earliest known drawing. Van Gogh. *Barn and Farmhouse*, Feb. 8, 1864. Pencil on paper; 20 × 27 cm (7 7/8 × 10 5/8 in.). Scholte–van Houten Collection.

Oct. 1, 1864
Zevenbergen, the Netherlands

Resides at Zandweg A40 while attending Jan Provily's boarding school for boys.

Boarding School, Zevenbergen. Van Gogh Museum, Amsterdam, Archives.

1866–1875

Sept. 3, 1866
Tilburg, the Netherlands

Lives at Korvel 57 with the Hannik family while attending the Rijks Hogere Burgerschool Tilburg Koning Willem II.

Van Gogh (likely third from right in the first row) on the steps of the Tilburg School. Vincents Tekenlokaal, Tilburg/Koning Willem II College, Tilburg.

Mar. 19, 1868
Groot-Zundert

Returns to live with his family.

Zundert Church. Van Gogh Museum, Amsterdam, Archives.

July 30, 1869
The Hague, the Netherlands

Lodges with Willem and Dina Roos at Lange Beestenmarkt 32 after being appointed junior apprentice at the art dealership Goupil & Cie.

Goupil Gallery, The Hague. Van Gogh Museum, Amsterdam, Archives.

May 12, 1873
London, England

Moves to an unknown suburb after being relocated to London branch of Goupil & Cie; en route, stays in Paris for several days.

End of Aug. 1873
Brixton, England

Moves to 87 Hackford Road, lodging with Ursula Loyer and her daughter Eugenie.

After Aug. 10, 1874
London

Moves into the home of John Parker and his family at 395 Kennington Road, South London.

Oct. 26, 1874
Paris, France

Temporarily transferred to the Goupil & Cie Paris branch.

Jan. 1875
London

Returns from Paris to London.

Mid-May 1875
Paris

Transferred back to the Paris branch of Goupil & Cie, living in a small room in Montmartre, address unknown.

Apr. 1, 1876
Etten, the Netherlands

After being fired from Goupil & Cie, goes to the Van Gogh family's new home at Roosendaalseweg 4, Etten.

Van Gogh. *Vicarage and Church at Etten*, Apr. 1876. Pencil, pen, and ink, on paper; 9.5 × 17.8 cm (3 3/4 × 7 in.). Van Gogh Museum, Amsterdam (Vincent van Gogh Foundation).

Apr. 14, 1876
Ramsgate, England

Lodges at 11 Spencer Square after taking a position as an assistant teacher at William Stokes's boarding school for boys.

11 Spencer Square.

Last week of June 1876
Isleworth, England

Moves to Isleworth (near London), Linkfield House, 183 Twickenham Road, where Stokes has opened a new school.

By November 19, Van Gogh is preaching and teaching Sunday school at the Congregational church in Turnham Green and in Petersham.

Van Gogh. *Letter to Theo van Gogh with the Sketch "Small Churches at Petersham and Turnham Green,"* Nov. 1876. Pencil, pen, and ink, on paper; 3.8 × 10 cm (1 1/2 × 3 15/16 in.). Van Gogh Museum, Amsterdam (Vincent van Gogh Foundation).

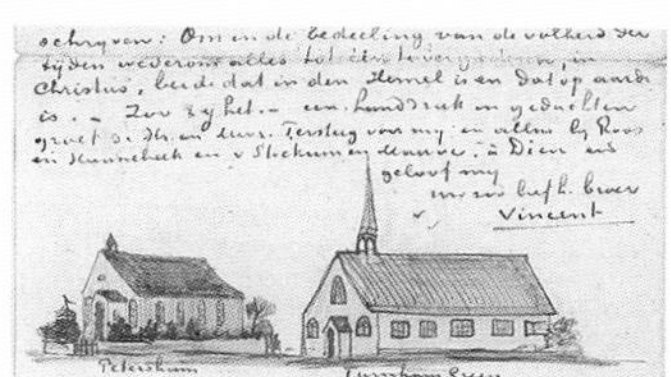

Vincent

Petersham

Turnham Green

Jan. 9, 1877
Dordrecht, the Netherlands

Moves to Tolbrugstraat A312 and begins working as a general assistant in the Blussé & Van Braam bookshop.

Scheffersplein, the market square in Dordrecht, with Blussé & Van Braam bookshop at center.

May 14, 1877
Amsterdam, the Netherlands

Lives with his uncle, Jan van Gogh, at Grote Kattenburgerstraat 3 while preparing for his theological studies.

Aug. 26, 1878
Laken, Belgium

Moves to Laken, outside Brussels, for a three-month trial period training to be an evangelist. Lodges with the Plugge family at 6, chemin de Halage.

Early Dec. 1878
Pâturages, Borinage, Belgium

Lodges until the end of December with the evangelist-colporteur Benjamin Vanderhaegen, 39, rue de l'Église.

End of Dec. 1878
Wasmes, Borinage, Belgium

Moves in with the farmer Jean-Baptiste Denis, 81, rue du Petit-Wasmes.

Home of Jean-Baptiste Denis. Van Gogh Museum, Amsterdam, Archives.

Early Aug. 1879
Cuesmes, Borinage, Belgium

Lodges with the evangelist-miner Édouard Joseph Francq, 5, rue du Pavillon.

July 1880
Cuesmes, Borinage

Moves into the home of miner Charles Decrucq, at 3, rue du Pavillon. Here, Van Gogh decides to become an artist.

The Decrucq home.

Oct. 1880
Brussels, Belgium

Moves to 72, boulevard du Midi.

Le boulevard du Midi. Archives de la Ville de Bruxelles.

Dec. 25, 1881
The Hague

Moves to The Hague after a furious argument with his father while visiting his family in Etten for Christmas.

Jan. 1, 1882
The Hague

Rents rooms at Schenkweg 138.

The view from Van Gogh's studio window. Van Gogh. *Carpenter's Yard and Laundry*, late May 1882, Kröller-Müller Museum, Otterlo (see p. 55, fig. 4). F939, JH150

July 4, 1882
The Hague

Moves to Schenkweg 136.

Sept. 11, 1883
Hoogeveen, Drenthe, the Netherlands

Stays in Albertus Hartsuiker's lodging house, Grote Kerksteeg 51.

Van Gogh. *Landscape in Drenthe*, Sept.–Oct. 1883. Pencil, pen, brush and ink, and watercolor on paper; 31.4 × 42.1 cm (12 3/8 × 16 9/16 in.). Van Gogh Museum, Amsterdam (purchased with support from the Vincent van Gogh Foundation and the Rembrandt Association). F1104, JH424

Oct. 2, 1883
Nieuw-Amsterdam/Veenoord, Drenthe, the Netherlands

Stays in lodging house run by Hendrik Scholte, District E, no. 34.

Van Gogh. *Drawbridge in Nieuw-Amsterdam*, 1883. Watercolor; 38.5 × 81 cm (15 3/16 × 31 7/8 in.). Collection Groninger Museum, the Netherlands. F1098, JH425

Dec. 5, 1883
Nuenen, the Netherlands

Lives with his parents in their new parsonage at De Berg F523.

Back of the parsonage with Van Gogh's studio on the right. Van Gogh Museum, Amsterdam (Vincent van Gogh Foundation).

May 1885
Nuenen

Moves out of the parsonage into a studio rented from Verger Schafrat.

Home of Schafrat, where he rents his studio. Van Gogh Museum, Amsterdam, Archives.

Van Gogh. *The Potato Eaters*, Apr.–May 1885. Van Gogh Museum, Amsterdam (Vincent van Gogh Foundation) (see p. 53, fig. 2). F82, JH764

Nov. 24, 1885
Antwerp, Belgium

Rents a room at 194, rue des Images.

View from a window between the first and second floors at 194, rue des Images. Van Gogh. *Houses Seen from the Back*, Dec. 1885–Feb. 1886. Oil on canvas; 43.7 × 33.7 cm (17 3/16 × 13 1/4 in.). Van Gogh Museum, Amsterdam (Vincent van Gogh Foundation). F260, JH970

Mid-Mar. 1886
Paris

Lives with Theo on the rue de Laval; the small, second-floor apartment does not have room for an easel, so Van Gogh works at the studio of Fernand Cormon at 104, boulevard de Clichy.

The artist's earliest known self-portrait. Van Gogh. *Self-Portrait*, Mar.–June 1886. Oil on canvas; 27.2 × 19 cm (10 11/16 × 7 1/2 in.). Van Gogh Museum, Amsterdam (Vincent van Gogh Foundation). F208, JH1195

June 1886
Paris

Moves with Theo into a larger apartment at 54, rue Lepic, Montmartre.

Rue Lepic, Paris. Private collection.

Henri de Toulouse-Lautrec (French, 1864–1901). *Vincent van Gogh*, 1887. Chalk on cardboard; 57 × 46 cm (22 7/16 × 18 1/8 in.). Van Gogh Museum, Amsterdam (Vincent van Gogh Foundation).

Van Gogh. *View from Theo's Apartment*, Mar.–Apr. 1887. Oil on canvas; 45.9 × 38.1 cm (18 × 15 in.). Van Gogh Museum, Amsterdam (Vincent van Gogh Foundation). F341, JH1242

**"A home of my own!"
—Van Gogh
Arrives in Arles**

On February 19, 1888, Van Gogh took an overnight train to the small Provençal city of Arles, likely with the intention of soon continuing on to Marseilles in search of brighter colors and a healthier environment in which he could regain his physical strength. Although it was not his intended final destination, Van Gogh was immediately struck by the "magnificent scenery" of Arles, and he drew three studies even before writing to Theo to let him know he had arrived. The artist felt he had discovered a stand-in for his imagined paradise of color, craft, and simplicity: "I feel I'm in Japan" (on or about Mar. 16, 1888, *Letters*, 585). Wandering through Arles and its vicinity, he was struck by the emerald landscapes, rich blue stretches of water, glorious yellow suns, and pale orange twilights, which made him feel as if he had stepped into one of the Japanese prints he had been avidly collecting.

For Van Gogh, finding "the equivalent of Japan" was about more than just finding the right light for his painting—it was about how to live. His conception of the Japanese way of life—informed by the popular stereotypes of late nineteenth-century Europe and novels such as Pierre Loti's *Madame Chrysanthème* (1888)—consisted of a disciplined regimen of work unfolding in private, uncluttered interiors. Van Gogh considered this type of existence to be essential for artists and a panacea for his life's difficulties: "An ideal of simplicity . . . is what society should give an artist, it seems to me, whereas nowadays one is *obliged* to live in the cafés or low inns. The Japanese have lived in very simple interiors, and what great artists have lived in that country!" (on or about Oct. 21, 1889, *Letters*, 812). The artist believed he could never reach this ideal by living in a hotel, and he began to search for a more permanent residence in Arles.

On May 1, 1888, Van Gogh wrote to Theo with the news that he had signed a lease on a house with four whitewashed rooms and a painted yellow exterior. Thrilled to finally have "a home of my own" (Sept. 4, 1888, *Letters*, 674), Van Gogh referred to his "yellow house" in at least seven letters, revealing that it was a meaningful designation, not just a physical description. This home possessed tremendous significance for the artist, symbolizing security, ownership, and freedom. Before long, he abandoned the stippled brushstrokes he had been borrowing from the Neo-Impressionists in Paris. In Arles, he developed the distinct style of brushstrokes, the heavy, impastoed paint application, and the vivid color juxtapositions that would become his signature. The brilliance of the southern sun, the "Japanese" vistas, and the independence of finally having a home he could consider his own all contributed to a surge of creativity for Van Gogh. Upon moving in, he described the Yellow House: "Inside, I can live and breathe, and think and paint" (Sept. 9 and about 14, 1888, *Letters*, 678).

Feb. 20, 1888
Arles, France

Rents a room in the Hôtel-Restaurant Carrel, 30, rue Cavalerie. Uses a small, covered roof terrace as his studio.

Hôtel-Restaurant Carrel. Van Gogh Museum, Amsterdam, Archives.

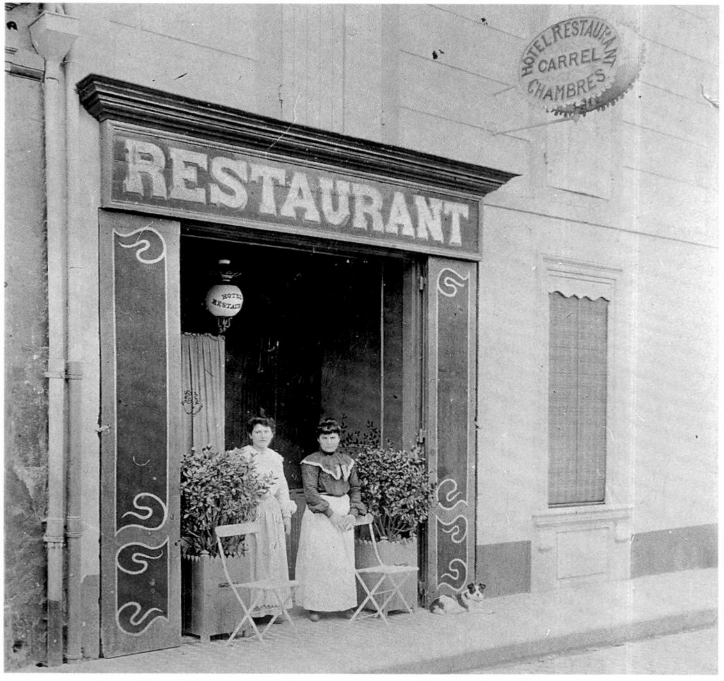

May 1, 1888
Arles

Signs lease for the Yellow House with estate agent Bernard Soulé.

May 7, 1888
Arles

Temporarily takes a room in the Café de la Gare, run by Joseph-Michel and Marie Ginoux, 30, place Lamartine.

Van Gogh. *Sunflowers*, c. Aug. 26, 1888. The National Gallery, London (see p. 40, fig. 3). This painting hung in Paul Gauguin's bedroom in the Yellow House. F454, JH1562

Van Gogh. *The Night Café*, Sept. 6–8, 1888. Yale University Art Gallery, New Haven, Connecticut (see p. 39, fig. 2). F463, JH1575

Sept. 17, 1888
Arles

Moves into the Yellow House, 2, place Lamartine.

The Yellow House. Van Gogh Museum, Amsterdam, Archives.

Van Gogh. *The Yellow House (The Street)*, Sept. 28, 1888. Oil on canvas; 72 × 91.5 cm (28 3/8 × 36 in.). Van Gogh Museum, Amsterdam (Vincent van Gogh Foundation). F464, JH1589

Oct. 16–17, 1888
Arles

After two and a half days of self-imposed bed rest, Van Gogh is inspired to paint his bedroom.

Van Gogh. *The Bedroom*, Oct. 16–17, 1888. Van Gogh Museum, Amsterdam (Vincent van Gogh Foundation) (see plate 20). F482, JH1608

Oct. 23, 1888
Arles

Paul Gauguin moves into the Yellow House.

Paul Gauguin (French, 1848–1903). *Vincent van Gogh Painting Sunflowers*, c. Dec. 1, 1888. Oil on canvas; 73 × 91 cm (28 3/4 × 35 13/16 in.). Van Gogh Museum, Amsterdam (Vincent van Gogh Foundation).

"A nightmare in these peaceful places" —Van Gogh's Final Bedrooms

Following a mental breakdown on December 23, 1888—during which he notoriously cut off part of his left ear—Van Gogh regained consciousness sometime the next day in an isolation room at the Arles hospital. Over the next four and a half months, Van Gogh spent most of his time in the hospital, with only two extended interludes back at the Yellow House: the first, lasting about a month, ended with another attack of mental illness; the second, lasting about ten days, ended with a citizens' petition demanding he be committed. Following these attacks, the artist could barely recall his actions and motivations, yet his few recollections reveal a profound nostalgia for his very first home, as he described in a letter to Theo on January 22, 1889: "During my illness I again saw each room in the house at Zundert, each path, each plant in the garden" (*Letters*, 741). In his letters to Theo, he expressed his strong desire to be working at his art and to find an environment in which to recover.

Van Gogh chose to live in Saint-Paul-de-Mausole, an asylum in Saint-Rémy-de-Provence, France. Upon his arrival on May 8, 1889, he spent his time painting its extensive gardens and grounds. He suffered another serious attack in mid-July, which confined him to his room for two months. Almost a year earlier in Arles, two days of self-imposed rest had inspired him to paint the first *Bedroom*; now under very different circumstances, this extended stay in bed also precipitated a burst of creativity, including the second and third versions of *The Bedroom*.

On February 22, 1890, Van Gogh visited Arles, which triggered another breakdown that left him unable to read or write. Back at the Saint-Rémy asylum, he was banned from his studio and forbidden the use of paints after he had attempted to ingest them. However, during peaceful intervals, he was allowed access to a sketchpad, chalk, and pencil in his bedroom. From memory, he made several sketches of peasants and cottages that he recalled from the Netherlands. In April, when he recovered from the attack, he immediately painted a series of cottages not of the type found in the South of France but rather like those he remembered from his childhood. With this return to the motifs of cottages found in his early paintings, but now translated into the brilliant color and brushwork that he had developed in France, Van Gogh realized that he needed a new direction for his mental health and his art.

A few weeks later, on May 16, 1890, Van Gogh was discharged from the asylum. A year after having arrived and less than a month after recovering from a mental breakdown, the artist decided that what he needed was not another hospital stay but rather a return to the North. On May 1 he had declared to Theo, "I'm almost sure that I'll soon get better in the north" (*Letters*, 865). Van Gogh traveled to Auvers-sur-Oise, France, and rented a room at the Auberge Ravoux, which would be his final residence. Back in what he considered more familiar territory, he felt relief from his previous anxiety. He had loved the South, but he also believed that it had contributed to an increasing unease, his "northern brain having been seized by a nightmare in these peaceful places" (May 25, 1890, *Letters*, RM21). Van Gogh found this little village beautiful, especially noting its thatched-roofed cottages, which were becoming rarer and no doubt reminded him of his earlier "human nests."

Dec. 24, 1888
Arles

After severing part of his ear and attempting to give it to Gauguin, admitted to the Old Hospital (also known as Hôtel-Dieu-Saint-Esprit) in Arles.

The courtyard of the hospital at Arles. Van Gogh Museum, Amsterdam, Archives.

Dec. 25, 1888
Arles

Disturbed by Van Gogh's recent behavior, Gauguin vacates the Yellow House and departs for Paris.

Jan. 8, 1889
Arles

Leaves the hospital and returns to the Yellow House.

Feb. 7, 1889
Arles

Taken back to the Old Hospital in Arles after a second attack.

Feb. 17, 1889
Arles

Leaves the hospital again.

Feb. 26, 1889
Arles

Confined to the hospital on police orders after a citizens' petition against him.

Van Gogh. *The Courtyard of the Hospital at Arles*, Apr. 1889. Oil on canvas; 73 × 92 cm (28 3/4 × 36 1/4 in.). Collection Oskar Reinhart «Am Römerholz», Winterthur. F519, JH1687

Apr. 30, 1889
Arles

Flooding in the Yellow House causes water damage to several of Van Gogh's works, including the first version of *The Bedroom*.

May 2, 1889
Arles

Sends a crate of paintings, including the first version of *The Bedroom*, to Theo in Paris.

May 8, 1889
Saint-Rémy-de-Provence, France

Admits himself to the asylum of Saint-Paul-de-Mausole.

Asylum of Saint-Paul-de-Mausole, Saint-Rémy.

View from Van Gogh's window in his room at Saint-Rémy. Van Gogh Museum, Amsterdam, Archives.

1889–1890

May 23, 1889
Saint-Rémy-de-Provence

Asks Theo to line the original *Bedroom*, which had sustained water damage.

June 9, 1889
Saint-Rémy-de-Provence

Asks Theo to send back the original *Bedroom*, instead of lining it, so that he can paint a copy.

June 16, 1889

Theo sends the original *Bedroom* from Paris to Saint-Rémy.

July 8, 1889
Arles

Visits Arles.

July 14 or 15, 1889
Saint-Rémy-de-Provence

Returns to the asylum.

Sept. 5, 1889
Saint-Rémy-de-Provence

Paints a second version of *The Bedroom*.

Van Gogh. *The Bedroom*, by Sept. 5, 1889. The Art Institute of Chicago, Helen Birch Bartlett Memorial Collection, 1926.417 (see plate 21). F484, JH1771

Sept. 28, 1889
Saint-Rémy-de-Provence

Paints a third version of *The Bedroom* as a gift for his mother and sister Willemien.

Van Gogh. *The Bedroom*, by Sept. 28, 1889. Musée d'Orsay, Paris, sold to national museums under the Treaty of Peace with Japan, 1959 (see plate 22). F483, JH1793

Dec. 6, 1889
Saint-Rémy-de-Provence

Sends Theo the third version of *The Bedroom* to be sent on to their mother and Willemien.

Dec. 18, 1889
Saint-Rémy-de-Provence

Sends Theo the original and second versions of *The Bedroom*.

Dec. 22, 1889
Saint-Rémy-de-Provence

The original and second versions of *The Bedroom* arrive at Theo's apartment in Paris.

Feb. 1890
Arles

Visits Arles again.

Feb. 22, 1890
Saint-Rémy-de-Provence

Returns to the asylum.

Van Gogh. *House and Figure*, Feb. 1890. Oil on canvas; 52 × 40.5 cm (20 1/2 × 15 15/16 in.). The Barnes Foundation, Philadelphia. F674, JH1920

May 16, 1890
Saint-Rémy-de-Provence

Is discharged from the asylum.

May 17, 1890
Paris

Arrives in Paris and stays with Theo in his apartment at 8, cité Pigalle.

May 20, 1890
Auvers-sur-Oise, France

Moves into the Auberge Ravoux, room 5.

The Ravoux family in front of the Auberge Ravoux.

Van Gogh's bedroom at the Auberge Ravoux. Van Gogh Museum, Amsterdam, Archives.

Van Gogh. *Portrait of Dr. Gachet*, June 3, 1890. Oil on canvas; 68 × 57 cm (26 3/4 × 22 7/16 in.). Musée d'Orsay, Paris, gift of Paul and Marguerite Gachet, children of the model, 1949. F754, JH2014

Van Gogh. *Farms near Auvers*, July 1890. Oil on canvas; 50.2 × 100.3 cm (19 3/4 × 39 1/2 in.). Tate Gallery, London, Bequeathed by C. Frank Stoop, 1933. F793, JH2114

July 29, 1890
Auvers-sur-Oise

Van Gogh dies.

The grave of Van Gogh, next to that of Theo, who died Jan. 25, 1891. Ryerson and Burnham Archives, Art Institute of Chicago.

THE EMPTY ROOM

—

GLORIA GROOM

The Empty Room

When someone like that dies . . . then it's a loss and leaves an empty place.
Van Gogh to Theo, May 4–5, 1885

The most famous image of a bedroom in the nineteenth century—and perhaps in art history—might also be the strangest. Devoid of any living presence, the space is dominated by an oversize bed and two side doors that can be seen as either completely closed or slightly ajar. This ambiguity is created by the doors' sharp but slightly skewed outlines, which seem to suggest that they flare outward, echoing the wide expanse of the floorboards. The exaggerated broadening of the foreground and the plunging perspective draw the viewer into the scene. The effect is of a stage set before the actors enter and give it meaning.[1] *The Bedroom* (plate 20), however, features the empty room itself in the leading role.

This essay explores what Steven Naifeh and Gregory White Smith have described as Vincent van Gogh's "synthesizing eye"—his ability to layer words and images in the pursuit of what he called "the finest expression."[2] By proposing links between the genesis of *The Bedroom* and Van Gogh's obsessive study of art and literature, I hope to uncover additional layers of meaning in this famous picture.

Bedroom as Art

The bedroom was not an unusual subject in art, especially if we make little distinction between a bed and the domestic interior in which it may have been situated. From the early Renaissance onward, the bedroom was a significant space in wealthy households, and the bed the most expensive and prized item.[3] We are all familiar with pictures that feature a bed as the perch of a reclining female nude, for example, Titian's *Venus of Urbino* (1538; Galleria degli Uffizi, Florence), Jean-Auguste-Dominique Ingres's odalisques, especially *La grande odalisque* (1814; Musée du Louvre, Paris), or Édouard Manet's notorious *Olympia* (1863; Musée d'Orsay, Paris). In these images and many others, the richly adorned bed was associated with amorous exploits and illicit liaisons, and this aspect of the subject continued to have popular appeal throughout the nineteenth century. It culminated in Henri de Toulouse-Lautrec's famous brothel paintings of the 1890s, especially several images tightly focused on a bed in which prostitutes embrace one another amorously.

Less known, perhaps, but no less rich is the long history of religious childbirth scenes, often set in elaborate bedrooms or domestic interiors decorated in the popular style of the day. These images most often depict the nativities of religious figures such as the Virgin Mary and John the Baptist. Among the most famous works in this genre, spanning the fourteenth and fifteenth centuries, are the fresco cycles of Giotto and Domenico Ghirlandaio, both titled *Birth of the Virgin* and located in the Arena Chapel in Padua and in Santa Maria Novella in Florence, respectively.[4] In Dutch art, this tradition included such exquisite works as Petrus Christus's *Virgin and Child in a Domestic Interior* (1460/67; Nelson-Atkins Museum of Art, Kansas City). It seems to be no coincidence that Van Gogh's first remarks about painting his bed—"Perhaps a naked woman, . . . perhaps a cradle with a child"—included both of these models.[5] It may indeed be the notion that he was working against the rich backdrop of these antecedents that contributed to his great pleasure in painting *The Bedroom*, which "amused [him] enormously."[6]

A generation before Van Gogh, Romantic artists in the first half of the nineteenth century occasionally depicted their bedrooms as places for privacy and study.[7] These images tended to represent the artist in the space, as seen in Léon Cogniet's *Artist in His Room at the Villa Medici, Rome* (fig. 1) or Adolph Menzel's series of small interiors (see fig. 2).[8]

In the second half of the century, the domestic interior continued to play an important role as backdrop for modern-life subjects, yet the bedroom—and particularly the empty bedroom—were simply not themes favored by the Impressionists.[9] Only in the 1890s, with the rise of new research focusing on the psyche of the individual, did the term *intérieur* become associated with one's inner nature; it was at this point that the bedroom took on special significance as a psychologically charged environment worth painting. As seen in the works of the Symbolist artists Édouard Vuillard and Edvard Munch, these rooms expressed meditation, dreams, and loss of consciousness (see fig. 3) or premonition of death (see fig. 4). Symbolist interiors conveyed emotions with an ambiguity hovering between narrative and abstraction, resulting in forms that could no longer be read as corresponding to the external world. Such goals were foreign to Van Gogh's own stated intentions when he painted *The Bedroom*. On the contrary, far from wanting to mystify the subject, he offered specific readings for his work.

A Place to Sleep

For most of his adult life, the artist expressed very complicated notions about beds and the *chambre à coucher*, or room to sleep in, which he often considered to be a luxury he could not afford or did not deserve. As a youth and young man, Van Gogh punished himself for his perceived failures by forgoing the comforts of a bedroom and instead sleeping under the stars, on the floor, or on a pallet in his many

Fig. 1 Léon Cogniet (French, 1794–1880). *The Artist in His Room at the Villa Medici, Rome*, 1817. Oil on canvas; 44.5 × 37 cm (17 1/2 × 14 9/16 in.). Cleveland Museum of Art, Mr. and Mrs. William H. Marlatt Fund.

Fig. 2 Adolph Menzel (German, 1815–1905). *The Artist's Bedroom in the Ritterstrasse*, 1847. Oil on cardboard; 56 × 46 cm (22 × 18 1/8 in.). Staatliche Museen zu Berlin, Alte Nationalgalerie.

Fig. 3 Édouard Vuillard (French, 1868–1940). *In Bed*, 1891. Oil on canvas; 74 × 92 cm (29 1/8 × 36 1/4 in.). Musée d'Orsay, Paris.

Fig. 4 Edvard Munch (Norwegian, 1863–1944). *Death in the Sickroom*, 1893. Oil on canvas; 134.5 × 160 cm (52 15/16 × 63 in.). Munch-Museet, Oslo.

1

2

3

4

5

6

Fig. 5 *La chambre mortuaire de Corot.* Reproduced in *L'illustration*, Mar. 6, 1875, p. 156. The Newberry Library, Chicago.

Fig. 6 *The Bedroom in which M. Gambetta Died.* Reproduced in *The Graphic*, Jan. 13, 1883, p. 1. Private collection, Oak Park, Illinois.

temporary lodgings.[10] Around 1880, when he decided that art was his true calling, he went to the other extreme, fixating on the idea of a permanent place to work and sleep. The bedroom became a symbol of stability, which he came to believe was an absolute necessity for the artistic life. In the Yellow House, his name for his home in Arles, France, the bedroom temporarily fulfilled this quest.

In a letter to his brother Theo dated September 9, 1888, he detailed the purchases made for his bedroom—"bed, the chairs, table, all in deal [whitewood]"—and also announced his intention to paint his own bed: "There'll be 3 subjects. Perhaps a naked woman, I haven't decided, perhaps a cradle with a child; I don't know, but I'll take my time."[11] This familial scene was never realized. Between September 9, when he began thinking about painting his bedroom and populating it with imaginary figures, and October 16 and 17, when he painted the first version of *The Bedroom*, Van Gogh changed his mind.

A bout of nervous exhaustion constrained the artist to two days of uninterrupted rest in this very room. Afterward, feeling invigorated and inspired, he wrote to Theo that "this [painting was] to take my revenge for the enforced rest that I was obliged to take."[12] Executed quickly and confidently, with few deviations from the pen-and-ink sketch and word pictures in his letter to his brother, *The Bedroom* was to be understood as an image "*of rest* or *of sleep* in general. In short, looking at the painting should *rest* the mind, or rather, the imagination."[13] In a similarly illustrated letter to Paul Gauguin the following day, Van Gogh repeated the idea that *The Bedroom* was to express "utter repose," adding, "with a simplicity à la *Seurat.*"[14]

On the walls, Van Gogh depicted portraits of two friends in addition to other artworks, which included Japanese prints and a landscape painting; he also included a rack on which to hang smocks and a straw hat. These details indicate that the empty room was inhabited by an artist. And it was this kind of room that he wanted to advertise to Theo and Gauguin, the two most important figures in his life at that time, expressing the way of life they could expect to find once they made the trip south. For Van Gogh, the bedroom documented his present condition and confidence in the future; like the Yellow House itself, it would bear witness to his "health" and his "peace of mind."[15]

The Empty Chair: Three Portraits

A devotee of the written word as much as of art, Van Gogh was as intensely engaged with newspapers and weekly journals as he was with contemporary literature, especially his beloved *romans parisiens* (novels set in Paris) (see plate 9).[16] He scoured magazines such as *L'illustration*, *The Graphic*, and the *London Illustrated News* for black-and-white engravings, which he would pin to the empty walls of his various residences and copy in his drawings.[17] He admired the prints as much for their illustrative quality as for their sentimental messages. Among these were images of empty bedrooms, which were featured because famous individuals had died in them (see figs. 5–6). Although these bedroom pictures built on a long artistic precedent of deathbed scenes, they are unusual in that, unlike their predecessors, they do not show the deceased. Although Van Gogh's preferences tended toward realism with a social purpose, such as depicting the plight of the poor, he was also keenly interested in biography, finding in the lives of others connections to his own. It thus seems likely that these images of empty bedrooms, with their accompanying stories of the famous deceased, would have interested the artist as he created and painted his chamber.[18]

One of Van Gogh's favorite prints was the two-page engraving after a watercolor by Samuel Luke Fildes depicting the desk and chair of Charles Dickens, which was published in *The Graphic* in its Christmas 1870 issue (fig. 7). From among the hundreds of images Van Gogh collected, he valued this one especially and tried to track down other copies for his friends.[19] Fildes had been working with Dickens on illustrations for *Edwin Drood* when the writer unexpectedly died of a stroke; visiting Dickens's home for the funeral and moved by the atmosphere of mourning, Fildes was inspired to depict the author's study just as it had been left at the time of his death.[20] Fildes's celebrated "portrait" of the absent author resonated with Van Gogh, who undoubtedly had it in mind during an incident in 1878 in Amsterdam: after a visit from his father, he wrote to Theo that, returning home from having seen him off at the train station, he wept "like a child" at the sight of his father's empty chair.[21]

7

Fig. 7 After Samuel Luke Fildes (English, 1843–1927). *The Room in which Charles Dickens Wrote*, reproduced in *Harper's Weekly*, Jan. 7, 1871, pp. 8–9. Originally published in *The Graphic* (Christmas 1870), after p. 24. Private collection, Oak Park, Illinois.

The engraving may have also served as partial inspiration for Van Gogh's "chair portraits" painted in November 1888, halfway through Gauguin's stay at the Yellow House (plates 23–24). Van Gogh's straw-bottomed, armless chair is of a type still in use today and is one of the twelve chairs he reported purchasing for the Yellow House. In Van Gogh's picture, Gauguin's more elaborate walnut chair is similar in design and placement to Dickens's chair in Fildes's image. Van Gogh referred to Gauguin as the "abbot," making an indirect association between his own father, a scholar-pastor with whom he had a complex relationship, and his friend. Gauguin's painted

8

9

chair—topped with books—further underscores his connection, in Van Gogh's eyes, both to his father and to Dickens, whom he idolized.

The Power of the Empty Room

When Van Gogh returned to *The Bedroom* in September 1889 to make a second and third version (plates 21–22), his stated intentions—as well as his life situation—were quite different. Gone was the optimism he felt in anticipation of the visits of other artists or his brother, whose portraits he might have added to his walls. By 1889 *The Bedroom* signaled to the artist what might have been. When working on the two later versions, and especially the smaller one for his mother and sister, it is as though he knew they would not be understood and thus did not allow himself to be so personally attached to the works. He distanced himself from the composition's autobiographical genesis, abandoning personal pronouns in his letters; "my bedroom" became "the interior" and "an empty bedroom." And yet the very fact that Van Gogh made two subsequent versions seems a testament to the picture's importance, a positive reminder of what he considered his best work.[22] Later statements reveal how much it meant to him.[23]

Regardless of the artist's own fluctuating opinions, the three *Bedroom* paintings remain among Van Gogh's most compelling pictures. These works stand out for their startling perspective and composition, their ambitious color scheme, and the rich story they tell about the artist during the year that separated their making. As suggested here, these works also achieve a fresh recasting of the subject in relation to existing visual traditions. With remarkable synthetic brilliance, Van Gogh used everything he came across, even popular black-and-white images of modest aesthetic value, to imbue his works with an extraordinary wealth of allusions. Rediscovering these references is one of the countless rewards of studying his work.[24]

Since the painter's death, in a fashion echoing that of the Victorian engravings of celebrity deathbeds, the artist's existing bedrooms have become memorials. In the 1940s, his cell at the Saint-Rémy-de-Provence asylum was converted into a gallery for reproductions of his paintings (fig. 8). His final bedroom at the Auberge Ravoux in Auvers-sur-Oise is today a museum (fig. 9).[25] But it is in the painted empty bedroom that he is most present.

Fig. 8 Dr. Edgar Leroy, the head of the Saint-Rémy-de-Provence asylum during the 1940s, in Van Gogh's former cell in 1949. Ryerson and Burnham Archives, Art Institute of Chicago.

Fig. 9 Van Gogh's bedroom at the Auberge Ravoux, Auvers-sur-Oise. Van Gogh Museum, Amsterdam, Archives.

I wish to thank Allison Perelman, Research Associate in the Department of European Painting and Sculpture, for her contributions to this essay. In the following notes, the artist and his brother are referred to as Van Gogh and Theo, respectively. The abbreviation *Letters*, followed by a number, refers to a specific letter in *Vincent van Gogh: The Letters*, ed. Leo Jansen, Hans Luijten, and Nienke Bakker (Van Gogh Museum/Huygens ING, 2009), http://vangoghletters.org/vg/.

1. Others have pointed out the "staginess" of Van Gogh's *Bedroom* representations, and although I came to my conclusions separately, I was struck by the following description of the room as metaphor: "The powerful simplicity of Van Gogh's painted *Bedroom*, its furnishings and its manner of representation force the actual room upon us. *The Bedroom* is like an empty stage-set, with entrances at left and right. It is like a miniature room, so real does the furniture seem, so palpable the space. It thrusts out at us and recedes into the wall with equal conviction. It is what home is, a bounded universe, an infinity turned upon itself." Brettell, "Van Gogh's Bedrooms at Arles," p. 150.

2. Naifeh and Smith, *Van Gogh*, p. 176.

3. I wish to thank independent art historian and curator Jean Goldman for her insights into the importance of the bedroom as a subject in Renaissance art. See also Blanc, "La chambre à coucher en France au moyen âge et à la renaissance,"pp. 40–67; and Chilton, *Bedroom*.

4. Giotto was one of Van Gogh's favorite artists and on his mind in 1888. See, for example, Van Gogh to Theo, Sept. 18, 1888, *Letters*, 683.

5. Van Gogh to Theo, Sept. 9, 1888, *Letters*, 677.

6. See Van Gogh to Gauguin, Oct. 17, 1888, *Letters*, 706.

7. Eugène Delacroix's painting of the tented bedroom of the comte de Mornay (c. 1833; Musée du Louvre, Paris) is a rare example of a painted empty bedroom. However, this work was a study for a larger painting (destroyed in World War I) with the comte de Mornay and Prince Anatole Demidoff portrayed in the room, so it was not Delacroix's final intention for the bedroom to be empty.

8. Van Gogh idolized both Delacroix and Menzel, but there is no evidence that links him to these interiors, either in Van Gogh's correspondence, the literature on the paintings, or their exhibition histories. According to Sabine Rewald, Menzel's interiors were pretexts for experiments in light effects. See Rewald, *Rooms with a View*, p. 18.

9. As Pamela Todd has noted, although the Impressionists often painted people in interiors, "Van Gogh's is the only one which shows an empty room; Bazille's portrait of Monet after his accident at the inn in Chailly the only one to show a man in bed." Todd, *Impressionists at Home*, pp. 145–46.

10. Perrot, *Histoire de chambres*, p. 187. While studying for theological exams that he was struggling to pass, Van Gogh employed a tutor, M. B. Mendes da Costa, who later recalled Van Gogh's behavior: "If he felt that he had forfeited the privilege of spending the night in bed, he would slip out of the house unnoticed and, upon returning late to find the door locked for the night, he forced himself to lie on the ground in a small wooden shed, without bed or blanket." Dr. M. B. Mendes da Costa, "Personal Reminiscences of Vincent van Gogh," *Het algemeen handelsblad*, Dec. 2, 1910; translated in Stein, *Van Gogh*, pp. 43–45. Firsthand accounts from neighbors of Van Gogh's self-deprivations are included in Secrétan-Rollier, *Van Gogh chez les gueules noires*; and Piérard, *Tragic Life of Vincent van Gogh*.

11. Van Gogh to Theo, Sept. 9, 1888, *Letters*, 677. In his thinking of subjects for a potential future painting, Van Gogh was recollecting another domestic interior, the "little nest" he had furnished for the prostitute Sien Hoornik and her newborn in the summer of 1882. As he wrote to his brother, Van Gogh felt the "unfortunate creature" gave him "hearth and home." Van Gogh to Theo, July 15 and 16, 1882, *Letters*, 246. See also Naifeh and Smith, *Van Gogh*, p. 284.

12. Van Gogh to Theo, Oct. 16, 1888, *Letters*, 705.

13. Van Gogh to Theo, Oct. 16, 1888, *Letters*, 705.

14. Van Gogh to Gauguin, Oct. 17, 1888, *Letters*, 706.

15. "By the end of this year I'm inclined to believe I'd have gained both my quite decent establishment and my health.... I would be a different man by the end of the year. I'd have a home and I'd have my peace of mind about my health." Van Gogh to Theo, May 4, 1888, *Letters*, 603.

16. On the artist's passion for *romans parisiens*, see Van der Veen, *Van Gogh, a Literary Mind*, p. 181.

17. See Hulsker, "Vincent as Collector," in Hulsker, *New Complete Van Gogh*, pp. 74–76.

18. In addition to memento mori images, these journals included illustrations of other kinds of empty bedrooms. See, for example, "Mr. Tweed's Sleeping-room," *Harper's Weekly*, Nov. 14, 1874, p. 932; "A Bedroom in the Barracks," *The Graphic*, July 31, 1880, p. 109; and "The Bachelor's Bedroom," *The Graphic*, Aug. 20, 1887, p. 193.

19. The artist's letters in which he refers to the Fildes print include Van Gogh to Theo, July 26, 1882; Van Gogh to Theo, on or about Dec. 11, 1882; Van Gogh to Anthon van Rappard, on or about Jan. 25, 1883; Van Gogh to Van Rappard, Feb. 23 and 26, 1883; and Van Gogh to Van Rappard, on or about Mar. 5, 1883, *Letters*, 251, 293, 304, 321, and 325, respectively.

20. Van Gogh paraphrased the genesis of Fildes's image, which was recounted in the Christmas issue of *The Graphic*, in a letter to Theo: "*Edwin Drood* was Dickens's last work, and Luke Fildes, having got in touch with D. through those small illustrations [for *Edwin Drood*], comes into his room ... sees his empty chair standing there, and so it was that one of the old Nos. of *The Graphic* had that striking drawing." Van Gogh to Theo, on or about Dec. 11, 1882, *Letters*, 293.

21. Van Gogh to Theo, Feb. 10, 1878, *Letters*, 140. One and a half years earlier, Van Gogh also copied the verses to a song about three empty chairs (representing three children who had died), which he included in a letter to Theo, Nov. 25, 1876, *Letters*, 99 (especially n. 4).

22. Van Gogh described *The Bedroom* as one of his best paintings. When he first returned to the Yellow House after his hospitalization in Arles, he wrote to Theo, "When I saw my canvases again after my illness, what seemed to me the best was the bedroom." Jan. 22, 1889, *Letters*, 741. Three months later, he wrote again about *The Bedroom*: "It's one of the best and I think that when you look at it you'll see more clearly what my studio, now foundered, could have been." Van Gogh to Theo, Apr. 30, 1889, *Letters*, 765.

23. In a letter to his sister about the third version of *The Bedroom*, Van Gogh wrote, "You'll probably find the interior the ugliest, an empty bedroom with a wooden bed and two chairs—and yet I've painted it twice on a large scale.... In telling you this you'll perhaps understand the painting quickly, but it's likely that it will remain ridiculous for others, not forewarned." Van Gogh to Willemien van Gogh, on or about Oct. 21, 1889, *Letters*, 812.

24. See the essays in this catalogue by David J. Getsy and Louis van Tilborgh, both of whom offer thoughtful interpretations of *The Bedroom* within the context of other works of the period and of Van Gogh's larger aspirations and life experiences. The three essays in this catalogue, together with the conservation study of the three versions of *The Bedroom*, demonstrate how endlessly multifaceted and layered Van Gogh's work is, such that no single vantage point ever exhausts the rich well from which the work emerges.

25. Chilton, *Bedroom*, pp. 147–49. This text discusses how a dead person's bedroom would be turned into a museum by preserving it in the same state as it was in when the person was living.

EXALTING THE UNREMARKABLE

—

DAVID J. GETSY

Exalting the Unremarkable: Van Gogh's *Poet's Garden* and Gauguin's Bedroom

The prospect of living with someone, however passionate or platonic, is always fraught with projections, hopes, and anxieties. Innumerable border scuffles are strategized and executed—a thousand little acts in a daily art of diplomacy. Safety and security (or their ideals) are ushered in with the idea that one will share one's habitus and habitat. Comforting and dividing, cohabitation is wrapped up with our beliefs in what gets us through our days, with what makes those days possible, and with the material confines that serve as glue to sociality.

Vincent van Gogh, in a period of ambition and hope, aspired to an ideal cohabitation that would involve not just life but work and art. His idea for a "Studio of the South" was both a commercial and a utopian endeavor, and he transformed his rental of a small house into a plan in which a new mode of painting would be cultivated and a brotherhood of painters nurtured. While others were considered, it was the older painter Paul Gauguin who became, in Van Gogh's mind, an essential cornerstone of the project. The two, together, would form the studio and live and work in concord.

At least, this was Van Gogh's hope in the months leading up to Gauguin's arrival. In May 1888, he signed a lease for a small, two-story residence (fig. 1) on the place Lamartine in the southern town of Arles, where he had been living for some months. It would be four months until he could move in. He was waiting for gas lighting to be installed, and, more importantly, he needed to acquire furniture. As he planned, Van Gogh wrote to Gauguin in Brittany, inviting him to the South. Gauguin would not arrive until the third week in October 1888, and Van Gogh spent the time leading up to his arrival painting the house, slowly purchasing some meager furnishings, and—crucially—decorating the interior. Van Gogh hung prints and filled the walls with his paintings made in anticipation of Gauguin's appearance.

This essay will focus on one of the major works done at this time—the painting that has come to be known as *The Poet's Garden* (plate 15), completed in mid-September 1888, in the collection of the Art Institute of Chicago.[1] Intended for Gauguin's bedroom, this painting can be understood to distill some of Van Gogh's hopes for the Studio of the South. After creating it, Van Gogh altered his initial plans for Gauguin's chamber, shifting to a new scheme in which *The Poet's Garden* would be joined by three additional paintings of the same subject sharing the same title.[2] As I will discuss, however, with this first work Van Gogh made a case—through the materiality and application of paint—for what art should do. *The Poet's Garden* is properly understood as a sort of manifesto, one that came to be directed at his confrère and imminent cohabitant.

The Poet's Garden was begun at a crucial point in the painter's preparations, after he had given much thought to what would be on the walls. During the four months of waiting, he undertook a suite of paintings that would key to various aspects of the interior. He aligned his work on the house with the practice of *décoration* that occupied many late nineteenth-century artists and critics.[3] A *décoration* involved a unity of ornamentation, art, furnishings, and design coordinated under an organizing principle. This integration of art and design was understood as a manifestation of the persona of the artist and, furthermore, as a vehicle for artistic innovation. Van Gogh, in dreaming of his Studio of the South, planned his *décoration* with Gauguin as its primary audience.[4]

In August 1888, after Gauguin declared his willingness to come to Arles, Van Gogh's initial plan for the *décoration* began to take shape. The impending move spurred his enthusiasm, and he started creating large, size 30 canvases, all intended to be placed on the newly whitewashed walls of the Yellow House. There was, however, some ambiguity in Gauguin's acceptance of Van Gogh's invitation, and an actual move date was left unspecified. In the days just prior to painting the Art Institute canvas, Van Gogh had written to Gauguin, pressing him on an arrival date.[5] It was this intense anticipation, mixed with doubt about whether Gauguin would actually come, that pushed Van Gogh in September to make some of his most ambitious and polemical paintings, such as *The Night Café* (fig. 2) and its initial chromatic inversion and daytime counterpart, *The Poet's Garden.*

Arriving at *The Poet's Garden*: Van Gogh's Changing Plans

Of particular concern was the upper floor's adjoining second bedroom, which Van Gogh hoped would be Gauguin's. Believing Gauguin to require more comfort than he did, Van Gogh gave much attention to this well-lit corner room. He wrote to his brother Theo, "There'll be the prettiest room upstairs, which I'll try to make as nice as possible, like a woman's boudoir, really artistic."[6] He had come up with a scheme to achieve this and had earlier written, "In the hope of living in a studio of our own with Gauguin, I'd like to do a decoration for the studio. *Nothing but large Sunflowers. . . .* The whole thing will be a symphony in blue and yellow."[7] In the initial plan, executed in late August, sunflower paintings (see figs. 3–4) were intended for many rooms of the house. Highly symbolic for the artist, the sunflower also reinforced the theme of the southern sun, making the interior evocative of this trait of the region that he so prized. Beyond this and other meanings, however, his reliance on the motif—he had originally envisioned between "half a dozen" and a dozen sunflower

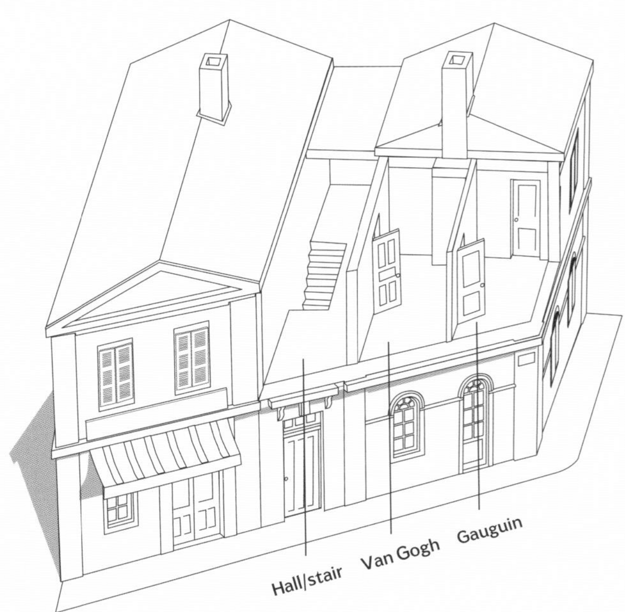

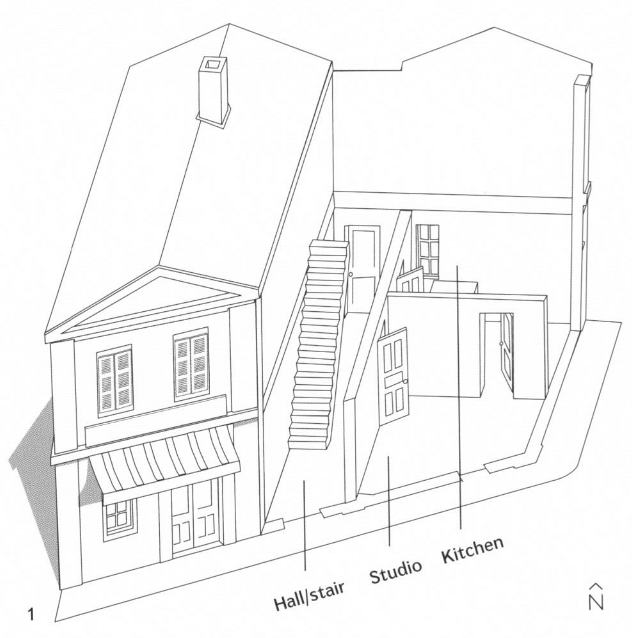

1

Fig. 1 *Top*, three-dimensional view of the Yellow House. *Middle*, section view of the second floor. *Bottom*, section view of the first floor. From Druick and Zegers, *Van Gogh and Gauguin*, p. 159.

paintings, of which he actually realized four—indicates that any individual symbolism the painting might have had singly was mitigated (by their planned repetition) in favor of their contribution to the overall *décoration*.[8] In particular, sunflower paintings were to fill the walls of Gauguin's bedroom.[9] Their number was reduced, however, after Van Gogh created *The Poet's Garden* series.[10] Throughout the autumn, he made these and other additions to the *décoration* of the house as a whole, including a selection of Japanese prints; lithographs by Honoré Daumier, Eugène Delacroix, and Théodore Géricault (all sent by Theo); and a group of portraits, some of which Van Gogh would eventually hang in his own room.

Before creating the first *Poet's Garden* canvas, the artist had been making paintings of the Yellow House and its surroundings. He had already done a major painting of the interior of a bar in town, *The Night Café*, over a few evenings in the first week of September. In the days immediately following, he shifted to a morning scene that would be its counterpart—*The Poet's Garden*.[11] The sun-drenched daytime garden inverted the intensified night-time scene of the café with its plunging perspective and exaggerated colors. He wrote soon after finishing the café painting that he had "tried to express the terrible human passions with the red and the green."[12] It was both the emotional tenor of *The Night Café* and its jarring use of complementary colors that Van Gogh reversed in *The Poet's Garden*, which is calm and quiet with its harmonious chromatic scheme and its idyllic scene. Such pairings of paintings in which the second would invert or comment on the first were central to how Van Gogh's plans for the *décoration* evolved. As Roland Dorn has discussed, this process allowed not only recombinations but also connections across works—wherever they ultimately were hung in the house.[13] This is the case with *The Poet's Garden*, which soon left its pairing with *The Night Café* behind as it became the foundation for the new plan for Gauguin's bedroom. This was among the last paintings the artist made before moving into the Yellow House.[14]

Excited by *The Poet's Garden*, Van Gogh made a new pendant for it a little over a week later.[15] It was a painting with a "round cedar or cypress bush" in the foreground and "a line of [oleander] bushes in the background." The painting (now lost) included two couples walking in the distance: a pair of women with parasols and an opposite-sex couple. This work is only known through two sketches in letters (see fig. 5).[16] In October he created another pair of paintings that, like the second canvas, include a male-female couple walking in the park—the *Public Garden with Couple and Blue Fir Tree: The Poet's Garden III* (fig. 6) and *Row of Cypresses with a Couple Strolling* (fig. 7). Together, these form a four-part cycle leading from the unpopulated early morning of the Art Institute canvas to the subsequent stages of the day, signaled by the increasing prominence of the two figures. He had painted the gardens before, but it was the Art Institute canvas that consolidated Van Gogh's belief that he should use the place Lamartine as part of the *décoration*.

Rendezvous in the Garden, Past and Present

In his letters, the artist explained his enthusiasm for making these new paintings by invoking the Renaissance. Since deciding to settle in Arles, he had attempted to justify to himself and others (such as Theo) exactly why he had chosen this small city. He associated the region with both Japan and the Netherlands, hoping that southern France would facilitate analogous approaches to light, perspective, and composition. Beyond these geographic associations, Van Gogh also looked back to the region's history and the poets with whom he associated it, such as Boccaccio (who had lived in Avignon and wrote about Arles). In June 1888, he wrote to the painter John Peter Russell of his intent to explain to him "something about Arles as it is—and as it was in the old days of Boccaccio."[17]

Some weeks into his stay in this new city, Van Gogh read an article on Boccaccio in the July/August 1888 issue of the *Revue des deux mondes*.[18] The piece discussed the conversations and correspondence of figures in the poet's literary and artistic milieu, such as Petrarch, Dante, and Giotto. Reading the accounts of Petrarch and Boccaccio's exchanges sparked Van Gogh's idea to layer onto his series of paintings a reference to the garden in which the poets purportedly conversed. Given the July 15 publication date of the *Revue* essay, it is likely that his engagement with the article only preceded the painting by a fairly short period (a few weeks to a month or so). Overall, the exact sequence of events cannot be fully determined, as Van Gogh did not mention the publication until a September 18 letter to Theo.[19]

Fig. 2 Vincent van Gogh (Dutch, 1853–1890). *The Night Café*, 1888. Oil on canvas; 72.4 × 92.1 cm (28 1/2 × 36 1/4 in.). Yale University Art Gallery, New Haven, Connecticut, bequest of Stephen Carlton Clark, B.A. 1903, 1961.18.34. F463, JH1575

2

Whatever the sequence may have been, the connection to the garden seems to have been activated by the presence of particular plants that Van Gogh observed in the place Lamartine. A few days after he had completed the Art Institute canvas, he wrote to Theo:

I have such luck with the house—with work—that I even dare believe that blessings won't come singly, but that you'll share them for your part, and have good luck too. Some time ago I read an article on Dante, Petrarch, Boccaccio, Giotto, Botticelli; my God, what an impression that made on me, reading those people's letters! Now Petrarch was just near here, in Avignon, and I see the same cypresses and oleanders.

3

4

Fig. 3 Vincent van Gogh (Dutch, 1853–1890). *Sunflowers*, 1888. Oil on canvas; 92.1 × 73 cm (36 1/4 × 28 3/4 in.). The National Gallery, London. Bought, Courtauld Fund, 1924. F454, JH1562

Fig. 4 Vincent van Gogh (Dutch, 1853–1890). *Sunflowers*, 1888. Oil on canvas; 92 × 73 cm (36 1/4 × 28 3/4 in.). Neue Pinakothek, Munich, 1912 Tschudi Contribution, inv. no. 8672. F456, JH1561

I've tried to put something of that into one of the gardens, painted with thick impasto, lemon yellow and lemon green. Giotto touched me the most—always suffering and always full of kindness and ardor as if he were already living in a world other than this.[20]

The plants were the main source of Van Gogh's enthusiasm, and they spurred further associations. In the same letter, he wrote, "My dear Theo, when you've seen the cypresses, the oleanders, the sun down here—and that day will come, don't worry—you'll think even more often of beautiful works by Puvis de Chavannes."[21] Coming on the heels of the association with Boccaccio, the reference to Puvis also hinged on the cypresses and oleanders. Rather than limiting himself to a single symbolic program for his series of garden paintings, Van Gogh layered and multiplied its meanings in his delight that this garden was across from the house that he had just moved into.

The intensity of these weeks in mid-September must be kept in mind when looking at *The Poet's Garden* series. While it is not directly iconographic or symbolic of the time of Petrarch and Boccaccio, it is infused with the artist's anticipation of new beginnings and the establishment of new traditions promised by the arrival of his housemate. It is for this reason that the innovations of the Renaissance came to Van Gogh's mind as he set to work on paintings intended for the space that would house the artists' fraternity for which he so fervently yearned. The letters of the poets that he read in the *Revue des deux mondes* article reinforced his hopes for an ideal community, and the garden came to be the imagined stage for this aspiration. As he would write to Gauguin several weeks later, "These parts of the world have already seen both the cult of Venus—essentially artistic in Greece—and the poets and artists of the Renaissance. Where these things have been able to flower, Impressionism can do so too."[22]

As the first painting of the series, the Art Institute canvas, especially, was tied up with the artist's conception of the garden outside the Yellow House as fertile ground for a new renaissance of painting, as he described in his letter to Gauguin:

The unremarkable public garden contains plants and bushes that make one dream of landscapes in which one may readily picture to oneself Botticelli, Giotto, Petrarch, Dante and Boccaccio. In the décoration *I've tried to tease out the essence of what constitutes the changeless character of the region.*[23]

Van Gogh was again making a case to Gauguin for why his impending move to Arles was a good one. Just at the time when his Studio of the South was about to become a reality, Van Gogh recalled (and probably reread) the article that discussed artistic collaboration and tied it to Petrarch's presence in the region. In that same letter of October 3, he wrote to Gauguin about the region's ties to "the old poet from here (or rather from Avignon), Petrarch, and at the same time the new poet living here—Paul Gauguin."[24] Thinking of the ways in which the younger Boccaccio turned to the older Petrarch for counsel, Van Gogh signaled (perhaps too obsequiously) the importance of Gauguin's arrival. This same letter is also the first reference to the series as *The Poet's Garden*; he also wrote to the artist Émile Bernard the same day using a very similar phrase.[25] This title, in other words, seems to have come to retroactively describe the first painting in the series.

In addition, the association with the poetry of Petrarch and Boccaccio has led some to interpret *The Poet's Garden* series as being about poetry's concern with the thematics of love.[26] The increasing prominence and seclusion of the strolling couples, keyed to the progress of the day, would seem to indicate that this theme structured the series. However, it is important to note that these are not necessarily the same couples, as there are clear differences in their clothes in each painting. Since Van Gogh prized working from observation, this multiplicity of pairings could be a subtle reference to (or merely the effect of) the nearby brothels, of which he was well aware and that also informed his understanding of the place Lamartine. A few days after finishing the Art Institute canvas, the artist wrote to Bernard about coming to Arles and the possibility of painting in the brothels.[27] Van Gogh's cognizance of their proximity to the Yellow House and the garden is repeatedly evident. He told Theo about the place, using the euphemism "good little ladies" (*bonnes petites femmes*):

But what scenery! It's a public garden where I am, just near the street of the good little ladies [...] But you'll understand that it's precisely that which gives a je ne sais quoi of Boccaccio to the place. That side of the garden is also, for the same reason of chastity or morality, empty of flowering shrubs such as the oleander. It's ordinary plane trees, pines in tall clumps, a weeping tree and green grass. But it has such intimacy! There are gardens like that by Monet.[28]

The second pair of paintings (figs. 6–7) that makes up the series depicts the couples alone on the side of the gardens with the coniferous trees. This landscaping, Van Gogh insinuated, avoided those trees and shrubs that could have provided cover for sexual encounters. Combined with the fact of the differing clothes, it becomes clear that there is not a unified or singular theme of love organizing the series. It seems, rather, to replay a recurring problem in Van Gogh's practice—how to balance a desire

Fig. 5 Vincent van Gogh (Dutch, 1853–1890). *The Public Garden ("The Poet's Garden")*, Sept. 26, 1888. Pen and ink on paper; 13.5 × 17 cm (5 5/16 × 6 11/16 in.). Private collection. F1465, JH1583

Fig. 6 Vincent van Gogh (Dutch, 1853–1890). *Public Garden with Couple and Blue Fir Tree: The Poet's Garden III*, 1888. Oil on canvas; 73 × 92 cm (28 3/4 × 36 1/4 in.). Private collection. F479, JH1601

Fig. 7 Vincent van Gogh (Dutch, 1853–1890). *Row of Cypresses with a Couple Strolling*, c. Oct. 21, 1888. Oil on canvas; 75 × 92 cm (29 1/2 × 36 1/4 in.). Location unknown (Nationalgalerie, Berlin, until 1937). F485, JH1615

for symbolic complexity and a belief in painting based on observation, not invention. Both the open spaces of the garden's landscape and the presence of couples can thus be seen to derive from the site that the artist chose.

Materializing Vision

Identifying Van Gogh's associations with the garden, however, does not foreclose or fully explain the meanings of these paintings.[29] One must be cautious about leaning too heavily on the title and on Van Gogh's associations of the series with the Renaissance. None of the four works, for instance, has any direct iconographic relationship to these contexts, and a discussion of topics such as Van Gogh's casting of Gauguin as Petrarch offers relatively little help in an analysis of the paintings themselves.[30] This is especially the case with regard to the first in the series. Van Gogh's excitement about *his* garden was driven by the ways he could deploy it, rhetorically, as an indication of the value of Arles, but the paintings are, more importantly, about the observation and transformation of what he could see if he crossed the street outside the front door of his new house and—more importantly—what he could see from the second bedroom's windows.

The choice to hinge the *décoration* of Gauguin's bedroom on this series is underwritten by this relation of proximity. Each day, Gauguin would wake to see both Van Gogh's painting of the morning garden and the windows that faced out onto the garden itself. As Van Gogh wrote to his sister Willemien, the bedrooms "look out on a very pretty public garden, and where you can see the sunrise in the morning."[31] It was this opportunity to have Gauguin compare the actual garden with his own painting that fueled Van Gogh's decision to make this work the grounds for a new plan. It became crucial to the message he was sending Gauguin about his own priorities with regard to working from observation in contrast to Gauguin's emphasis on imagination and invention. Whereas he told his sister that the garden was "very pretty," it is important to remember that he had described it to Gauguin as "unremarkable," setting up the contrast between his own painting's intensification and its prototype outside the window.[32]

The first *Poet's Garden* (plate 15) canvas did transform and amplify what could be seen in the public gardens. It depicts an expanse of grass studded with wildflowers and hedged in by trees and bushes, offering a view of the setting "under a pale yellow lemon sky."[33] Indeed, the colors of the sky are intense, and they echo tones used throughout the foreground, with its range of greens. The composition is divided into demarcated zones, with the foreground's spread of grass leading to the middle ground's smaller area, bound by the round bush on the left and the weeping tree on the right with the oleander at the direct center. Beyond that, a row of trees begins to dissolve into an almost aerial perspective as the dark greens give way to lighter oranges and browns. These trees are overtaken by the yellow sky, thick with impasto. On the far left, a blue steeple over the tree line picks up the light blue of the flowers dotted across the grass.

In its organization, *The Poet's Garden* follows the structure of most landscape paintings, in which an expanse of space and its visual recession moves from foreground to background. By convention, such works are sectioned into proportional horizontal bands in which the lowermost represents the most proximate space to the viewer's/painter's perspective. Following the image's depiction of space, one moves upward along the canvas's horizontal bands from foreground to middle ground to background (often rendered as sky). Most paintings of landscape follow this structure, in which the viewer's gaze is directed to move vertically up the painting as it engages with the illusion of spatial recession extended behind the picture plane. In *The Poet's Garden*, the relationship between the image created by the pictorial array and the flat material object's division into horizontal zones is an active one. Beyond the construction of an image of landscape, the move upward along the horizontal bands of the painting's surface also brings with it an increase in the literal depth of the paint's impasto. The flat picture of the garden's receding expanse, in other words, is interpenetrated with a literal projection of materiality out from that surface that grows as one's eyes track upward along the painting's surface to focus on the representation of sky.

In the band that represents the grass nearest to the position of the painter or viewer, the handling is light and the paint thin. Patterns of grass are visually generalized through the use of vertical brushstrokes with almost no literal depth. The vertical orientation of the brushstrokes continues until the tree line well into the middle ground, but they become more pronounced, thicker, and more varied when the forms of trees or bushes are outlined and demarcated. The weeping tree at right, for instance, has strong outlines and passages of short, broken brushstrokes throughout the dark green of the drooping branches, their weight reinforced by the dark values of the shaded lower foliage. By contrast, the bush to the left seems to emit energy through the use of thicker brushstrokes organized in a radial pattern. The progressive thickening of the brushstrokes continues to the tree line, where the predominantly vertical pattern gives way to a multidirectional one. The uppermost reaches of the tree line begin to meld into the yellow sky. That sky, however, returns to regularity with the use of emphatic horizontal brushstrokes applied thickly.

5

6

7

Fig. 8 X-ray image of *The Poet's Garden* (plate 15). The Art Institute of Chicago, 1933.433.

As noted in the conservation report on this painting, X-ray examination reveals how much this spatial organization was structured into the composition as a whole (see fig. 8).[34] The space around the two middle-ground trees has been carefully plotted out. Their dark outlines indicate thin areas in the paint surface, probably from holding the space for the trees in reserve when the first layer of foreground was painted. This planning is further indicated by vertical paint strokes at regular intervals along the bottom edge that are evident to the naked eye when the picture is unframed. They operate like and resemble a ruler's measured divisions, and their presence reinforces the emphasis on verticality that characterizes the lowermost band of the landscape painting and its depiction of the grass.

8

Overall, Van Gogh established a syntax in his use of vertical, diagonal, and horizontal regular brushstrokes. The strong distinction between the verticality that characterizes the nearby grass and the horizontality with which he painted the heavily impastoed sky is important in thinking through the effects of materiality in *The Poet's Garden*. It is the immediate foreground that could be seen most closely and most directly, and it was here that Van Gogh gave an indication of empirical measurement. The grass, after all, was underfoot. It could be seen, touched, and inspected. The painting, however, orchestrates a series of contrasts between the canvas's lowermost and uppermost bands. The vertical brushstrokes of the lower, foreground section are thinly applied, bleeding one into the next.

The horizontal brushstrokes of the background sky, on the other hand, are prominent, visible, and individualized. This was intentional on Van Gogh's part. He described the painting to Theo, writing, "There's a lemon-coloured sky above it all, and then the colours have the richness and intensities of autumn. Then it's done in much heavier impasto, plain and thick" (see fig. 9).[35] The medium-thick impasto of the trees was painted directly onto the ground layer, but the sky was underpainted with a thin layer of pale yellow that Van Gogh almost entirely covered over with a layer of the yellow, thick, horizontal strokes.[36] Unlike the still visible bright-green underlayer of the foreground and its scattering of thin, almost watery strokes, the sky's paint is piled up as part of Van Gogh's efforts to achieve both chromatic brightness and articulated material density. It would be unmistakable as paint—"plain and thick."

The syntax of the paint's thickness and directionality encourages the viewer to recognize that both the pictorial image and its material substance are in dialogue with each other. The experience of looking *into* the represented space (and following the bands from near to far, bottom to top, thin to thick) is an experience of tracking the increasing pictorial recession while simultaneously encountering the accumulating material presence of paint as one looks into the represented distance. As a result, the sky—which is not a thing and in its immensity cannot be touched, measured, or even outlined—has in Van Gogh's painting a real, impasto-heavy, physical thickness, which incites an almost tactile response.

This performance of paint's materiality in *The Poet's Garden* was Van Gogh's message to Gauguin. In his enthusiasm for what the Studio of the South could do, he wanted to make this canvas for Gauguin's bedroom as a reminder of painting's ability to transform and deepen the experience of the observable world. It is the ineffable and the immaterial—sky itself—that the work makes most tangible. The riotous yellows of the sky, in contrast to the thinness of the nearer grass, appear *more present* in their literal, material depth. This is an image of the painter's work of amplification, with Van Gogh showing how the aim is to make material that is beyond our quotidian grasp. That is, the artist made a case for observation but also showed how it is the painter's task to transform and intensify it. Here he did so by making the thick and tactile sky call attention to itself in contrast to the thin grass underfoot. In short, *The Poet's Garden* was for Van Gogh a statement about the painter's *vision*, which he claimed should be founded on observation and transformation.

This was, as discussed below, an ongoing concern in Van Gogh's ambitions. Within days of making *The Poet's Garden*, he would destroy for the second time his attempt to paint

Christ in the Garden of Gethsemane. He explained to Theo that he could not paint it if it was not based on observation: "Because here I see real olive trees."[37] He later wrote to Bernard about this failed work, "I mercilessly destroyed an important canvas—a Christ with the angel in Gethsemane—as well as another one depicting the poet with a starry sky—because the form hadn't been studied from the model beforehand, necessary in such cases—despite the fact that the colour was right."[38] The artist believed in working from and being inspired by the direct observation of nature. He did, however, amplify and alter those observations, and he even wrote to Theo about how he edited out some of the small bushes in *The Poet's Garden* in order to increase the painting's clarity. He continued to couch

9

Fig. 9 Detail of the top left of *The Poet's Garden* (plate 15) showing the horizontal impasto of the sky. The Art Institute of Chicago, 1933.433.

this as a form of accuracy to the observed site and its character: "Now it's true that I've left out some trees, but what I've kept in the composition is really like that. . . . Now that's the garden that's right in front of my house, after all. But this corner of a garden is a good example of what I was telling you, that to find the real character of things here, you have to look at them and paint them for a very long time."[39]

Intensely looking outward at nature rather than inward at imagination, Van Gogh argued, was how painters could make their works most vital and expressive. This, he knew, was a main source of contention with Gauguin, who argued that painters should work from invention and imagination. Van Gogh capitalized upon *The Poet's Garden*'s exaltation of that "unremarkable" public garden to make an anticipatory response to Gauguin.

Van Gogh had both the Art Institute's *Poet's Garden* and its pendant framed in walnut—the material out of which Gauguin's bed and elaborate chair were made.[40] Its use for all of these furnishings not only contributed to unifying the *décoration* but also communicated to Gauguin that *The Poet's Garden* was intended specifically for him. Writing to Theo just after the completion of the fourth painting in the series and just days before Gauguin's arrival, Van Gogh summarized how much he was addressing these works to Gauguin as a means to initiate their dialogue about painting:

I nevertheless pressed ahead as far as I could with what I had on the go, in a strong desire to be able to show him something new. And not to fall under his influence (because of course he'll have an influence on me, I hope) before being able to show him beyond any doubt my own originality. He'll see that anyway from the décoration *as it is now.*[41]

These were the emotions and aspirations that were tied up with the series from the first. Van Gogh's anticipation combined both hope for synergistic collaboration and fear of losing his own voice.[42]

Over the course of the nine weeks of Gauguin's cohabitation with Van Gogh, the two engaged in intense—and increasingly contentious—dialogues about the priorities and future of modern painting. *The Poet's Garden* was but the initial move in a contest that evolved from collaborative to agonistic. As happens with intense expectation, reality often does not live up to hopes and dreams.

Apart Together: Van Gogh and Gauguin at Home

It is important to remember that the Yellow House was no ideal space for living or for art. The ground-floor studio, while of a somewhat good size, was shared by the two painters. More intimately, the two small bedrooms on the upper floor were adjoining, so that Gauguin had to daily (and nightly) pass through Van Gogh's bedroom to get to his own. Especially given their different nightlife proclivities, this would have meant recurring negotiations about living space. Van Gogh's anxieties about social interaction were fueled by his observation of Gauguin's activities and a degree of jealousy about them. He wrote to his brother that the French painter was "particularly intrigued" by the women of Arles and, later, that he "has some success with the Arlésiennes."[43] Van Gogh, by contrast, had often stated that sexual activity distracted from the artist's task.[44] With this in mind, Gauguin's nocturnal departures would have been met with Van Gogh's disapproval as well as worry that his friend's time away from him also weakened their joint project.[45]

For Gauguin's part, he arrived at his new home to find it completely decorated (somewhat obsessively so) with Van Gogh's own canvases and prints by artists he admired. Van Gogh even came to include a painting of his own bedroom among the works in the house's *décoration* (plate 20).[46] In this way, *The Bedroom* reiterated the message that painting, according to Van Gogh, should focus on what could be observed directly. The strong-willed Gauguin was met with his new housemate's urging everywhere he looked. From this perspective, works like *The Poet's Garden* and *The Bedroom* were not just arguments about painting but were also evidence of Van Gogh's suffocating enthusiasm.

Surrounded by Van Gogh's canvases and having to endure his pleading yet judging attention every night when he came home to

10

Fig. 10 Vincent van Gogh (Dutch, 1853–1890). *Woman Reading a Novel*, Nov. 1888. Oil on canvas; 73 × 92.1 cm (28 3/4 × 36 1/4 in.). Private collection. F497, JH1632

Fig. 11 Vincent van Gogh (Dutch, 1853–1890). *Memory of the Garden at Etten (Ladies at Arles)*, 1888. Oil on canvas; 73.5 × 92.5 cm (28 15/16 × 36 7/16 in.). State Hermitage Museum, Saint Petersburg. F496, JH1630

Fig. 12 Paul Gauguin (French, 1848–1903). *Arlésiennes (Mistral)*, 1888. Oil on jute; 73 × 92 cm (28 3/4 × 36 3/16 in.). The Art Institute of Chicago, Mr. and Mrs. Lewis Larned Coburn Memorial Collection, 1934.391.

his own bedroom, Gauguin became increasingly dissatisfied with the arrangement. He talked of establishing a "studio of the tropics" that would be more in line with his own ambitions. Van Gogh began to see his own lofty anticipations—the ones that had infused *The Poet's Garden*—turn from hope to precariousness. Again, he looked to painting as a means to engage Gauguin in a dialogue, and a tipping point in their relationship can be located in the two pictures of chairs (plates 23–24) from the Yellow House that he executed rapidly in the middle of November, about a month after Gauguin's arrival.[47] While *The Poet's Garden* series distilled Van Gogh's anticipatory aims into the *décoration* of the home, these paintings drew on the lived reality of its furnishings to give voice to his growing awareness of the profound differences between himself and Gauguin.

He painted Gauguin's chair (plate 24) against a background of green and red, restaging Gauguin's use of these antagonistic hues. The horizontal line created by the join of the floor and the wall creates a stark bilateral division, flattening out the space and offering little sense of perspective or depth. This, too, evoked some of Gauguin's methods and the ways in which he replaced spatial recession with flat, mostly unmodulated fields of contrasting color. Van Gogh overlaid the bottom half of this division with reflections from a gaslight on the wall, spreading yellow glimmers across the red floor tiles.

Van Gogh set both chairs in the ground-floor studio in which the two artists worked. The red tiles can be seen in both pictures, but Van Gogh's painting of his own chair (plate 23) departs significantly from the other work in its color and depiction of space. He placed it against a daylight blue wall instead of a nighttime green wall, and diagonals dominate. Whereas the other image emphasizes flatness, this one showcases the ways in which he could amplify perspective (as in *The Bedroom*). The colors are far more harmonious, and Van Gogh's signature yellow gives both solidity and lightness to the chair. Van Gogh painted Gauguin's chair after dark, perhaps when the other painter was out at the local café; his own enjoys a flood of natural light.

Van Gogh's chair is one of twelve he had purchased in September.[48] Rush-bottomed and without arms, it evokes both simplicity and traditions of rural craft. With its curving lines, Gauguin's chair was the most intricate in the house, and it had been acquired specifically for the guest bedroom. On it sits a candle and books, indicating Van Gogh's continued faith in Gauguin as a source of inspiration. His own chair, however, holds a pipe and tobacco. Behind it is a box bearing his signature and containing onions. While these attributes would seem to show the artist's continued self-subordination to the example of Gauguin, the different ways of using color and space are also an assertion of his own artistic independence. Much like *The Poet's Garden*, Van Gogh placed emphasis on the painter's amplification and enhancement of the observable, quotidian world. These two chairs became a substitute portrait and self-portrait that, together, showed Van Gogh's ability to emulate Gauguin's practice while also keeping to his initial ambition to work from observation of all that surrounded them in the Yellow House and its environs.[49]

The Poet's Garden, *The Bedroom*, and the two chair paintings all take the exaltation of the unremarkable as their starting point. Van Gogh placed an emphasis on the amplification of observed reality, whereas Gauguin sought to introduce imagination and new imagery, likening his role as artist to that of prophet, able to see the unseen.[50] In *The Poet's Garden*, Van Gogh retained the traditional structure of landscape painting and maintained the importance of observation. Nevertheless, he transformed what he observed, stressing the *importance of paint itself* to make the "unremarkable garden" into something remarkable. Each day, Gauguin would wake to Van Gogh's painting, more vivid than the actual garden just outside the window. Just as the Studio of the South was becoming a reality, Van Gogh chose to make a case for the importance of observation as a means of achieving evocative and symbolic content. He wanted to keep his work rooted in reality, and he made the polemical move of showing Gauguin how the painting of the world outside could both resemble and exalt that which could be seen. But, as John House noted, "The paradox is, of course, that at this moment Gauguin was looking in quite the opposite direction for the roots of inspiration—not outwards to nature, but inwards to his own vision."[51]

11

12

Van Gogh did attempt to learn from Gauguin, and he wrote to his sister that Gauguin encouraged him "to work purely from the imagination."[52] Under Gauguin's influence, he explained, he tried to paint from memory (rather than direct observation), resulting in *Woman Reading a Novel* (fig. 10) and *Memory of the Garden at Etten (Ladies at Arles)* (fig. 11). The *Memory of the Garden at Etten* looked back to *The Poet's Garden*, using the place Lamartine as its setting. In that same letter he continued, "There you are, I know it isn't perhaps much of a resemblance, but for me it conveys the poetic character and style of the garden as I feel them." Emphasizing the dialogue with *The Poet's Garden*, he also told Willemien that he intended to hang this new painting in his own bedroom. Following this experiment, however, the artist returned to his commitment to observation, however amplified and intensified it became.[53] As has been argued, Gauguin recognized the ways in which these two garden paintings were directed at him. He responded to both with *Arlésiennes (Mistral)* in mid-December 1888 (fig.12), in which he more boldly redefined pictorial space, flattening out the stages of receding depth that structured Van Gogh's canvases. In that painting, he not only remade the scene from Van Gogh's *Memory* but also quoted—and anthropomorphized as a self-portrait—the bush from *The Poet's Garden*.[54]

Van Gogh already knew that he and Gauguin had differences before his friend arrived, and his anticipation of cohabitation led him to make a painting to stake out a position for himself. The preparations for the Yellow House were interwoven with hope and anxiety for Van Gogh, and just as moving into it became a reality, he made a manifesto in paint about how the observable world could be an endless resource for the painter without, however, leading to pure imagination and fabrication.

Van Gogh would reiterate this aim in one of the next major works he created after his intense period of working outdoors on the paintings of the garden of the place Lamartine—his *Bedroom*. Also intended as part of the *décoration* of the house, *The Bedroom* similarly amplified the experience of observation and set up a comparison between that which could be immediately seen and the painting that transformed it. He wrote coyly to Gauguin about this painting, saying that "it amused me enormously doing this bare interior."[55] But Van Gogh knew that—like the garden across the street—Gauguin would, in his daily life in the Yellow House, be confronted again and again by the comparison between the painting and what it depicted. He had walked through that bedroom every day on the way to his own, after all.

The significance of *The Poet's Garden* for this moment in Van Gogh's history has not been fully acknowledged previously, and it has often been overshadowed by other paintings that seem to dramatize the psychological complexity that has come to be associated with his work. That is, paintings like *The Night Café* and *The Bedroom* are receptive to readings that emphasize the painter's emotions and anxieties, and they have made the landscape of *The Poet's Garden* seem, to many, to be less revealing by comparison. Added to this has been the tendency to see all of the *Poet's Garden* paintings as a single endeavor. The initial painting in the series, I contend, is worthy of attention precisely because it evinces such a concerted effort by Van Gogh. It does this intentionally, with evidence not of anxiety but of conviction. This conviction, however, had its primary manifestation neither in subject matter nor in form but rather in the orchestration of paint's materiality.

I would like to thank Gloria Groom for encouraging me to write this essay and Kristin Hoermann Lister for her insights. My research assistant from the School of the Art Institute of Chicago's graduate program, Maggie Carrigan, was exemplary and contributed to the research for this essay. In the following notes, the artist and his brother are referred to as Van Gogh and Theo, respectively. The abbreviation *Letters*, followed by a number, refers to a specific letter in *Vincent van Gogh: The Letters*, ed. Leo Jansen, Hans Luijten, and Nienke Bakker (Van Gogh Museum/Huygens ING, 2009), http://vangoghletters.org/vg/.

1. The date is confirmed in a letter from Van Gogh to Theo, Sept. 16, 1888, *Letters*, 681.

2. There are paintings of the gardens at the place Lamartine that precede and follow the tightly linked series of four works that Van Gogh intended for the second bedroom and that have been grouped accordingly under his title *The Poet's Garden*.

3. A key source for Van Gogh was Bracquemond, *Du dessin et de la couleur*.

4. See Van Uitert, "Vincent van Gogh in Anticipation of Paul Gauguin"; and the extensive discussions in Druick and Zegers, *Van Gogh and Gauguin*; Dorn, "Vincent van Gogh and the Concept of *Décoration*"; and Dorn, *Décoration*.

5. Van Gogh to Theo, on or about Sept. 11, 1888, *Letters*, 680.

6. Van Gogh to Theo, Sept. 9, 1888, *Letters*, 677.

7. Van Gogh to Theo, Aug. 21 or 22, 1888, *Letters*, 666. Emphasis in the original.

8. See Van Gogh to Émile Bernard, on or about Aug. 21, 1888, *Letters*, 665, which mentions "half a dozen paintings of sunflowers"; and Van Gogh to Theo, Aug. 21 or 22, 1888, *Letters*, 666, which raises the number to "a dozen or so panels."

9. "But you'll see these big paintings of bouquets of 12, 14 sunflowers stuffed into this tiny little boudoir with a pretty bed and everything else elegant. It won't be commonplace." Van Gogh to Theo, Sept. 9, 1888, *Letters*, 677.

10. It is believed that two sunflower paintings continued to be included in Gauguin's bedroom after *The Poet's Garden* series commenced. This is based on a later letter in which Van Gogh mentions that two sunflower paintings (figs. 3–4) were hung together in the bedroom. Van Gogh to Theo, Jan. 28, 1889, *Letters*, 743. See further in Dorn, *Décoration*, p. 60.

11. Dorn, "Van Gogh and the Concept of *Décoration*," pp. 379–80. The morning scene of *The Poet's Garden* should also be seen in relation to the evening setting of the café's exterior in *The Café Terrace on the Place du Forum, Arles, at Night* (1888; Kröller-Müller Museum, Otterlo [F467, JH1580]). See also Dorn, *Décoration*, pp. 370–75.

12. Van Gogh to Theo, Sept. 8, 1888, *Letters*, 676.

13. As Dorn noted, "This [practice] permanently allowed alterations, regroupings within the *Décoration*. The first, that is, the genetic pendant relationship, is therefore not necessarily pointing to the factual decorative use." See Dorn, "Van Gogh and the Concept of *Décoration*," p. 380; and more generally, Dorn, *Décoration*, pp. 71–110.

14. In a letter of September 16, Van Gogh mentioned that it was his "plan to go live in the house tomorrow" and discussed the completed *Poet's Garden*, saying, "That's the first painting this week," citing as well his *Café Terrace* (see n. 11) and *Self-Portrait* (p. 59, fig. 8 [F476, JH1581]). Van Gogh to Theo, Sept. 16, 1888, *Letters*, 681.

15. On September 26, he wrote to Theo of the pendant's completion. Van Gogh to Theo, Sept. 26, 1888, *Letters*, 689.

16. Figure 5 was sketched in a letter from the artist to Theo, Sept. 26, 1888 (*Letters*, 689). The other sketch (JH1584) was in a letter to Eugène Boch, Oct. 2, 1888, *Letters*, 693. The latter, more abbreviated sketch from the October 2 letter only includes the pair of women.

17. Van Gogh to John Peter Russell, on or about June 17, 1888, *Letters*, 627.

18. Henry Cochin, "Boccace d'après ses oeuvres et les témoignages contemporains," *Revue des deux mondes,* July 15, 1888, pp. 373–413.

19. Van Gogh to Theo, Sept. 18, 1888, *Letters*, 683.

20. Van Gogh to Theo, Sept. 18, 1888, *Letters*, 683.

21. Van Gogh to Theo, Sept. 18, 1888, *Letters*, 683.

22. Van Gogh to Gauguin, Oct. 3, 1888, *Letters*, 695.

23. Van Gogh to Gauguin, Oct. 3, 1888, *Letters*, 695.

24. Van Gogh to Gauguin, Oct. 3, 1888, *Letters*, 695.

25. Van Gogh to Émile Bernard, Oct. 3, 1888, *Letters*, 696. The phrase in the letter to Gauguin of October 3 (see Van Gogh to Gauguin, Oct. 3, 1888, *Letters*, 695), is "jardin d'un poète," and in the one of the same date to Bernard is "jardin du poète."

26. See Van Uitert, "Van Gogh in Anticipation."

27. Van Gogh to Émile Bernard, Sept. 19–25, 1888, *Letters*, 684.

28. Van Gogh to Theo, Sept. 18, 1888, *Letters*, 683.

29. For a discussion of the theme of the garden among Van Gogh's contemporaries and of the more specific "poet's garden," see Van Uitert, "Van Gogh in Anticipation." As Van Uitert notes, such comparisons are limited, since "neither the extent of his knowledge nor exactly where he found the title can be precisely ascertained" (p. 196).

30. Van Gogh's general familiarity with the literary context is discussed in Johnson, "Vincent van Gogh and the Vernacular." However, Johnson overextends his analysis, basing it on an ungrounded assertion that each of the four paintings relate directly to one of the poets mentioned in Cochin's article. This results in interpretations that do not correlate with the evolution of the series nor with the paintings themselves.

31. Van Gogh to Willemien van Gogh, Sept. 9 and about 14, 1888, *Letters*, 678. He also wrote to Theo, "Opening the window in the morning, you see the greenery in the gardens and the rising sun and the entrance of the town." Van Gogh to Theo, Sept. 9, 1888, *Letters*, 677.

32. Van Gogh to Gauguin, Oct. 3, 1888, *Letters*, 695.

33. Van Gogh to Theo, Sept. 26, 1888, *Letters*, 689.

34. Kristin Hoermann Lister, conservation report for *The Poet's Garden*, Mar. 20, 1990, on file in the Department of Conservation, Art Institute of Chicago.

35. Van Gogh to Theo, Sept. 16, 1888, *Letters*, 681.

36. Kristin Hoermann Lister, conservation report for *The Poet's Garden*, Mar. 20, 1990, on file in the Department of Conservation, Art Institute of Chicago.

37. Van Gogh to Theo, Sept. 21, 1888, *Letters*, 685.

38. Van Gogh to Émile Bernard, on or about Oct. 5, 1888, *Letters*, 698. See discussion in Druick and Zegers, *Van Gogh and Gauguin*, pp. 142–44; and Edwards, *Van Gogh's Ghost Paintings*.

39. Van Gogh to Theo, Sept. 26, 1888, *Letters*, 689.

40. See Van Gogh to Willemien van Gogh, Sept. 9 and about 14, 1888, *Letters*, 678.

41. Van Gogh to Theo, Oct. 21, 1888, *Letters*, 709.

42. For more on this relationship and its combination of collaboration and rivalry, see Van Uitert, "Vincent van Gogh and Paul Gauguin," pp. 149–68.

43. Van Gogh to Theo, Oct. 27 or 28, 1888; and Van Gogh to Theo, on or about Dec. 1, 1888, *Letters*, 714 and 723, respectively.

44. In a long letter to Bernard, Van Gogh detailed his observations about a number of painters' sexual appetites and their effects on their art. He advised Bernard that "if you don't fuck too hard, your painting will be all the spunkier for it." As for himself, he wrote, "Personally, I find continence is quite good for me. It's enough for our weak, impressionable artists' brains to give their essence to the creation of our paintings. Because in thinking, we expend cerebral activity." Van Gogh to Émile Bernard, on or about Aug. 5, 1888, *Letters*, 655.

45. For a speculative, but illuminating, discussion of the ways in which sexuality was an element of Van Gogh's attachment to and desire for Gauguin's partnership, see Nagera, *Vincent van Gogh*, esp. pp. 132–50.

46. Van Gogh painted the first version of *The Bedroom* as part of the suite of size 30 canvases intended for the décoration. See Van Gogh to Theo, Oct. 16, 1888; and Van Gogh to Gauguin, Oct. 17, 1888, *Letters*, 705 and 706, respectively. That it was on display in the Yellow House is attested to in Van Gogh to Theo, on or about Oct. 29 1888, *Letters*, 715.

47. For the November date for these paintings, see Van Gogh to Theo, on or about Nov. 19, 1888, *Letters*, 721.

48. On the number of chairs, see Van Gogh to Theo, Sept. 9, 1888, *Letters*, 677.

49. See the more extensive analysis of these paintings in Druick, "Van Gogh and Gauguin," pp. 127–28; Druick and Zegers, *Van Gogh and Gauguin*, pp. 209–10. For another interpretation, see the essay by Louis van Tilborgh in this catalogue.

50. I benefited from Joan Greer's discussion of these issues at the Universities Art Association of Canada 2013 conference. As Greer noted, the distinction between Van Gogh and Gauguin is informed by their religious backgrounds: Van Gogh's Protestantism emphasized the humanity of Christ and, by extension, the empirical, whereas Gauguin's Roman Catholicism stressed the visionary. See also Silverman, *Van Gogh and Gauguin*.

51. House, "Post-Impressionist Visions of Nature," p. 580.

52. Van Gogh to Willemien van Gogh, on or about Nov. 12, 1888, *Letters*, 720.

53. In the period after the Studio of the South, Van Gogh did take more liberties with his compositions, for instance, with regard to the amalgamation of sources in *Starry Night* (1889; Museum of Modern Art, New York [F612, JH1731]), as is argued in Soth, "Van Gogh's Agony," pp. 301–12. The question of Van Gogh's emphasis on observation versus Gauguin's on imagination informed not just these developments but also the former's continued engagement with the latter's work, as Cornelia Homburg has argued with regard to Van Gogh's painting after Gauguin's *L'Arlésienne, Portrait of Madame Ginoux* (1888), in "Affirming Modernity," pp. 127–38.

54. This argument is made by Dario Gamboni in *Paul Gauguin*, pp. 86–89. See further Gamboni, *Potential Images*, pp. 88–90; and Druick and Zegers, *Van Gogh and Gauguin*, pp. 252–53.

55. Van Gogh to Gauguin, Oct. 17, 1888, *Letters*, 706. The day before, he had written to Theo about *The Bedroom* that "looking at the painting should *rest* the mind, or rather, the imagination," further indicating how the painting was part of Van Gogh's debate with Gauguin about imagination and observation. Van Gogh to Theo, Oct. 16 1888, *Letters*, 705.

THE BEDROOM

LOUIS VAN TILBORGH

The Bedroom: Van Gogh's Quest for Affection and Peace of Mind

When nineteenth-century artists depicted their homes, they tended to focus only on their studios, or, if fortune was smiling on them, they would throw open the doors of their well-appointed drawing rooms as well. In the autumn of 1888, though, Vincent van Gogh invited the world into the small, bare bedroom on the top floor of the house he had just moved into in Arles (plate 20). Although he was not the first artist to document such an intimate place, it was a rare subject.[1] The result is still astonishing. He had spruced the room up with a big bed and a few of his own paintings on the walls, but it was still a banal subject by the standards of the day. All the same, he had transformed it into "a thing of world class," to quote the Dutch painter and art critic Jan Veth, writing in 1893.[2]

Veth spoke of "artless" painting, but even if he is correct, there is no lack of refinement. The viewer is seduced, led into the scene without realizing it. The eye is drawn first to the bright splash of fresh, hot-pepper red just off center, and then the irresistible, receding perspective, combined with the empty foreground, pulls us into the scene. Although his jackets and beloved straw hat are hanging on the rack, there is no sight of the occupant, but we have been given permission to poke around in this personal, intimate space, perhaps just a little embarrassed as we do so. We can examine his toiletries (soap, a clothes brush, a hairbrush, and bottles containing what could be mouthwash and hair lotion) and raise an eyebrow at the bed for two.

The room, though, looks more like a monk's cell than a warm and welcoming love nest. Personal items are limited to the bare essentials, and it seems that comfort is unwelcome. The occupant will not find a soft rug beneath his feet when he steps out of bed, but a cold tiled floor. At the same time, there is nothing pitiful about the room. Everything is tidy and peaceful, and this impression is strengthened by Van Gogh's relatively calm brushwork. The bed is neatly made, unlike the one in Henri Evenepoel's *The Pink Bed (My Bedroom)* of 1896 (fig. 1), and there are no shoes or chamber pots cluttering up the floor.[3] The things on the dressing table stand tidily side by side, and the towel in this male household has not been tossed carelessly onto one of the kitchen chairs but hangs neatly where it always hangs, from a nail.

The Bedroom has been called Van Gogh's "most complex objectified self-image," a view of his sleeping quarters that tells us something about his "character, life-style and ambitions."[4] That "one can guess a man by seeing his rooms" had been a common conviction at least since the days of the Realists, and although from a biographical point of view such an approach is useful to understanding Van Gogh as a person, it seems unlikely that this was Van Gogh's point artistically when he painted *The Bedroom*.[5] All he said about the picture was that he wanted "to be suggestive here *of rest* or *of sleep* in general."[6] In his work, he searched openly for a broadly human expression rather than a narrowly individual one, and, except for his self-portraits, he wanted his art to transcend biographical peculiarity, which is clear from his early views on the subject: "When an artist shows his work to people he has the right to keep to himself the inner struggle of his own private life."[7] Or, as he put it in the same letter, more pithily and expressively: "An artist's work and his private life are like a woman in childbed and her child. You may look at her child, but you may not lift up her chemise to see if there are any bloodstains on it, that would be indelicate on the occasion of a maternity visit."[8]

Nowadays, though, thanks to Van Gogh's correspondence, we know so much about what took place under that chemise that there is a tendency to present what he wrote down about his life, feelings, and circumstances as part of his intentions when interpreting his works of art. That happened with *The Bedroom*, and this is hardly surprising. Depicted is the most intimate room in his home, and since we also see a bed with two pillows we have to resist the temptation to probe into his private life and to think, prompted by his letters, that he wanted to tell us something about his love life—or rather, the lack of one. The actual subject of the empty interior was "loneliness and desire for physical company," or so Carol Zemel asserted in 1997.[9] I myself have written, together with others, that Van Gogh "wanted to stress in his painting the atmosphere that only a companion and a stable family life could have brought."[10] Richard Brettell put it differently in 1986 but meant the same: "One might say its [the room's] potential for being filled, that must have mattered."[11]

However, without realizing it, we were simultaneously right *and* wrong. Even though at first Van Gogh really did want to express just "rest" with his *Bedroom*, lovers of historical irony will be pleased to learn that a year later he twisted the meaning of the work in a direction somewhat closer to the one outlined above. In 1889 he made two variants of the canvas (plates 21–22), and in them the portraits over the bed were turned into a self-portrait and a picture of a woman. Now, it seems, he was prepared to say something about the human need for a companion, and the main thrust of this essay is to clarify this change in his thinking and intentions. It will involve quite a tight focus on his evolving ideals regarding his own path through life, but first we must take a look at the three versions of *The Bedroom*, the circumstances under which they were born, and precisely what Van Gogh said about them in his letters.

An Unplanned Masterpiece

Van Gogh began work on the first version of *The Bedroom* (plate 20) on October 16, 1888. He became so enthusiastic while he was painting it that he wrote to his brother Theo about it that same day, adding a "little croquis" to the letter to give him "at least an idea of the direction the work is taking" (plate 19).[12] He finished the picture the following day and wrote about it again that evening, only in passing in a new letter to Theo, but at length in one to his colleague Paul Gauguin, together with another sketch of it (p. 71, fig. 2).[13] These two letters, almost entirely devoted to the description of a new work with the aid of explanatory sketches, are rather exceptional in Van Gogh's correspondence. They show how elated he was at the result:

1

Fig. 1 Henri Evenepoel (Belgian, 1872–1899). *The Pink Bed (My Bedroom)*, 1896. Oil on canvas; 32.5 × 41 cm (12 3/4 × 16 1/8 in.). Private collection.

Fig. 2 Vincent van Gogh (Dutch, 1853–1890). *The Potato Eaters*, 1885. Oil on canvas; 82 × 114 cm (32 1/4 × 44 7/8 in.). Van Gogh Museum, Amsterdam (Vincent van Gogh Foundation). F82, JH764

"It amused me enormously doing this bare interior."[14]

This was no fleeting euphoria in the first flush of the moment, for in a letter to Theo at the beginning of the following year, looking back on what he had achieved during his early days in Arles, he started by singing the praises of his *Sunflowers* (see p. 40, figs. 3–4) but then told his brother that "what seemed to me the best was the bedroom," so he evidently considered these to be the best works since his last shipment to Theo in Paris in mid-August 1888.[15] He later qualified the latter as "certainly one of the best," and when it was damaged by water he decided almost immediately to make a second version.[16] He did not get around to it until his Saint-Rémy-de-Provence period (plate 21)—September 1889—and, because he had also decided to make "reductions of the best canvases" for his mother and sister, he painted a smaller one for them as well the same month (plate 22).[17] The fact that he continued to treasure this picture for so long indicates that he did not regard it so much as the best of 1888 but as the best of his entire oeuvre.[18] If one searches in his correspondence for works that he treasured far beyond their date of origin, one finds three works that Van Gogh took to heart: *The Potato Eaters* of 1885 (fig. 2), *Sunflowers* (p. 40, fig. 3), and *The Bedroom* of 1888 (plate 20). Although he admitted that criticism of the first one was justified, these three works were in his own eyes his true chefs d'oeuvre, and they are still counted among his finest achievements.[19] Yet there are major differences between them. *The Potato Eaters* was a deliberate, premeditated attempt to produce a masterpiece; *Sunflowers* was also intended to be one, but while he was painting it he relied more on intuition than reason; *The Bedroom* was not planned as a masterpiece at all.

It came into the world after Van Gogh's "enforced rest" in mid-October.[20] He had worked as a man possessed the previous week and was "almost knocked out."[21] He slept for sixteen hours at a stretch from Sunday to Monday, but although his eyes were still "strangely tired" despite "two and a half days" of rest, he picked up his brush again on October 16.[22] His fourth and last version of *The Poet's Garden* (p. 43, fig. 7) could hardly be put off any more, but the mistral made it impossible to work out of doors, and that seems to have given him the idea to paint the spot to which his exhaustion had tied him for days on end: his bedroom.[23]

It was a brilliant idea. The unusual subject drew the best out of him, and that too can be attributed to the unusual circumstances. Less effort often yields surprisingly good results, and in his state as a "sleepwalker," Van Gogh probably gave his intuition freer rein than was usual for a subject that he found so interesting.[24] One simply produces better work "as if in a dream, and without suffering so much for it," as he had put it the previous week.[25] Having already half-convinced himself of the need to leave his will out of the creative process, he forced nothing, thus rising above himself.[26]

Van Gogh, however, repeated none of these remarks when he explained the smaller version of the painting (plate 22) to his sister Willemien in 1889. Unlike the original, this work and its predecessor (plate 21) are in the gestural style with more linear brushstrokes, which he had developed in Saint-Rémy, so the visual impact is far livelier and thus no longer restful. He suspected that many would find the subject "unimportant and ugly" and said that he had—referring probably to the motif rather than the style—tried to achieve "an effect of simplicity as described in Felix Holt."[31] This is a reference to the 1866 book *Felix Holt, the Radical* by George Eliot. It is the story of a middle-class man who embraced the sober, simple way of life of a skilled member of the working class. Van Gogh, in other words, was suggesting that his bare, plain

2

The sketches in his letters to Theo and Gauguin showed "how simple the idea" was: a nonsubject, "simply my bedroom," with "nothing in" it.[27] He thought it important to stress the room's emptiness, but however simple the room may have been, the scene was laden with meaning due to the stylization of his palette. "The colour has to do the job here, and through its being simplified by giving a grander style to things.... The shadows and cast shadows are removed; it's coloured in flat, plain tints like Japanese prints."[28] The aim of the manipulation of "all these very different tones" was "to express *utter repose*."[29] He wanted "to be suggestive here *of rest* or *of sleep* in general." Looking at the painting, he emphasized, "should *rest* the mind, or rather, the imagination."[30]

bedroom symbolized the deliberate rejection of all elegance and luxury.[32] He returned to this theme later in the letter: "I'd certainly like other artists to have, like me, the taste, the need for simplicity. In current society, though, an ideal of simplicity makes life more difficult, and he who has it, this ideal—he merely ends up, as in my case, unable to do what he wants." He then mentioned another model for his own modest way of life: "The Japanese have lived in very simple interiors, and what great artists have lived in that country!"[33] Although he misunderstood the aesthetic of the Japanese interior by likening it to Holt's way of life, the emphasis on a simple, sober life has been taken as the "key to the painting[s]."[34]

But is it? Van Gogh's explanation of 1888 is notably at odds with the one of 1889. Why did he start out by talking about rest and sleep only to say nothing about them a year later? And if he considered "the need for simplicity" as a way of life so important, why did he not mention it in 1888? It is a complex question, and in order to answer it we must take a closer look at Van Gogh's different circumstances at the moment of making the three versions of the bedroom, as well as at his evolving ideals regarding his own path through life, of which his search for simplicity was a part. The cultural-historical viewpoint of this essay employs the most productive and at the same time perhaps also the riskiest weapon available to the historian interested in biography: empathy.[35] It yields new and unexpected results.

The Course of Van Gogh's Life

Van Gogh's need to live a simple and sober life should be traced back not only to *Felix Holt* or Japan, but above all to his Protestant roots.[36] As Max Weber explained in *The Protestant Work Ethic and the Spirit of Capitalism* (1904–05), it was the fundamental duty of a true Protestant to pursue a life of austere virtue, avoiding joy and luxury as much as possible in order to demonstrate one's worthiness in the eyes of God. Unlike the Catholic monastic, however, a Protestant should strive for asceticism not by withdrawing from society but by living in society's very midst.[37] Rather than saying prayers between the walls of a cell, the faithful should earn God's grace through daily work, and to be more specific, not so much through work itself as through the way it is carried out. A believer's goal should be progressive improvement, step by step, as economically and rationally as possible, resulting in a sharp-eyed and clear-headed life.

3

Although it had its origins in the sixteenth and seventeenth centuries, this doctrine had lost none of its force in the nineteenth. It had taken on a life of its own, as it were, almost independent of religious affiliation, and had even intensified. The church as the guardian of rituals and dogmas was under pressure, and as a result faith was increasingly being identified with the protection of cherished values. It was a process that was taking place everywhere, most especially in England, where the Protestant work ethic was an integral part of what for ages were anachronistically known as "Victorian values."[38] "Blessed is he who has found his work. He has a work, a Life-purpose; he has found it, and will follow it!" Thomas Carlyle wrote in his *Past and Present*, which Van Gogh read and quoted. "All true Work is sacred; in all true Work, were it but true hand-labour, there is something of divineness."[39]

This doctrine placed an enormous weight on the shoulders of every Protestant adolescent. A young person's very first task was to decide which occupation would put one's God-given talents to the best possible use, and Van Gogh became acutely aware of this around the age of twenty, when he was working in the London branch of the art dealers Goupil & Cie. Shortly after his arrival there, he was impressed by middle-class Victorian norms and values, the essence of which had actually already been passed on to him by his parents, but which now, in his English surroundings, took on added force. He began to doubt whether the profession his father had chosen for him was actually the one to which he was most suited. Should he not pursue a more elevated "Life-purpose"?

On arriving in London in 1873, he felt himself to be "a true cosmopolitan," but within a year he was longing for the very opposite: an internalized and ascetic life.[40] From then on he filled his letters with references to scenes of saints, monks, pilgrims, philosophers, and American Puritans, and in doing so he became "one of those people who has seen the world from close up and has chosen to withdraw from it," as Theo later described to their sister Elisabeth.[41] At first he did not really know how to deal with this desire, apart from studying the Bible and neglecting his duties at work. After he was dismissed from Goupil in 1876, he pinned his hopes on a career in the church, but when he proved a failure as a lay preacher in the Borinage, an area of Belgium, he fell into the grip of a personal crisis. This crisis did not end until around 1880 when, after much hesitation, he embarked on a career as an artist.

He now believed that he had really found his calling in life, and like a "Christian labourer," he set out to live as simply and industriously as the main characters in the novels of Eliot, among them *Adam Bede, Silas Marner*, and *Felix Holt*.[42] In most of her books, she extolled the virtues of solitary craftsmen working away steadily in small communities with an Evangelical background (see fig. 3), and in his new career Van Gogh felt that he could match their moral path through life. By stepping "out of the world and [looking] to a quieter life with a craft," he believed that he could best demonstrate the conscious and clear-headed life demanded by the Protestant work ethic.[43] Previously he had tried to do so by moving back in with his parents in the village of Etten in the southern Dutch province of Brabant, but he did not find his ideal working environment until 1882, when he rented a place in The Hague. That first-floor apartment was in a genuine working-class district and, to his great joy, it looked out over a carpenter's yard and a garden (see fig. 4).

He lived up to his belief that he belonged to the working class by fitting out his apartment with "furniture in true 'village constable style,'" as his family called plain, long-lasting household goods, and he noted buying "real kitchen chairs, . . . and a really sturdy kitchen table."[44] The furnishings had to exude an air not only of simplicity and reliability but also of "peace" and "order." Soon afterward he moved to slightly roomier quarters in the same apartment block, which he described as "plain" and "bright." The shelves were given a good scrubbing when he moved in, and his "drawing boards, portfolios, boxes, sticks, &c." were neatly arranged.[45] Even though he had taken on a "cleaner," blessed as he was with two left hands when it came to domestic chores, the message was clear: order and neatness were necessary to a hardworking, fruitful, and respectable life.[46]

But it was necessary not only to abandon so-called "civilization [and] to learn a craft," but also to "marry a woman," because the prevailing Christian view was that life's purpose could not be completely fulfilled without love and, ultimately, a family.[47] In theory, then, Van Gogh was a true follower of his parents' values and of the standards that held sway in the first half of the nineteenth century, but he did realize that he was a bit late in adopting them: men were expected to be married by the time they were thirty in those days.[48] This helps to explain why at the age of twenty-eight, despite an unshakable refusal, he continued to pursue his cousin Kee Vos, a widow seven years his senior with a young son, in the hope that she would accept his proposal of marriage. He had "a strong, passionate love" for her, which he believed would also help him to practice his profession: "I think that nothing sets us down in reality as much as a true love."[49] However, he was blind to the fact that his class-conscious family already regarded him as an outsider, because of his financial dependence on Theo, as well as his idea that "work lies in the heart of the people."[50]

The refusal of virtually everyone to give him a helping hand with his courtship of his cousin hit him hard, and soon afterward he sought comfort and intimacy with another older woman, the pregnant prostitute Sien Hoornik. After a while they began living together, and he even wanted to marry her, but he ran into even fiercer opposition to that idea. However much he protested that he was doing nothing more than what his own class had laid down as an ideal—finding fulfillment in life, getting married and starting a family, as well as extending a helping hand to those less fortunate—his parents and the circle around them now really did turn their backs on him. He had truly become an outcast; he had stooped "beneath [his] station," as the saying went.[51] Even Theo was against the marriage, and Van Gogh eventually dropped the idea. At the end of 1883, he left Sien and her children after a difficult eighteen months together.

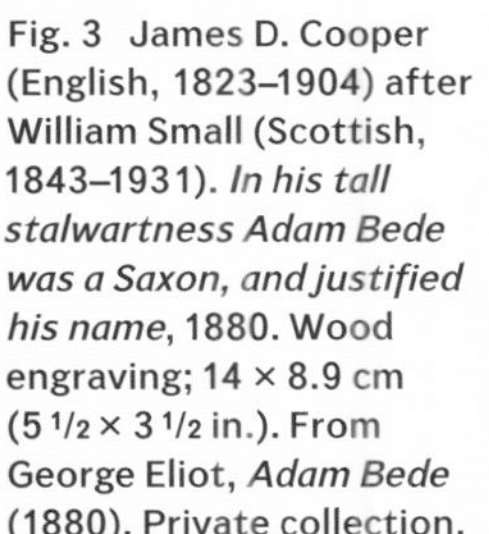

Fig. 3 James D. Cooper (English, 1823–1904) after William Small (Scottish, 1843–1931). *In his tall stalwartness Adam Bede was a Saxon, and justified his name*, 1880. Wood engraving; 14 × 8.9 cm (5 1/2 × 3 1/2 in.). From George Eliot, *Adam Bede* (1880). Private collection.

Fig. 4 Vincent van Gogh (Dutch, 1853–1890). *Carpenter's Yard and Laundry*, late May 1882. Pencil, black chalk, pen, and brush in black ink, brown wash, opaque watercolor, scratched, traces of squaring, on laid paper; 28.6 × 46.8 cm (11 1/4 × 18 7/16 in.). Kröller-Müller Museum, Otterlo. F939, JH150

4

A Moral, Purposeful Life Ebbs Away

Van Gogh blamed his family for the failure of his simple, well-ordered, craftsman-like existence with a wife and children, and it scarred him. He had finally found his direction in life after an unhappy start, and even though his chosen path was an unconventional one, he defended this choice fiercely, almost blindly. He felt that he had done nothing other than seek a suitably purposeful, moral life of the kind that his own class had held up to him as the norm. By now, though, he had been banished from that class, and from then on his distrust of the bourgeoisie turned into total rejection. To his despair, however, he still had to depend on its financial generosity. In Nuenen, the Netherlands, where he was now living, a second attempt to marry an older woman, which was probably opportunistic, ended in disaster, and he began to lash out at everyone. In 1884 he even blamed Theo, who had been his financial lifeline for two years, saying, "You can't give me a *wife*, you can't give me a *child*, you can't give me *work*. Money—yes. But what good is it to me if I have to do without the rest?"[52]

In The Hague he had already started casting around for a solid basis for his unusual social position as an artist and, thanks to the novels of French Realist authors, he began taking an interest in the golden age of the first Paris bohemians.[53] After a visit to the painter George Breitner in 1883, he was a little shocked, however, at what a bohemian life meant in practice. Breitner's apartment, he wrote, "was furnished mainly with various matchboxes (empty), and then with a razor or something, and a cupboard with a bed in it," which led him to conclude "that one can count oneself lucky if one is in relatively normal surroundings in today's society, and doesn't have to seek refuge in a coffee-house life which will make one begin to see things ever more cloudily and confusedly."[54] Bohemianism, in other words, entailed a dereliction of the proper attitude toward work, which gave him cause for thought, as a disciplined work ethic was still as sacred to him as it had been in 1880.

Given his isolated position, it was not surprising, however, that he was finding it more and more difficult to meet the demands of an elevated life, and the first thing to fall by the wayside was the facade of decent, genteel poverty in the mold of figures like Felix Holt. It was replaced by opportunism and a certain indifference. He stopped caring as much, and he dropped the pretense of keeping up appearances. His studio in Nuenen—which he began using in 1884 and later moved into—looked "really bohemian," according to his friend Anton Kerssemakers, with "a great heap of ashes around the stove, which had never known a brush or stove polish, a small number of chairs with frayed cane bottoms," and in contrast to the way Van Gogh had cared for his work in The Hague, his studies were not properly arranged and tidied away but instead lay scattered on the floor.[55]

In reality he was still far from being a true bohemian. He may have behaved and dressed oddly, and he had developed a healthy distaste for the bourgeoisie, but he still worked like a mule and also continued to feel fortified in his ideals by the example of the working man's life of family and labor, from which he took his subjects, culminating in his *Potato Eaters* (fig. 2 above). "I feel for *the brood and the nests*—particularly those *human* nests, those cottages on the heath and their inhabitants."[56] But this love of subjects that matched his own ideals of a simple, elevated, and industrious life was proving untenable. Theo was urging him to modernize, and the pressure to choose subjects that would sell was growing, until eventually he decided that it was time to change course, although it was not easy.[57] At the end of 1885, he left for Antwerp and later Paris, where he exchanged his old repertoire of hardworking peasants and laborers for brightly colored still lifes of flowers and semitouristic portraits of the windmills in the popular Montmartre district.

It was a defeat when seen from his earlier perspective, but after years of worrying about his duty, he seems to have been happy to relax and take things easier. Living in Montmartre, where the bohemian life of the past had in fact become commercialized, he abandoned his old ideal of a sober and industrious life and instead embraced joie de vivre.[58] At any rate he advised his sister at the end of 1887 to "enjoy yourself as much as you can and have as many distractions as you can." Loftier goals were now also suspicious: "Why are religion or law or art so sacred?"[59] Although we have far less information about his life at this time than when he was back in the Netherlands, we do know that in the winter of 1886–87 he eagerly surrendered to the "coffee-house life" that he had considered such an abomination three years earlier. Probably together with his comrades he visited Aristide Bruant's cabaret, the gaiety of which is depicted so vividly by Henri de Toulouse-Lautrec (fig. 5), and depictions of himself smoking and drinking at a bar were undoubtedly an accurate picture of the life he was leading.[60] He had "the most impossible and highly unsuitable love

5

Fig. 5 Henri de Toulouse-Lautrec (French, 1864–1901). *The Refrain of the Chair in the Style of Louis XIII at the Cabaret of Aristide Bruant*, 1886. Conté crayon, oil on paper; 78.4 × 50.4 cm (30 7/8 × 19 13/16 in.). Hiroshima Museum of Art.

Fig. 6 Vincent van Gogh (Dutch, 1853–1890). *Study for "Reclining Female Nude,"* Jan.–June 1887. Pencil on paper; 24 × 31.6 cm (9 7/16 × 12 7/16 in.). Van Gogh Museum, Amsterdam (Vincent van Gogh Foundation). F1404, JH1213

affairs," and it does not come as a surprise that there was a sharp drop in his output in this period.[61] We know about his infatuation with the Italian Agostina Segatori, but it was probably preceded by an affair with a streetwalker, who can be seen in several of his artworks (see fig. 6).[62] It was when he was around twenty that he had first embarked on what Gauguin later called "nocturnal excursions of a hygienic sort," which is how he later got to know Sien Hoornik, but these meetings with ladies of easy virtue, which in those days were seen as a necessary, unspoken evil, now became a part of his artistic life, together with the new, salacious way of talking about women that he shared with friends like Émile Bernard and Lautrec.[63]

This bohemian life had taken its toll by the end of 1887. Van Gogh was hardly painting or drawing anymore, and was "very, very upset, quite ill and almost an alcoholic through overdoing it, while [his] strength was abandoning [him]."[64] That was how he depicted himself in a self-portrait (fig. 7), with "something like, say, the face of—death."[65] In those days, people in their forties were already considered old, and because he had neglected himself for so long he felt, at the age of thirty-four, that he was already "a little old man, you know, with wrinkles, with a bristly beard, with a number of false teeth, &c."[66] He was "well on the way to catching a paralysis" and, in order to make something of life before it was too late, he decided to start all over again.[67] Difficult times demanded drastic measures.

Working and Living Together: A New Alternative

At the beginning of 1888, Van Gogh left Paris for the provincial town of Arles, where distractions would be at a minimum in surroundings that he thought met the modern imperative "to see colour under a stronger sun and in a more Japanese clarity."[68] He might have already been taken to task by his and Theo's doctor, David Gruby, who was popular among artists and writers, and above all practical.[69] He now clung to the life raft of regularity, which meant a return to the old, strict work regime he had followed before going to Paris—work, work, and nothing but work. He stopped drinking and "smoking so much," and as a result once again lived as he had in The Hague, "like a monk, . . . bound up in his work and not inclined to waste his time."[70] In the South of France, he actually imagined that he was living in the equivalent of a colorful, supposedly primitive Japan, and, probably after reading Pierre Loti's *Madame Chrysanthème*, he hit upon the apt idea of depicting himself as a Buddhist monk (bonze), or simple disciple (fig. 8), with closely cropped hair and almond-shaped eyes.[71]

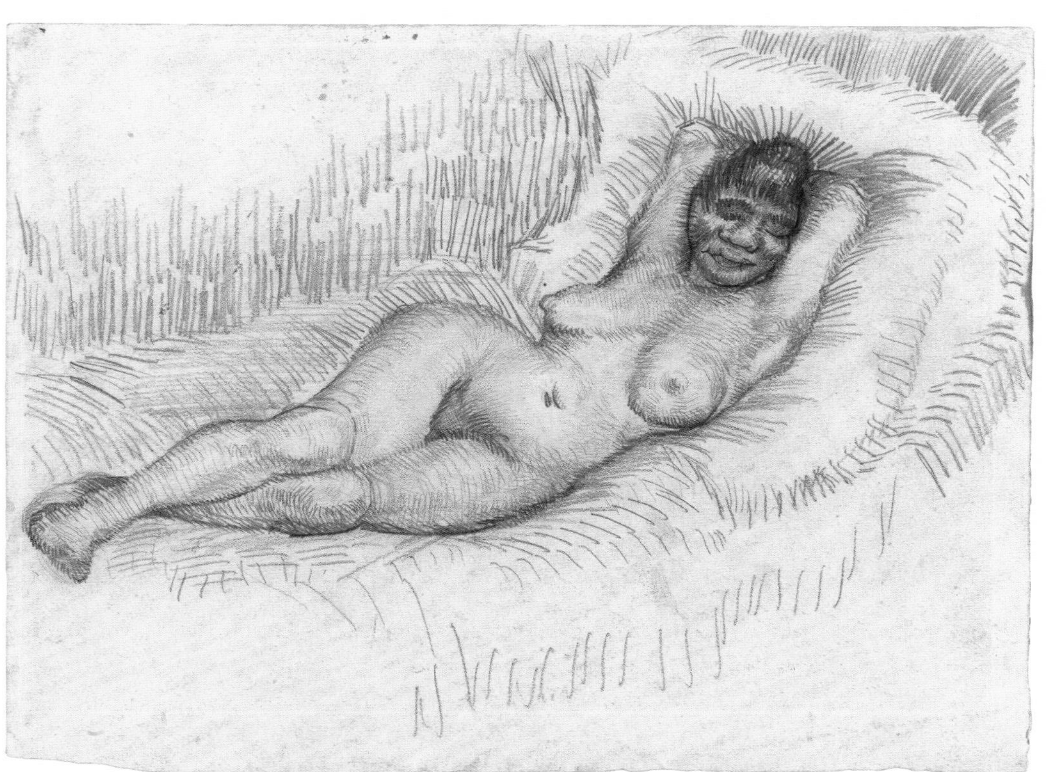

6

Van Gogh had long ago given up all hope of starting a family, and embarking on improper love affairs of the Parisian kind (even assuming that this would have been possible in Arles) would have conflicted with his well-ordered existence devoted entirely to work. He thus made do instead with regular fortnightly visits to the brothel.[72] Although these precautions

Fig. 7 Vincent van Gogh (Dutch, 1853–1890). *Self-Portrait as a Painter*, 1887–88. Oil on canvas; 65.1 × 50 cm (25 5/8 × 19 11/16 in.). Van Gogh Museum, Amsterdam (Vincent van Gogh Foundation). F522, JH1356

Fig. 8 Vincent van Gogh (Dutch, 1853–1890). *Self-Portrait Dedicated to Paul Gauguin*, 1888. Oil on canvas; 61.5 × 50.3 cm (24 3/16 × 19 13/16 in.). Harvard Art Museums/Fogg Museum, Bequest from the Collection of Maurice Wertheim, Class of 1906, 1951.65. F476, JH1581

brought order back into his life, they felt psychologically like stopgaps. Previously he had worked out of a sense of duty with a loftier moral goal, but that idea had ebbed, and this state of mind, combined with the lack of clear prospects for the future, now left him feeling empty. "I'm definitely better now, but hope, the desire to achieve, is broken and I work from necessity, so as not to suffer so much mentally, to distract myself."[73]

His need for an ordered, industrious life was also not helped by his temporary lodgings—a hotel that he shared mainly with shepherds. After two months, he started looking around for a roof of his own. On the first of May, he signed the lease to a suitable house on the north side of town, just beyond the city walls, consisting of "4 rooms, or more precisely, two, with two little rooms."[74] Not having any household goods or furniture, he used it at first as a studio and storage space, but four months later, when the situation at the hotel had become "intolerable" and not "compatible with thoughtful work," he furnished the house with the aid of an extra contribution from Theo, who had just inherited some money.[75]

From the very outset, Van Gogh had planned to live in the house with other artists. Whereas he used to think that he was doomed to failure without "true love," without a wife and children, he had evidently come to the conclusion at the end of his time in Paris that, if he could not reach the "natural" way of life, he only had a future as a painter if he belonged to a community of artists.[76] He could now put that plan into action, and he staked all he had on a collaboration with Gauguin. Van Gogh moved into the house in mid-September, and together with his friend's promise to come and stay in the near future, this suddenly opened up new possibilities: "It's beginning to appear on the horizon: Hope."[77]

With his own roof over his head, Van Gogh, the reluctant adventurer and bohemian, could finally put down roots; if he could do so for long enough, he thought, there was a realistic chance that France would indeed become his second home. In his house, he lost himself in "the reassuring, familiar look of things" and, as he had done in The Hague, he hired a cleaner who kept the "tiles nice and red and clean."[78] The great advantage of his new home, though, was that it would give him all the peace and quiet he needed to develop his personal artistic vision; as a result, Theo's years of generosity would with any luck be repaid with a considerable increase in the value of his paintings. It was for that reason that he wanted to decorate the house from top to bottom with works of art he had made in Arles, turning it into "AN ARTIST'S HOUSE," but "not precious, on the contrary, *nothing precious.*"[79]

Furnishing the House

In order to make the house look as artistic as possible, Van Gogh took great trouble over the two bedrooms on the upper floor.[80] He felt that the guest room was "the prettiest" one, "almost elegant," and by decorating it with his pictures of sunflowers he would make it "as nice as possible, like a woman's boudoir."[81] "Wide double beds" were installed in both rooms, but Gauguin's was made of walnut, while Van Gogh chose the cheaper pinewood for himself. That would suit the furnishing of his room better, which had to be "exceedingly simple."[82] As he had done in The Hague, he chose simple, "sturdy" furniture, "square and broad." He bought rush-bottomed kitchen chairs for himself, but he gave Gauguin an armchair to match the more feminine nature of his room (see plate 24).

Van Gogh undoubtedly wanted Gauguin to have the more attractive room because he needed to make him feel as comfortable as possible. His friend was a former stockbroker who had lived in style and still adopted the air of a man of the world, and Van Gogh wanted to oblige him. His idea of furnishing Gauguin's room like a boudoir may have been prompted by another side of his friend's nature. Van Gogh found him "a very spirited painter," that is, endowed with a powerful poetic imagination, which was considered to be feminine in those days.[83] It was a talent that was absolutely essential for depicting southern, more "primitive" parts of the world convincingly, and according to Van Gogh, Gauguin had demonstrated that he was a real master at that with his *Mangoe Trees, Martinique* (fig. 9), which Theo had purchased.[84] It is a painting of Martinique, but Van Gogh hoped that the special talent that it displayed could also be employed in the surroundings they would now share—Provence. When Gauguin announced that he would be coming, Van Gogh even made a portrait of him as "the Poet," for which he used an acquaintance, the Belgian artist Eugène Boch, as the stand-in, because he had the same sort of Dantean features (plate 13).[85]

Although Van Gogh described his own room to Theo as "exceedingly simple," that was not strictly true. His double bed, like one from a better-quality hotel room, was more suited for Gauguin's lifestyle. For Van Gogh, however, that bed was a luxury, utterly at odds with his ideal of the simple life, so it took a bit of explaining to justify the expensive purchase to Theo. "It gives a look of solidity, durability, calm, and if it takes a bit more bed-linen, that's too bad."[86] Since Van Gogh had turned his back on "unsuitable love affairs" in favor of a life devoted to work, he would never have bought the bed with a view to the possibility of an intimate relationship with a woman.[87] But that did not apply to Gauguin, and it very much looks as if he acquired it simply because his friend had to have one.

7

8

9

Fig. 9 Paul Gauguin (French, 1848–1904). *The Mangoe Trees, Martinique*, 1887. Oil on canvas; 86 × 116 cm (33 7/8 × 45 11/16 in.). Van Gogh Museum, Amsterdam (Vincent van Gogh Foundation).

10

Fig. 10 Venus of Arles (Roman copy of an Aphrodite by Praxiteles), end of the 1st century B.C., restored by François Girardon. Marble; height, 194 cm (76 3/8 in.). Musée du Louvre, Paris.

Fig. 11 Toyohara Kunichika (Japanese, 1835–1900). *Actor Ōtani Tomoemon V as Michikaze*, from an untitled series of actor portraits, 1869. Wood-block print (*nishik-e*), ink and color on paper; vertical *ōban*; 39.4 × 26.5 cm (15 1/2 × 10 7/16 in.). Museum of Fine Arts, Boston, William Sturgis Bigelow Collection, 11.16151.

He himself would probably have been perfectly happy with a cheap, single bedstead made of iron, but he did not want to risk Gauguin thinking that he was unmanly. His friend had a reputation as a womanizer and was a great subscriber to the widely held belief that free love, untrammeled by any restrictions, was the norm in warmer places such as Arles.[88] Van Gogh shared that view, which he reflected in the furnishings of the guest room in order to convince his colleague that he was not wasting his time by coming to Provence.

The women of Arles were famed for their beauty and their daring, even dangerous ideas about love, and although Van Gogh had already depicted local lovers soon after arriving in the town, his interest in this theme blossomed at a later date, when he started thinking about how he should receive Gauguin in his home.[89] He began painting views of parks, which he presented as modern variants of artist Adolphe Monticelli's *fêtes galantes*. Indirectly referring to the famous Venus of Arles in the Musée du Louvre (fig. 10), a nineteenth-century copy of which he had seen in the Musée Lapidaire in Arles, he insisted to Gauguin that "these parts of the world have already seen both the cult of Venus—essentially artistic in Greece—and the poets and artists of the Renaissance."[90] At first he had wanted to decorate Gauguin's room solely with his still lifes of sunflowers but did not have enough of them, so he planned to add four such park scenes, giving all of them the honorific title *The Poet's Garden*.[91] He had already painted two of them (plate 15 and see p. 43, fig. 5) and now made two more especially for the occasion (p. 43, figs. 6–7). In three of them the main subjects are lovers, and in this way he hoped to show Gauguin that Provence was the ideal place for his genius to flourish.[92] As a connoisseur of free love and poet of the "primitive" south, Gauguin would be at home there.

We know from a letter from Saint-Rémy that Van Gogh did not much like seeing his "own paintings" in his bedroom, probably because he fretted about whether they were any good, which kept him awake.[93] Nevertheless, he hung two in his bedroom in Arles, *Eugène Boch* (which Van Gogh referred to as *The Poet*) (plate 13) and *The Lover (Portrait of Lieutenant Milliet)* (plate 14).[94] Once again, he did this with Gauguin in mind. *The Lover* was a portrait of the Zouave Paul-Eugène Milliet, who "makes love so easily that he almost has contempt for love."[95] By hanging it with *The Poet*, he again wanted to show that Gauguin's way of life could easily be part of their "studio-refuge right at the entrance to the south."[96] He had also placed them in positions where his guest could not fail to see them. Gauguin's bedroom could only be reached by passing through Van Gogh's; in other words, *The Poet* and *The Lover* smiled at Gauguin every day.[97]

The Bedroom—Three Versions, Three Interpretations

If Van Gogh's personal taste and need for simplicity in his bedroom were tempered by his desire to make Gauguin feel at home, he made it clear again that his 1888 painting was not intended to be an "objectified self-image."[98] That is a term that can only be applied to *Van Gogh's Chair* (plate 23), the companion piece to *Gauguin's Chair* (plate 24). He called those studies "rather funny," because he was employing earlier imagery of a chair as a person.[99] These still lifes were portraits of the two inhabitants, presenting their artistic identities in an unusual way. The solid, rather rustic, rush-bottomed chair symbolized Van Gogh's own artistic vision, which was based on the simple, industrious life that he had chosen back in 1880, and to which he had returned after leaving Paris, whereas Gauguin's feminine armchair portrayed him as the spirited painter blessed with great sensitivity and thus the right person to paint southern, exotic countries.[100] The humor spills over into the compositions, because both chairs are too cramped by the frames, in a manner that seems borrowed from Japanese prints like those by Toyohara Kunichika, who had become famous for tautly framed close-up portraits (see fig. 11).

Now, to come back to what has been discussed above, Van Gogh never suggested in his correspondence that *The Bedroom* was a disguised self-portrait like *Van Gogh's Chair*, but he did say that it represented rest and sleep, and that explanation turns out to be very understandable. He ended his letter about the work to Theo with the idea that "looking at the painting should *rest* the mind, or rather, the imagination"—which clarifies a great deal.[101] Van Gogh was expressing his hope that the canvas would convey the same meaning he had found in the bedroom itself, which had recently served him as a haven after too much nerve-wracking labor over his paintings. Although he had moved into the house as early as mid-September, it was not until a month later that he experienced the anticipated, therapeutic effect of his house as a haven, during the period of "enforced rest" described above.

1

By staying at home and getting a good night's sleep, on October 16 he had recovered the peace of mind he had shattered by working too hard, and he wanted to celebrate in *The Bedroom* that it is natural and beneficial for mankind to have such havens. That is the message at the heart of the picture—rest as a *condition humaine*. The canvas, he went on, "will contrast, for example, with the Tarascon diligence [fig. 12] and the night café [p. 39, fig. 2]."[102] In the latter painting he had expressed the idea "that the café is a place where you can ruin yourself, go mad, commit crimes," and in the picture of the stagecoaches he appears to have reflected on Alphonse Daudet's novel *Tartarin de Tarascon* (1872), in which a Provençal coachman complains about his unbearable life, always on the road.[103] This seems to confirm that *The Bedroom* did indeed stand for the opposite of a chaotic life, that is to say, a place where one could really rest after hard work. Anyone who would want to build a future needed that, and it is hardly a coincidence that the day Van Gogh started work on *The Bedroom*, which expressed his sense of having found a restful haven, was also the day on which he registered himself as the official occupant of the house on the place Lamartine.[104]

Van Gogh used his paint in such a way that the effect is indeed one of rest, which is why he was so pleased with the result. The composition is defined by three large areas of color, each one in a predominant tint: the floor, the walls, and the greatly magnified foot of the bed. He eliminated shadows because they would be too restless, and for the same reason he barely even attempted to suggest that the floor was tiled. The maze of lines created by the many joins would have been inconsistent with the need for a calm image. His brushwork is deliberately restrained, at least by his standards. There did have to be a sense of contrast, of course, but he depicted only a few objects with his customary dynamic style—the pillows, the blanket, and the landscape on the rear wall.

His palette was the greatest contributor to the serene effect, but in order to fully appreciate this, one has to realize that the painting is now discolored.[105] It is only by revisualizing the original color scheme (pp. 90–91, figs. 20–21) that one can understand his previously quoted comment that "the colour has to do the job here, and through its being simplified by giving a grander style to things, to be suggestive here *of rest* or *of sleep* in general."[106] He used all the contrasts of complementary colors (violet against yellow, red against green, orange against blue, supplemented with white against black), and although some of these contrasts are admittedly harsh, by also including hues of different gradations, the final effect was harmonious.[107]

That becomes even clearer if one considers his models, the modern Japanese prints he had avidly collected in Paris.[108] In these works we often see the new synthetic colors that had become common around 1860. They stand out for their fairly extreme use of red, as well as violet and lilac (see figs. 13–14), and Van Gogh borrowed those for *The Bedroom*. However, in contrast to his Japanese models, he balanced them with their complementary colors and also used different kinds of hues, as noted above, to create the effect of "unshakeable repose," which was indeed a remarkable achievement.[109]

To Van Gogh's way of thinking, this association with the Japanese model was strengthened by arranging the composition in such a way that the simply furnished room looks almost empty: an interior with "nothing in it," as he himself wrote, or "a little room that has run to the back," as a Dutch critic so neatly put it in 1895.[110] He had read in Loti's *Madame Chrysanthème* and seen in its illustrations that Japanese rooms and monasteries were kept as empty as possible (see fig. 15), and he evidently wanted his own interior to communicate the same quality.[111] He did not make that connection in his letters to Theo and Gauguin, but he did in his letter to his sister Willemien on the occasion of his second repetition of *The Bedroom* (plate 22), in which he referred to the life of the "Japanese . . . in very simple interiors."[112] But there is one essential difference. In 1889 he wanted to stress that the simple room in his painting derived from his old "need for simplicity," referring to a way of life, whereas earlier, in 1888, he had wanted to emphasize that the picture embodied a Japanese aesthetic ideal, which had led him to furnish his house and studio in accordance with the very latest modernist views.

Fig. 12 Vincent van Gogh (Dutch, 1853–1890). *Tarascon Diligence*, 1888. Oil on canvas; 71.4 × 92.5 cm (28 1/8 × 36 7/16 in.). The Henry and Rose Pearlman Foundation, on long-term loan to the Princeton University Art Museum. F478a, JH1605

Fig. 13 *A Modern Narihira*, late nineteenth century. Center and right sheets from an *ōban* triptych; each, 36.4 × 23.9 cm (14 5/16 × 9 7/16 in.). Van Gogh Museum, Amsterdam (Vincent van Gogh Foundation).

Fig. 14 *A New Print with Children's Games*, 1850/1900. Crepon print; 36.5 × 25 cm (14 3/8 × 9 13/16 in.). Van Gogh Museum, Amsterdam (Vincent van Gogh Foundation), inv. No. N 30.

Fig. 15 Luigi Rossi (Italian, 1853–1923). Illustration of a Japanese interior. From Pierre Loti, *Madame Chrysanthème* (Paris, 1888), p. 133.

Thus style and content merged into a single entity, which for Van Gogh was the highest creative achievement. He wrote about attaining this ideal unity of style and content again in Saint-Rémy when he depicted the view from his room of a wheat field battered to destruction by a storm, a subject that probably attracted him as an allusion to his own existence turned upside down by a bad illness (fig. 16), and it made him think almost automatically of *The Bedroom*. "It's a landscape of extreme simplicity—in terms of coloration as well. It would be suitable as a pendant to that study of the bedroom.... When the thing depicted is stylistically absolutely in agreement and at one with the manner of depiction, isn't that what creates the quality of a piece of art?"[113]

Looking Back on His Life

The bedroom, however, began to take on another meaning when the grand venture of a communal house for artists ended in disaster. Originally a symbol of rest as a *condition humaine*, the picture now became a painful reminder of an unfulfilled ideal. "You'll see more clearly what my studio, now foundered, could have been," he wrote to his brother in 1889, when he was about to send the first version of *The Bedroom* and other Arles paintings to Paris before entering the asylum in Saint-Rémy.[114] In the long term, the haven had not given him what it had promised—a future, a goal to live for.

That is why the later versions of *The Bedroom* (plates 21–22) do not have the same meaning as the original of 1888. The idea of expressing the bliss of "unshakeable repose" was pushed aside by the sobering observation in 1889 that his "need for simplicity" had once again not yielded the results he desired: "He who has it, this ideal—he merely ends up, as in my case, unable to do what he wants."[115] After Paris he had tried to get his life back on track by reverting to his old ascetic and industrious way of life, albeit in a different, less "natural" way than before. Lacking a wife and family to support him in his goals, he had endeavored to work with other artists, but this fresh attempt had failed too, and that was a feeling he could not shake off. The extent of his disappointment emerges from the meaning he attached retroactively, in 1890, to *Gauguin's Chair* (plate 24). More than a year after Gauguin's tumultuous departure from Arles, he stated in a letter to the critic Albert Aurier that the painting embodied his colleague's "empty place."[116]

Van Gogh expressed the new meaning of *The Bedroom* through the portraits on the wall. They are different from those in the original, and he probably got the idea of changing them from the scene itself. The double bed is of course still emphatically present and, although he had initially not given it a meaningful role, he could no longer resist the power of suggestion that this was a love nest. For the walls in the two later *Bedroom* pictures were no longer decorated with *The Poet* (plate 13) and *The Lover* (plate 14) but with a self-portrait, loosely based on either the one now in the National Gallery of Art, Washington, D.C. (plate 26) or another in the Musée d'Orsay, Paris (1889 [F627, JH1772]), and the portrait of a woman, suggesting that the pair of them were sharing the bed.

The woman is blonde in the Chicago work, and it seems likely that this image is a reference to a poem by Émile Zola, "Ce que je veux," about desire for a queen with blonde hair. In 1881, probably at the time of his attempt to win over Kee Vos, he had taken the poem as the point of departure for a drawing (now lost).[117] Zola's "reine d'amour" (queen of love) stood for romantic love, and the Chicago painting as a whole was probably meant to say that artists like him needed a simple, ascetic life in combination with "a strong, passionate love" that would help them achieve their artistic ideals.[118]

Van Gogh may still have been searching for a general expression in this picture rather than a strictly individual one, but that was not the case with his last variation (plate 22). Of the three versions, it is the only one specifically intended for a private audience and with an autobiographical function. It was meant for his sister and his mother, and he probably made it "with them in mind," as he wrote at the time.[119] The self-portrait hanging in the background of the third *Bedroom* was based on the *Self-Portrait with Clean-Shaven Face* (1889; private collection [F525, JH1665]); he transformed the blonde woman into the recent portrait that he had painted of the wife of the chief orderly in the asylum, Charles-Elzéard Trabuc (fig. 17). He was fascinated by her, "as a faded woman, an unfortunate, quite resigned one, and really not much, and so insignificant that I have a great desire to paint that dusty blade of grass."[120] From this we know almost for certain that this Jeanne Trabuc reminded him of Sien Hoornik (see fig. 18), who also had "that *je ne sais quoi* of withering, that drubbed by life quality."[121] By basing the landscape background in that picture loosely on a watercolor with a prominent pollarded willow that he had made shortly after starting to live with Sien, there can be no doubt of what he was referring to—his attempt after Kee Vos to marry and have a family of his own, yet another venture that had ended in disappointment.[122] Without suggesting that he intended to accuse his family again for his failure to get married, he certainly wanted the picture to express that this had been his ideal and that he had failed to achieve it.

This idea of failure dogged him for the rest of his life. Or as he put it to Theo in 1890, not long before he committed suicide: "I believe that

12

13

14

15

16

17

18

Fig. 16 Vincent van Gogh (Dutch, 1853–1890). *Landscape from Saint-Rémy*, 1889. Oil on canvas; 70.5 × 88.5 cm (27 3/4 × 34 13/16 in.). Ny Carlsberg Glyptotek, Copenhagen, SMK 1840. F611, JH1723

certainly it's better to bring up children than to expend all one's nervous energy in making paintings, but what can you do, I myself am now, at least I feel I am, too old to retrace my steps or to desire something else. This desire has left me, although the moral pain of it remains."[123] Without a wife and family, he had not fulfilled the moral duty of creating the oasis of calm and order that he had foreseen in 1880 when he chose the path of an artist. He felt that his life had been far too adventurous, too unstable, without roots, so to speak, but in twentieth-century scholarship the Victorian within him was barely even recognized any more. He had lived, or so Brettell asserted in 1986, "a chaotic and disorderly life," so the "real bedroom at Arles [could] never [have been] so clean, never so restful" as Van Gogh suggested in his painting.[124]

But Van Gogh had most definitely striven for a kind of Victorian order in his daily life. One can perhaps conclude that he was too nervous, too restless to find peace of mind anywhere, but if you have empathy for the evolution of his plans and dreams, the first version of *The Bedroom* really does allow you to believe in the sincerity, the authenticity of the feeling that he had on October 16, 1888, when he finally thought that he had found a peaceful haven in his new home that would help him secure a future. His dream was fulfilled, it seemed, but his hope for rest as an enduring *condition humaine* was soon afterward shattered and scattered, prompting new interpretations of the motif. It shows that the meaning of a work of art is not chiseled in stone: it can move in directions new and unexpected—even to the artist.

Fig. 17 Vincent van Gogh (Dutch, 1853–1890). *Portrait of Jeanne Lafuye Trabuc*, 1889. Oil on canvas; 64 × 59 cm (25 3/16 × 23 1/4 in.). State Hermitage Museum, Saint Petersburg, formerly collection of Otto Krebs. F631, JH 1777

Fig. 18 Vincent van Gogh (Dutch, 1853–1890). *Woman Sewing, with a Girl*, Mar. 1883. Chalk, pen, brush and ink, and watercolor on paper; 55.6 × 29.9 cm (21 7/8 × 11 3/4 in.). Van Gogh Museum, Amsterdam (Vincent van Gogh Foundation). F1072, JH341

This essay could not have been written without the inspirational discussions that I had with Evert van Uitert, Teio Meedendorp, Hans Luijten, and Ella Hendriks and the preparatory work by Sander Hintzen, who conjured up literature and documents from a great variety of sources. I am also very grateful to Margherita Andreotti, Gloria Groom, Maia M. Rigas, and Charline Petit-Fournier in Chicago and Véronique Abel, Nienke Bakker, Alexandra van Dongen, Ijsbrand Hummelen, Benjamin Mordehai Janssens, Gerard Rooijakkers, Belinda Thomson, and Chris Uehlenbeck on the other side of the ocean, who were kind enough to ponder specific issues and come up with suggestions, of which I made grateful use. The translation from the Dutch is by Michael Hoyle. In the following notes, the artist and his brother are referred to as Van Gogh and Theo, respectively. The abbreviation *Letters*, followed by a number, refers to a specific letter in *Vincent van Gogh: The Letters*, ed. Leo Jansen, Hans Luijten, and Nienke Bakker (Van Gogh Museum/Huygens ING, 2009), http://vangoghletters.org/vg/.

1. For a more extended treatment of this topic, see the essay by Gloria Groom in this catalogue.

2. Veth, *Hollandsche teekenaars van dezen tijd*, p. 50: "Zijn zolderkamertje wordt, als hij argeloos het portretteeren zal, een ding van wereldorde" (When he artlessly paints the portrait of his little attic room, it will be a thing of world class). This article was first published as "Studiën over Moderne Kunst," *De nieuwe gids* 7 (1893), pp. 427–31.

3. Although Van Gogh was allowed to use the water closet at the neighbor's on the avenue Montmajour, which had the same landlord (see *Letters*, 602, n. 19), he certainly had a chamber pot in his bedroom like Evenepoel. However, he decided to keep it out of sight.

4. Chu, "Emblems for a Modern Age," p. 93.

5. Henri Thulié, "Du roman: L'action," *Réalisme*, Mar. 15, 1857, p. 701, quoted in Armstrong, "Duranty on Degas," p. 172.

6. Van Gogh to Theo, Oct. 16, 1888, *Letters*, 705.

7. Van Gogh to Theo, Mar. 11, 1882, *Letters*, 211. I hasten to add here that Van Gogh at the same time embraced the idea that painting was "a corner of nature seen through a temperament," to quote Zola's famous definition, but this is something else. It refers to execution and sentiment rather than iconography.

8. Van Gogh to Theo, Mar. 11, 1882, *Letters*, 211.

9. Zemel, *Van Gogh's Progress*, p. 196.

10. Van Uitert, Van Tilborgh, and Van Heugten, *Vincent van Gogh*, p. 172.

11. Brettell, "Van Gogh's Bedrooms at Arles," p. 145.

12. Van Gogh to Theo, Oct. 16, 1888, *Letters*, 705.

13. Van Gogh to Theo, Oct. 17, 1888; and Van Gogh to Gauguin, Oct. 17, 1888, *Letters*, 707 and 706, respectively.

14. Van Gogh to Gauguin, Oct. 17, 1888, *Letters*, 706.

15. Van Gogh to Theo, Jan. 22, 1889, *Letters*, 741.

16. Van Gogh to Theo, Sept. 5–6, 1889, *Letters*, 800. For the water damage, see the essay by Inge Fiedler et al. in this catalogue.

17. Van Gogh to Theo, Sept. 28, 1889, *Letters*, 806.

18. See Van Tilborgh, *Van Gogh and the Sunflowers*, esp. pp. 50–65.

19. Van Gogh did not use the term "chef d'oeuvre" himself, though. For nineteenth-century ideas about the notion of a chef d'oeuvre, see Cahn, *Masterpieces*, pp. 131–56; and Ashton, *Fable of Modern Art*, esp. pp. 7–47.

20. Van Gogh to Theo, Oct. 16, 1888, *Letters*, 705.

21. Van Gogh to Theo, Oct. 15, 1888, *Letters*, 704.

22. Van Gogh to Gauguin, Oct. 17, 1888, *Letters*, 706.

23. *Row of Cypresses with a Couple Strolling* (location unknown [F485, JH1615]) was begun after *The Bedroom*; see Van Gogh to Theo, Oct. 21, 1888, *Letters*, 709.

24. Van Gogh to Gauguin, Oct. 17, 1888, *Letters*, 706.

25. Van Gogh to Theo, Oct. 8, 1888, *Letters*, 699.

26. On this, see Van Tilborgh and Van Uitert, "Van Gogh in Search of His Own Voice," pp. 15–18.

27. Van Gogh to Theo, Oct. 16, 1888, *Letters*, 705.

28. Van Gogh to Theo, Oct. 16, 1888, *Letters*, 705.

29. Van Gogh to Gauguin, Oct. 17, 1888, *Letters*, 706.

30. Van Gogh to Theo, Oct. 16, 1888, *Letters*, 705. Emphasis in the original.

31. Van Gogh to Willemien van Gogh, on or about Oct. 21, 1889, *Letters*, 812.

32. On George Eliot's *Felix Holt*, see *Letters*, 812, n. 12.

33. Van Gogh to Willemien van Gogh, on or about Oct. 21, 1889, *Letters*, 812.

34. Lövgren, *Genesis of Modernism*, p. 137.

35. For a defense of empathy, see Holmes, "Quest for the Real Coleridge," pp. 61–63. There are many biographies of Van Gogh, the most important of which, so to speak, is the complete edition of his letters published in 2009. For supplementary information and interpretations, see Hulsker, *Vincent and Theo van Gogh*; Van der Veen, *Van Gogh*; Naifeh and Smith, *Van Gogh*; Van Tilborgh and Meedendorp, "Life and Death of Vincent van Gogh," pp. 456–62; and Grant, *Letters of Vincent van Gogh*.

36. What follows is in part taken from a lecture given by Van Tilborgh and Van Uitert, "Van Gogh and His Religious Inspired Craftsmanship." See also Silverman, "Weaving Paintings," pp. 137–68, although her interpretation differs from the one given above.

37. Weber, *Protestant Ethic and the Spirit of Capitalism*, pp. 56–89. See also Sennett, *Respect*, pp. 57–58, 107–11.

38. On this, see Houghton, *Victorian Frame of Mind*; Himmelfarb, *De-Moralization of Society*, esp. pp. 4–52; and Harrison, *The Bible, Protestantism, and the Rise of Natural Science*, pp. 1–10.

39. Ludovico, *Selected Writings of Thomas Carlyle*, pp. 369, 399.

40. Van Gogh to Caroline van Stockum-Haanebeek, Feb. 9, 1874, *Letters*, 18.

41. Theo to Elisabeth van Gogh, Oct. 13, 1885, quoted in Tilborgh, "Van Gogh: A Dutch Traveller in France," p. 148.

42. Van Gogh to Theo, Mar. 23, 1877, *Letters*, 109.

43. Van Gogh to Theo, on or about Oct. 16, 1883, *Letters*, 397. For the influence that this idea of craftsmanship had on his working method, see Van Tilborgh and Van Uitert, "Van Gogh in Search of His Own Voice," pp. 23–26.

44. Van Gogh to Theo, on or about Jan. 3, 1882, *Letters*, 196.

45. Van Gogh to Theo, July 6–7, 1882, *Letters*, 245.

46. Van Gogh to Theo, June 1–2, 1882, *Letters*, 234. Employing a cleaner may have been a little hypocritical, given Van Gogh's attempt to identify with craftsmen, but it would have been second nature at the time to a middle-class man living on his own; see Stokvis, *Het intieme burgerleven*, p. 128.

47. Van Gogh to Theo, on or about May 16, 1882, *Letters*, 228. Furthermore, the family was considered to be a natural phenomenon, and so it enforced his denial of the public domain; for the increasing value of the family in this nineteenth-century debate on nature versus culture, see Sennett, *Fall of Public Man*, pp. 90–91. On Van Gogh's love affairs, see the handy summary by Luijten, *Van Gogh and Love*.

48. Stokvis, *Het intieme burgerleven*, pp. 57–58.

49. Van Gogh to Theo, July 6, 1882; and Van Gogh to Theo, Nov. 7, 1881, *Letters*, 244 and 180, respectively. It is clear that Van Gogh wanted to start a family with her from a drawing from that period in which he depicted a woman with her features breast-feeding a baby. See Meedendorp, *Drawings and Prints*, p. 80.

50. Van Gogh to Theo, May 12 or 13, 1882, *Letters*, 226.

51. Van Gogh to Theo, on or about May 16, 1882, *Letters*, 228.

52. Van Gogh to Theo, on or about Dec. 10, 1884, *Letters*, 474. Emphasis in the original.

53. See, for example, *Letters*, 274, n. 5, for a reference to the novels of Henri Murger, such as *Buveurs d'eau* (1854).

54. Van Gogh to Theo, on or about July 11, 1883, *Letters*, 361.

55. The original Dutch of the quotations is from Anton Kerssemakers's recollections noted down in 1912; and Benno Jules Stokvis, *Nasporing omtrent Vincent van Gogh in Brabant* (n.p., 1926); see Van Gogh–Bonger, *Verzamelde brieven van Vincent van Gogh*, vol. 3, pp. 93–94 and 98.

56. Van Gogh to Theo, Oct. 4, 1885, *Letters*, 533.

57. On this development, see Van Tilborgh, "From Realist to Modernist," pp. 53–67.

58. Bohemian Montmartre is discussed in Seigel, *Bohemian Paris*, pp. 336–65.

59. Van Gogh to Willemien van Gogh, late Oct. 1887, *Letters*, 574.

60. Van Gogh may very well be the fourth person from the left in the background of figure 5, together with some of his former colleagues from Cormon's academy: Louis Anquetin, Henri de Toulouse-Lautrec, Albert Grénier, and Armand de Terratz.

61. Van Gogh to Willemien van Gogh, late Oct. 1887, *Letters*, 574. For more on this, see Hendriks and Van Tilborgh, *Vincent van Gogh*, pp. 274–77.

62. On the streetwalker, see Hendriks and Van Tilborgh, *Vincent van Gogh*, pp. 274–76.

63. For the quotation, see Gauguin's *Avant et après*, cited in *Letters*, 736, n. 19. See also Stokvis, *Het intieme burgerleven*, p. 87, for contemporary attitudes about visiting brothels, which were tolerated by liberals and the Christian community because masturbation was regarded as an even greater evil.

64. Van Gogh to Gauguin, Oct. 3, 1888, *Letters*, 695.

65. Van Gogh to Willemien van Gogh, between June 16 and 20, 1888, *Letters*, 626.

66. Van Gogh to Willemien van Gogh, late Oct. 1887, *Letters*, 574. See Stokvis, *Het intieme burgerleven*, p. 58.

67. Van Gogh to Theo, May 4, 1888, *Letters*, 603.

68. Van Gogh to Theo, Sept. 18, 1888, *Letters*, 682.

69. On Gruby, see *Letters*, 603, n. 6. For another example of his practical advice, see Raphaël Blanchard, "Notices biographiques David Gruby," p. 63.

70. Van Gogh to Theo, May 4, 1888; and Van Gogh to Theo, May 28 or 29, 1888, *Letters*, 603 and 616, respectively.

71. Van der Veen has pointed out that the bonzes in Loti's book were, like Van Gogh, "entirely earthbound" and regularly went to a brothel. Van der Veen, *Van Gogh*, p. 199.

72. Van Gogh to Theo, May 28 or 29, 1888; Van Gogh to Émile Bernard, June 26, 1888; and Van Gogh to Theo, Aug. 19 or 20, 1888, *Letters*, 616, 632, and 664, respectively. He later wrote that he had stopped going altogether because he was impotent. Van Gogh to Theo, July 9 or 10, 1888, *Letters*, 638. Naifeh and Smith believe that Van Gogh had affairs, but there is not the slightest evidence of that, despite the fact that, due to the popularity of Walt Whitman's *Leaves of Grass*, he seemed to agree with his message of "a world of health, of generous, frank carnal love" (Van Gogh to Willemien van Gogh, on or about Aug. 26, 1888, *Letters*, 670). Naifeh and Smith, *Van Gogh*, p. 638.

73. Van Gogh to Theo, on or about July 22, 1888, *Letters*, 645.

74. Van Gogh to Theo, May 1, 1888, *Letters*, 602.

75. Van Gogh to Theo, Sept. 18, 1888, *Letters*, 682.

76. See *Letters*, 575, nn. 2, 7; and *Letters*, 584, n. 6.

77. Van Gogh to Theo, Oct. 3, 1888, *Letters*, 694.

78. Van Gogh to Theo, Sept. 23 or 24, 1888; and Van Gogh to Theo, Sept. 9, 1888, *Letters*, 686 and 677, respectively. For this cleaner, see Van Gogh to Theo, July 9 or 10, 1888; Van Gogh to Theo, Sept. 9, 1888; and Van Gogh to Theo, Jan. 17, 1889, *Letters*, 638, 677, and 736, respectively.

79. Van Gogh to Theo, Sept. 9, 1888, *Letters*, 677. Emphasis in the original.

80. For the decoration of his house, see Dorn, *Décoration*.

81. Van Gogh to Theo, Sept. 9, 1888, *Letters*, 677.

82. Van Gogh to Theo, Sept. 9, 1888, *Letters*, 677.

83. Van Gogh to Willemien van Gogh, July 31, 1888, *Letters*, 653. See also Van Lindert and Van Uitert, *Een eigentijdse expressie*, pp. 108–11.

84. For Van Gogh's outspoken admiration of this work, see *Letters*, 612, n. 1.

85. Van Uitert, *Vincent van Gogh in Creative Competition*, pp. 33–35; and Van Gogh to Theo, Sept. 3, 1888, *Letters*, 673.

86. Van Gogh to Theo, Sept. 9, 1888, *Letters*, 677. Van Gogh had initially asked Theo to send him his bed from their Paris apartment, and given the size of his room it could only have been a single; see Van Gogh to Theo, May 4, 1888, *Letters*, 603.

87. Van Gogh to Willemien van Gogh, late Oct. 1887, *Letters*, 574.

88. On these ideas, see Childs, *Vanishing Paradise*, pp. 21–38.

89. On the reputation of the Arlésiennes, see Dymond, "Displaying the Arlésienne," p. 150. For his first painting with lovers, see Van Gogh to Émile Bernard, Mar. 18, 1888, *Letters*, 587.

90. Van Gogh to Gauguin, Oct. 3, 1888, *Letters*, 695.

91. For the planned still lifes of sunflowers in Gauguin's room—six works on three walls—see Van Gogh to Theo, Sept. 9, 1888; and Van Gogh to Willemien van Gogh, Sept. 9 and 14, 1888, *Letters*, 677 (especially n. 8) and 678, respectively. The paintings *Sunflowers* (p. 40, fig. 3) and *Sunflowers* (p. 40, fig. 4) were the only two still lifes considered to be good enough, and in the end he failed to make more of them, which he regretted. Van Gogh to Theo, Sept. 25, 1888, *Letters*, 687.

92. The second *Poet's Garden*, now lost, is known only from sketches (Van Gogh to Theo, Sept. 26, 1888 [p. 43, fig. 5]; and Van Gogh to Eugène Boch, Oct. 2, 1888, *Letters*, 689 and 693, respectively). The second pair was *Public Garden with Couple and Blue Fir Tree: The Poet's Garden III* (p. 43, fig. 6) and *Row of Cypresses with a Couple Strolling* (p. 43, fig. 7). See also the essay by David J. Getsy in this catalogue.

93. Van Gogh to Willemien van Gogh, Sept. 19, 1889, *Letters*, 804.

94. These were the only two works in the bedroom; see Van Gogh to Eugène Boch, Oct. 2, 1888, *Letters*, 693. The two prints and the landscape were not part of the decoration. Van Gogh had added them in his picture simply for aesthetic reasons. See also the essay by Inge Fiedler et al. in this catalogue.

95. Van Gogh to Theo, Sept. 18, 1888, *Letters*, 683.

96. Van Gogh to Theo, Sept. 18, 1888, *Letters*, 682.

97. Van Gogh thought of painting the head and foot of his bed: "Perhaps a naked woman, I haven't decided, perhaps a cradle with a child." Van Gogh to Theo, Sept. 9, 1888, *Letters*, 677. I think this would also have been with a view to Gauguin's arrival. Van Gogh realized that his guest might very easily have "some success with the Arlésiennes." Van Gogh to Theo, on or about Dec. 1, 1888, *Letters*, 723. But at the same time he felt the need to rescue him, as it were, by making him feel that he would be far better off with his wife and children. See, among others, Van Gogh to Theo, Oct. 10 or 11, 1888, *Letters*, 702.

98. Chu, "Emblems for a Modern Age."

99. Van Gogh to Theo, on or about Nov. 19, 1888, *Letters*, 721. For an example of this imagery, see the essay by Gloria Groom in this catalogue, which reproduces and discusses an image by Samuel Luke Fildes (p. 33, fig. 7), showing Dickens's empty chair, that Van Gogh much admired. See also *Letters*, 251, n. 11.

100. The books with the yellow and white (originally pink) covers probably stand for the need to depict contemporary issues in society; see Hendriks and Van Tilborgh, *Vincent van Gogh*, pp. 290–91, 502–07. Van Gogh set this nocturnal scene in the studio, where gaslight had recently been installed. Next to the pile of books he included a lit candle, which was still necessary if one wanted to read. For a symbolic interpretation of this candle, see the essay by David J. Getsy in this catalogue (pp. 46–47).

101. Van Gogh to Theo, Oct. 16, 1888, *Letters*, 705.

102. Van Gogh to Theo, Oct. 16, 1888, *Letters*, 705.

103. See Van Gogh to Theo, Sept. 9, 1888, *Letters*, 677; see also *Letters*, 703, n. 1; and Van Tilborgh, "Dutch Traveller in France," p. 155.

104. On this registration, see *Letters*, 602, n. 3.

105. See the essay by Inge Fiedler et al. in this catalogue.

106. Van Gogh to Theo, Oct. 16, 1888, *Letters*, 705.

107. On this, see Georges Roque, "Chevreul's Colour Theory and Its Consequences for Artists," http://www.colour.org.uk/Chevreul, pp. 19–21; and the essay by Inge Fiedler et al. in this catalogue.

108. For Van Gogh's collection, see Van Rappard-Boon, Van Gulik, and Van Bremen-Ito, *Japanese Prints*, which contains many prints of the second half of the nineteenth century. Surprisingly, until now they have not been highlighted as possible sources for Van Gogh's color experiments in Arles.

109. Van Gogh to Theo, Oct. 16, 1888, *Letters*, 705.

110. Dulk, "Tentoonstellingwerken Vincent van Gogh."

111. On this, see *Letters*, 628, n. 20; and 639, n. 11.

112. Van Gogh to Willemien van Gogh, on or about Oct. 21, 1889, *Letters*, 812.

113. Van Gogh to Theo, June 9, 1889, *Letters*, 779.

114. Van Gogh to Theo, Apr. 30, 1889, *Letters*, 765.

115. Van Gogh to Theo, Oct. 16, 1888; and Van Gogh to Willemien van Gogh, on or about Oct. 21, 1889, *Letters*, 705 and 812, respectively.

116. Van Gogh to Albert Aurier, Feb. 9 or 10, 1890, *Letters*, 853.

117. *Letters*, 244, n. 4. The poem dates from 1859, but Van Gogh probably knew it from *La vie moderne* 3 (Jan. 29, 1881).

118. Van Gogh to Theo, July 6, 1882, *Letters*, 244.

119. Van Gogh to Theo, Sept. 28, 1889, *Letters*, 806. Although he says that about all the repetitions made for his mother and sister, I think he is only referring to this painting here, since none of the others differ from the original in such a fundamental way.

120. Van Gogh to Theo, Sept. 10, 1889, *Letters*, 801.

121. Van Gogh to Theo, on or about Dec. 23, 1881, *Letters*, 193.

122. The watercolor is *Pollard Willow* (1882; Van Gogh Museum, Amsterdam [F947, JH164]).

123. Van Gogh to Theo and Jo van Gogh-Bonger, on or about July 10, 1890, *Letters*, 898.

124. Brettell, "Van Gogh's Bedrooms at Arles," p. 150, who evidently based this on Gauguin's *Avant et après* (see *Letters*, 736, n. 19), but there the artist only speaks of Van Gogh's disorder in his box of colors.

MATERIALS, INTENTION, AND EVOLUTION

INGE FIEDLER, ELLA HENDRIKS,
TEIO MEEDENDORP, MICHEL MENU,
AND JOHANNA SALVANT

Materials, Intention, and Evolution: Van Gogh's *Bedrooms*

Bringing together Vincent van Gogh's three versions of *The Bedroom* (plates 20–22) for this exhibition provides us not only the rare experience of seeing all three paintings together, but also the unique opportunity to assemble all of the research performed to date in Amsterdam, Chicago, and Paris.[1] In this essay, we outline our discoveries, first by exploring the differences in the materials and techniques used in each version. We also draw upon new analytical techniques that have enabled us to map the distribution of Van Gogh's pigments over the entire surface of his paintings, as well as identify the red lake pigments that we now know have faded.[2] With this new technology we can present a digital recolorized visualization that brings us closer to the original color schemes of the Amsterdam and Chicago pictures.[3] This is especially significant for our understanding of these paintings, which, as Van Gogh emphasized in his letters, relied heavily on color for their impact. Finally, by combining the physical evidence of the artworks themselves—their early damage, handling, and treatment—with attention to the artist's letters, we are able to shed light on two other important aspects of this series, revealing the remarkable uniqueness of each work in terms of process and palette and affirming once and for all the order in which they were made.

Based on Van Gogh's letters, we know that the first *Bedroom* was painted in Arles on October 16–17, 1888, and that the other two, based on the Arles original, were executed at Saint-Rémy-de-Provence in September 1889, the first repetition completed by September 5 and the second by September 28.[4] The Arles version is the picture now in the Van Gogh Museum in Amsterdam. The second version, on the same scale as the first, is the one now in the Art Institute of Chicago, and the final version, reduced in scale, is the one now at the Musée d'Orsay in Paris. While this sequence is now universally accepted, this was not always the case, and some of the evidence presented here has not previously been related to the issue of chronology.[5]

In accordance with Van Gogh's own nomenclature for these works, we will often refer to the first picture as a "study" (*étude*) and to the other two as "repetitions" (*répétitions*).[6] In the case of the smaller version, the artist also used the term "reduction" (*réduction*). Especially in his early years, in keeping with the academic practice of his day, Van Gogh used the term "étude" to distinguish a work from a fully fledged "painting" (i.e., *tableau*), signifying that it was of high quality and often a final or definitive version of a theme. But later in France, Van Gogh used these terms in a much less rigid fashion, assigning to them a very personal meaning within his own unique creative process.[7] "Study," in the end, became the general term for practically all his paintings, but some of them were obviously more important than others. Size mattered, especially to distinguish smaller "études d'après nature" from more ambitious attempts, which he called "serious studies" or, in the case of more deliberate works, "compositions." For instance, when thinking about exhibiting his work in Paris, he wrote to his brother Theo in September 1888: "The studies shouldn't be confused with compositions. . . . Because there's still hardly more than the sower and the night café that are attempts at composed paintings."[8] In Saint-Rémy he made a couple of attempts at what may be referred to as "tableaux" by making repetitions of quickly painted size 30 études that he was proud of but which he thought still needed stylization—in the end sometimes preferring the initial, freshly observed study to the tableau.[9]

Compositional Changes, Paint Application, Texture, and Materials

This time it's simply my bedroom, but the colour has to do the job here, and through its being simplified by giving a grander style to things, to be suggestive here of rest *or* of sleep *in general.*
Van Gogh to Theo, Oct. 16, 1888

One of the paintings Van Gogh made to decorate the rooms in the Yellow House in Arles was of his bedroom, and from his letters we know that he was very satisfied with how the painting turned out. In the artist's correspondence there are two sketches (or *croquis*, as Van Gogh referred to them) illustrating this first version. The first sketch appears in a letter written to Theo on October 16, 1888 (fig. 1, plate 19), while he was busily working on the painting. It is not known whether the sketch was made that day or a day earlier, since in the beginning of the letter he mentions having already started working on the painting. Indeed, on that day the painting seems to be quite advanced, because he indicates that he is planning on finishing it the next day. The sketch differs from the picture in several respects. There are no prints below the portraits on the wall, there is a portrait instead of a landscape by the head of the bed, there are two bottles on the table rather than three, the hat is hanging on the left of the rack rather than on the right, and only in the sketch is there a basin and sponge under the table. This seems to suggest that Van Gogh had not yet settled on the details and was basing the sketch on the way his bedroom actually looked at that moment.[10]

The sketch is on a sheet of notepaper with proportions different from those of the canvas, which forced him to compress the composition vertically, making the room look wider. The left-hand chair is further back, and more of the wall on that side is visible, showing more clearly that the door to the adjoining room is ajar.[11] The most significant distortion is that Van Gogh made the room look like a regular rectangular space, whereas in fact it was trapezoidal, with the rear wall not at right angles to the sides but on a slant (see p. 38, fig. 1).[12]

That created a problem with the table. The sketch clearly shows it in a corner and up against the rear wall, yet we can see far more of its left side than would be possible if it were obeying the laws of perspective in a rectangular space. The trapezoidal shape is not really evident in the painting either, but Van Gogh hit on an elegant solution by making the legs of the table longer, which frees it from the back wall and firmly establishes its diagonal position in the room. A hint of the complex perspectival construction of the room is given by the glimpse of the right-hand corner of the ceiling at the top. It is only when one realizes that the right-hand wall is longer than the one on the left that the space becomes easier to understand. It was impossible, for instance, for the head of the bed to be placed up against the back wall; the side of the bed had to be against the right-hand wall, by the doorpost, leaving a triangular space between the bed and the back wall large enough for a clothes rack.[13] Van Gogh had relied for a long time on his perspective frame to help him resolve awkward compositions like this, but he seems to have abandoned it back in June when he visited Saintes-Maries-de-la-Mer, and he did not resort to it for *The Bedroom.*[14]

In the second sketch (fig. 2), included in the letter he wrote the following day, October 17, to Paul Gauguin, Van Gogh drew the painting in what is nearly its final composition. The room is still shown as rectangular, and the table is still up against the corner, though the artist has shifted the table's relation to the corner by moving the vertical line demarcating the corner to a position behind the table rather than alongside it. Most important, he added the prints below the portraits on the right-hand wall, hung his hat on the right side of the rack, and replaced the portrait above it with a landscape. The basin and sponge under the table have disappeared.

Technical Comparison of the Three Versions of *The Bedroom*

I'm adding another line to tell you that this afternoon I finished the canvas of the bedroom. . . . This bedroom is something like that still life of French novels with yellow, pink, green covers, you'll recall. But I believe that the execution is simpler and more virile. No stippling, no hatching, nothing, the tints flat, but in harmony.
Van Gogh to Theo, Oct. 17, 1888

At first glance, the three *Bedroom* paintings appear very similar; however, closer inspection reveals compositional differences, subtle nuances in the way each is painted, and differences in the depiction of some of its components, especially the paintings hung on

---

From a letter dated Oct. 16, 1888 (fig. 1 and plate 19). *Vincent van Gogh: The Letters*, ed. Leo Jansen, Hans Luijten, and Nienke Bakker (Van Gogh Museum/Huygens ING, 2009), 705.

My dear Theo—
At last I'm sending you a little croquis to give you at least an idea of the direction the work is taking. Because today I've gone back to it.
My eyes are still tired, but anyway I had a new idea in mind, and here's the croquis of it. No. 30 canvas once again.
This time it's simply my bedroom, but the colour has to do the job here, and through its being simplified by giving a grander style to things, to be suggestive here *of rest* or *of sleep* in general. In short, looking at the painting should *rest* the mind, or rather, the imagination.
The walls are of a pale violet. The floor—is of red tiles.
The bedstead and the chairs are fresh butter yellow.
The sheet and the pillows very bright lemon green.
The bedspread scarlet red.
The window green.
The dressing table orange, the basin blue.
The doors lilac.
And that's all—nothing in this bedroom, with its shutters closed.
The solidity of the furniture should also now express unshakeable repose.
Portraits on the wall, and a mirror and a hand-towel and some clothes.
The frame—as there's no white in the painting—will be white.
This to take my revenge for the enforced rest that I was obligated to take.
I'll work on it again all day tomorrow, but you can see how simple the idea is. The shadows and cast shadows are removed; it's coloured in flat, plain tints like Japanese prints.
It will contrast, for example, with the Tarascon diligence and the night café. [. . .]
Ever yours,
Vincent

From a letter dated Oct. 17, 1888 (fig. 2). *Vincent van Gogh: The Letters*, ed. Leo Jansen, Hans Luijten, and Nienke Bakker (Van Gogh Museum/Huygens ING, 2009), 706.

My dear Gauguin,

[. . .] Look here, I wrote to you the other day that my vision was strangely tired. Well, I rested for two and a half days, and then I got back to work. But not yet daring to go outside, I did, for my decoration once again, a no. 30 canvas of my bedroom with the whitewood furniture that you know. Ah, well, it amused me enormously doing this bare interior.

With a simplicity à la *Seurat.*

In flat tints, but coarsely brushed in full impasto, the walls pale lilac, the floor in a broken and faded red, the chairs and the bed chrome yellow, the pillows and the sheet very pale lemon green, the bedspread blood-red, the dressing-table orange, the washbasin blue, the window green. I had wished to express *utter repose* with all these very different tones, you see, among which the only white is the little note given by the mirror with a black frame (to cram in the fourth pair of complementaries as well). [. . .]

Ever yours,
Vincent

Fig. 1 Van Gogh's *Letter to Theo van Gogh with the Sketch "The Bedroom"* (plate 19). Van Gogh Museum, Amsterdam (Vincent van Gogh Foundation).

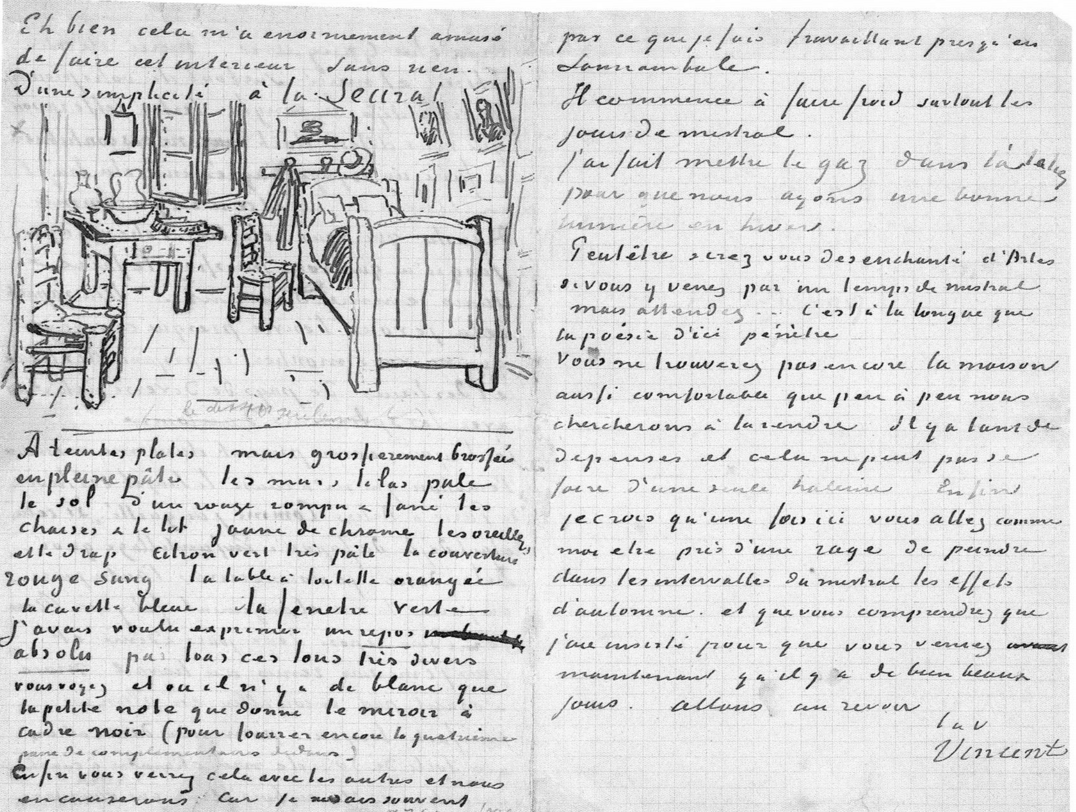

Eh bien cela m'a énormément amusé
de faire cet intérieur sans rien
d'une simplicité à la Seurat
A teintes plates mais grossièrement brossées
en pleine pâte les murs lilas pâle
le sol d'un rouge rompu et fané les
chaises et le lit jaune de chrome les oreillers
et le drap citron vert très pâle la couverture
rouge sang la table à toilette orangée
la cuvette bleue la fenêtre verte
J'avais voulu exprimer un repos absolu
par tous ces tons très divers
vous voyez et où il n'y a de blanc que
la petite note que donne le miroir à
cadre noir (pour fourrer encore la quatrième
paire de complémentaires dedans.)
Enfin vous verrez cela avec les autres et nous
en causerons car je ne sais souvent

par ce que je fais travaillant presqu'en
somnambule.
Il commence à faire froid surtout les
jours de mistral.
J'ai fait mettre le gaz dans l'atelier
pour que nous ayons une bonne
lumière en hiver.
Peutêtre serez vous desenchanté d'Arles
si vous y venez par un temps de mistral
mais attendez... C'est à la longue que
la poésie d'ici pénètre
Vous ne trouverez pas encore la maison
aussi confortable que peu à peu nous
chercherons à la rendre Il y a tant de
dépenses et cela ne peut pas se
faire d'une seule haleine. Enfin
je crois qu'une fois ici vous allez comme
moi être pris d'une rage de peindre
dans les intervalles du mistral les effets
d'automne. et que vous comprendrez que
j'ai insisté pour que vous venez
maintenant qu'il y a de bien beaux
jours. allons au revoir
t à t
Vincent

9766

Fig. 2 Vincent van Gogh (Dutch, 1853–1890). *Sketch of the Bedroom*, from a letter dated Oct. 17, 1888. Pen and black ink on machine-made wove paper; 9 × 14.2 cm (3 9/16 × 5 9/16 in.). Thaw Collection, the Pierpont Morgan Library, New York. JH1610

the walls. These individual variations highlight that Van Gogh was not trying to make an exact or precise duplicate of the original version. This is more apparent when all three works are viewed together and especially if one was to actually trace or overlay them; it then becomes clear that the various elements in the room are all placed slightly differently.[15]

For example, the Amsterdam and Chicago paintings show the corner of the ceiling, whereas this feature is absent in the Paris picture. This is most likely due to the fact that the squatter proportions of the Paris canvas precluded this feature's inclusion. Another significant difference is in the pictures depicted on the walls in each version; none are the same. There are also striking variations in the treatment of the floor. The combination of bright green and light reddish brown of the floor in the Chicago version is markedly different from that of the original Amsterdam study and the smaller Paris painting. Both of the latter appear closer to Van Gogh's original color description of the tiled floor "in a broken and faded red." The positions and angles of the chairs are unique to each version; so, too, is the way the still life on the table is painted.

Fig. 3 Map of the Chicago *Bedroom* showing charcoal underdrawing and painted sketch lines. Opposite page, legend showing magnified details.

3 Chicago

There is also a marked difference in the way the bright-green-and-yellow shuttered window is painted. In the Amsterdam study the window appears to be almost completely shut, while in the Chicago painting both sides are slightly open, and in the Paris version only the right side appears slightly open. The height and width of each window vary as well.

There is very little information in the artist's letters about his working methods, including how he transferred the composition when making his repetitions. In the case of the two later versions of *The Bedroom*, it is likely that Van Gogh did them freehand, because careful examination found no evidence of a tracing or a grid pattern. He normally relied on having the original painting on hand to make another version or repetition, and this was certainly the case for the two later pictures, as can be surmised from the exchange of letters that took place between Van Gogh and Theo.[16]

Preliminary Sketching of Composition

Examination of the paintings with the aid of a stereomicroscope as well as various analytical techniques can supplement the scarce documentary evidence by allowing the paintings themselves to reveal visual clues of their maker's working methods. With careful observation we determined the different types of materials that Van Gogh used for the initial sketching in of the composition onto the primed canvas, and we also identified areas that were initially left in reserve, that is, left to be painted in at a subsequent stage. This process involved significant variations in how each version was planned.

In the original Amsterdam study, it appears that only thin painted lines were used to initially define the composition. In the Chicago repetition, the presence of dark charcoal particles was observed microscopically along the edges of many of the forms, particularly in areas where breaks in the brushwork were evident and priming was left exposed, indicating that Van Gogh used charcoal as well as painted lines to sketch the initial composition.[17] This includes areas around the window, furniture, and some of the picture frames (see fig. 3). Some of the dark charcoal underdrawing material was also observed to be mixed in with the paint, probably caused by the brush picking up loose charcoal particles when it was loaded with paint. In contrast, no such compelling evidence of charcoal underdrawing was observed in either the Amsterdam or Paris versions.[18]

In all three works, thin, sometimes quite fluid, painted lines of different colors were used to define the contours of the main elements (see figs. 3–5) and, in the Chicago picture, to reinforce the initial charcoal underdrawing.[19] In the Amsterdam study, Van Gogh employed a wide variety of painted colored lines for laying out the composition, such as light green for the window, orange for the bed frame, light blue–gray for the pillows and sheets, a translucent red lake for the table and the left chair, and

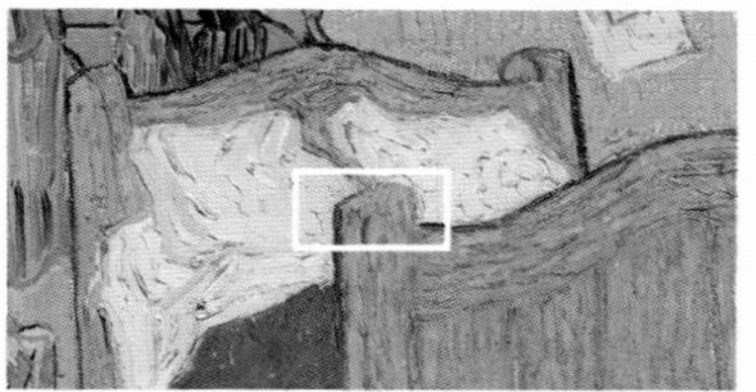

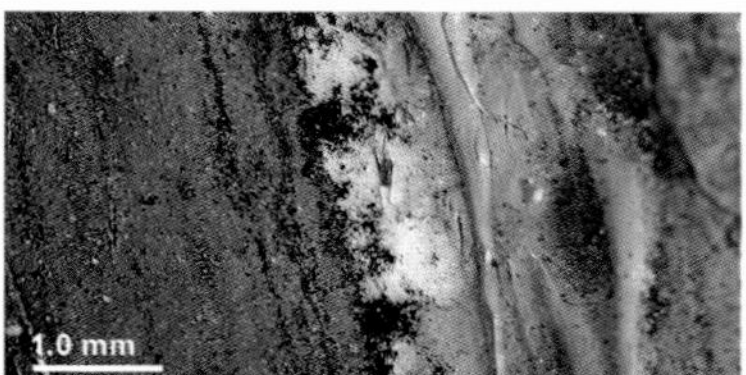

Charcoal underdrawing

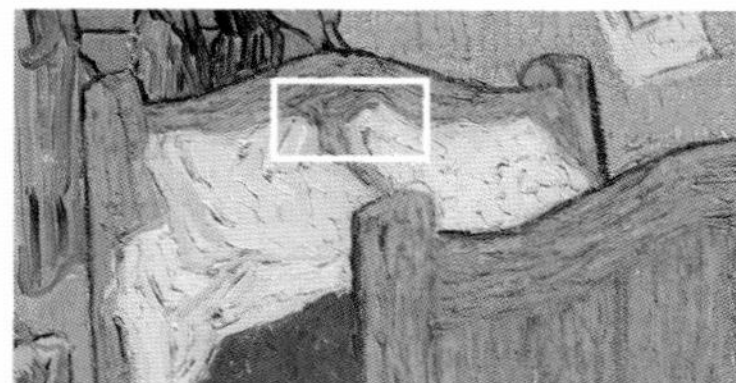

Painted sketch lines
■ Brownish green

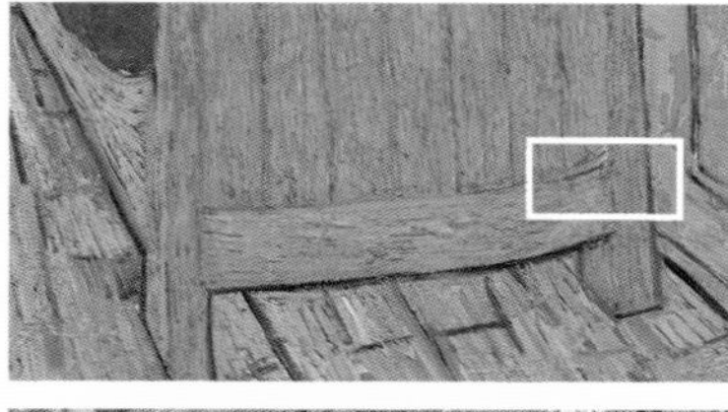

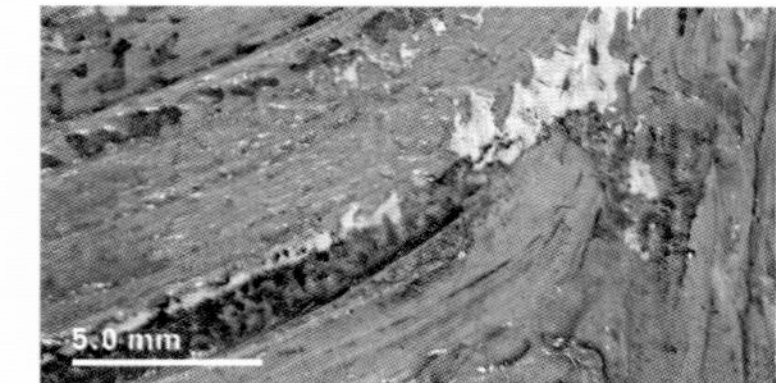

Painted sketch lines
■ Greenish gray

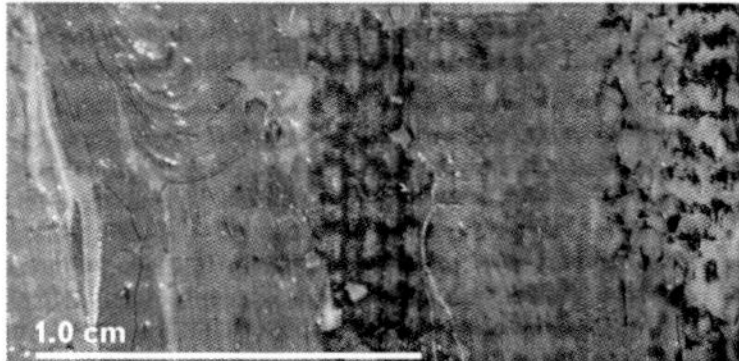

Painted sketch lines
■ Dark grayish blue

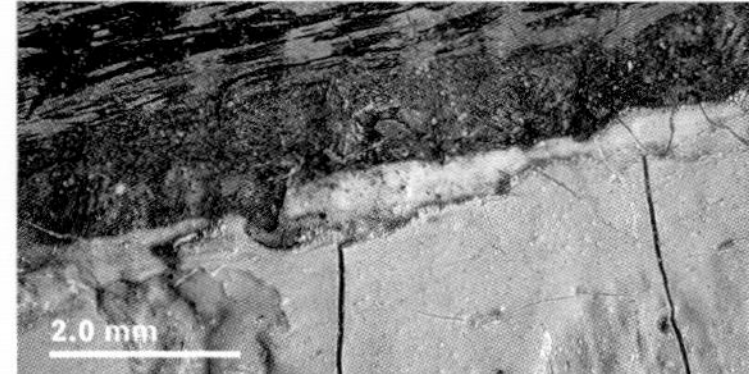

Painted sketch lines
■ Bluish green

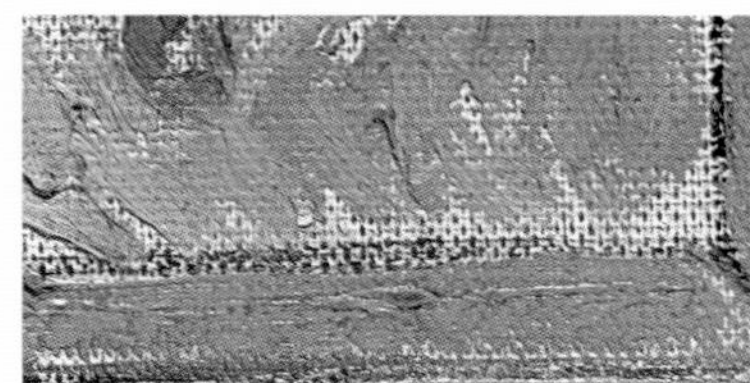

Painted sketch lines
■ Greenish blue

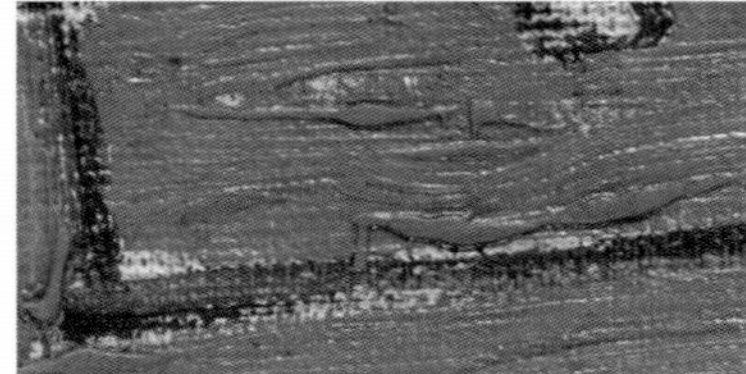

Painted sketch lines
■ Grayish blue

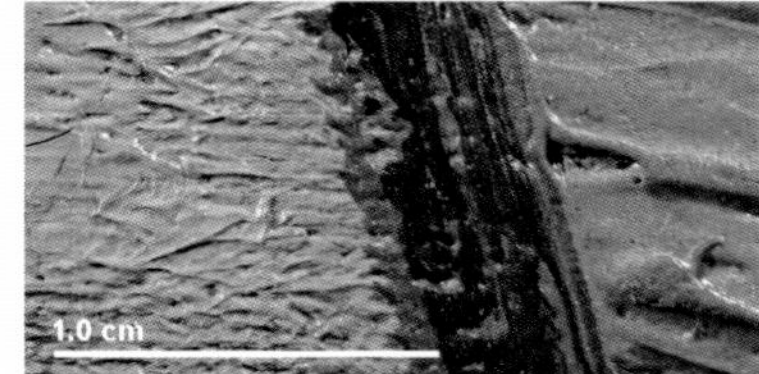

Painted sketch lines
■ Green

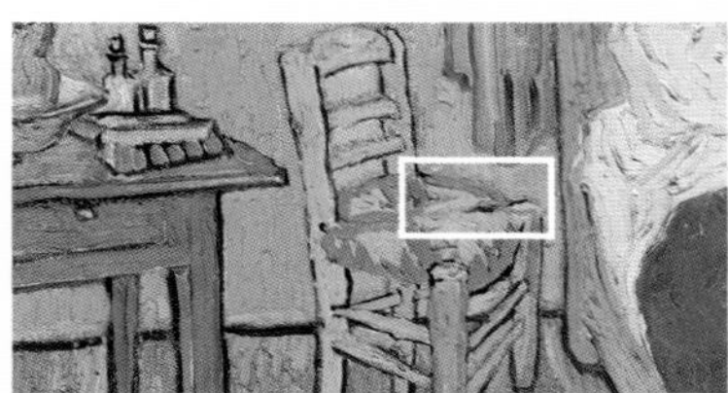

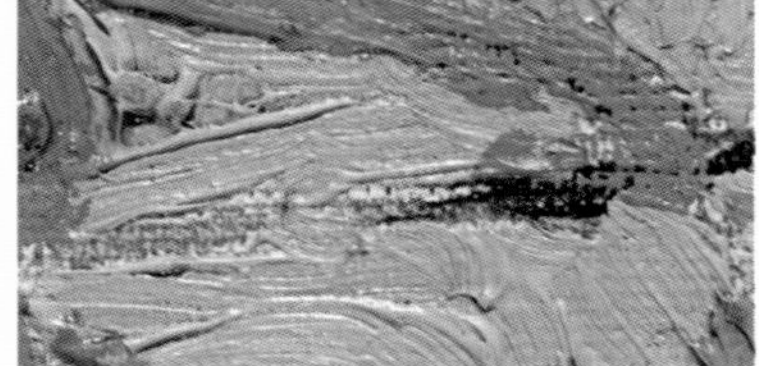

Painted sketch lines
■ Light-to-medium gray

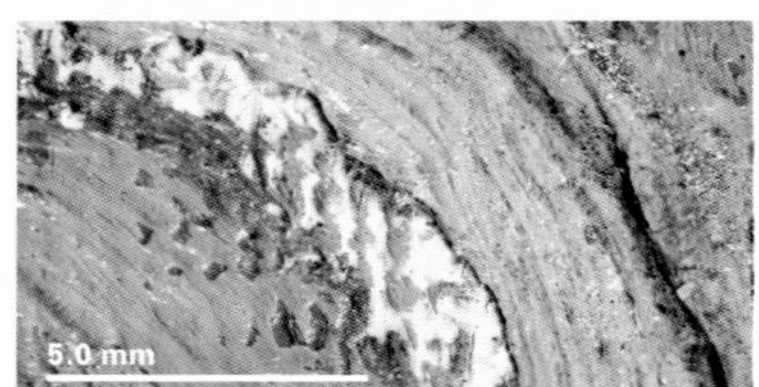

Painted sketch lines
■ Olive green

Fig. 4 Map of the Amsterdam *Bedroom* showing painted sketch lines. Opposite page, legend showing magnified details.

4 Amsterdam

Fig. 5 Map of the Paris *Bedroom* showing painted sketch lines. Opposite page, legend showing magnified details.

5 Paris

Painted sketch lines
■ Light green

Painted sketch lines
■ Blue wash

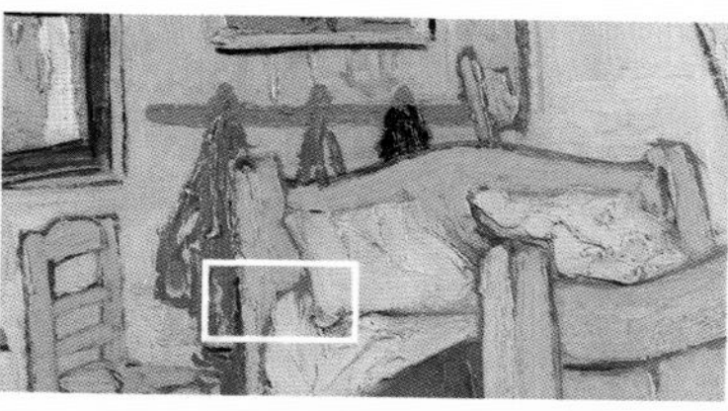

Painted sketch lines
■ Orange

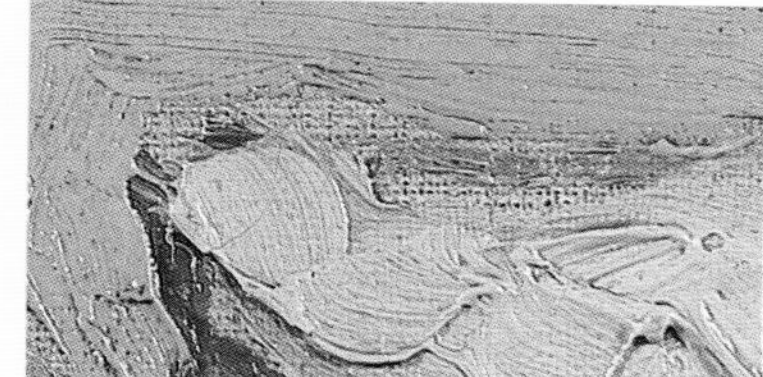

Painted sketch lines
■ Light blue-gray

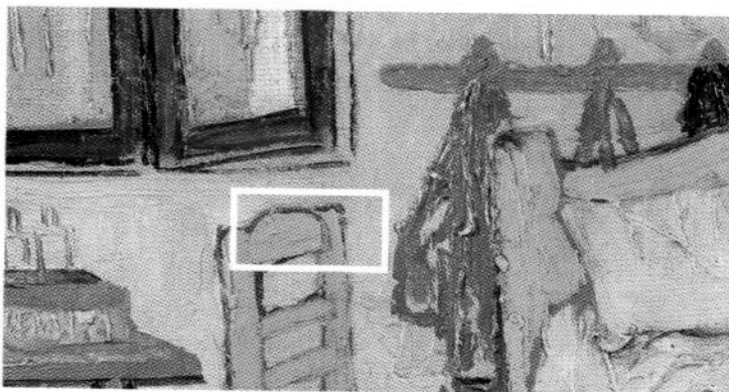
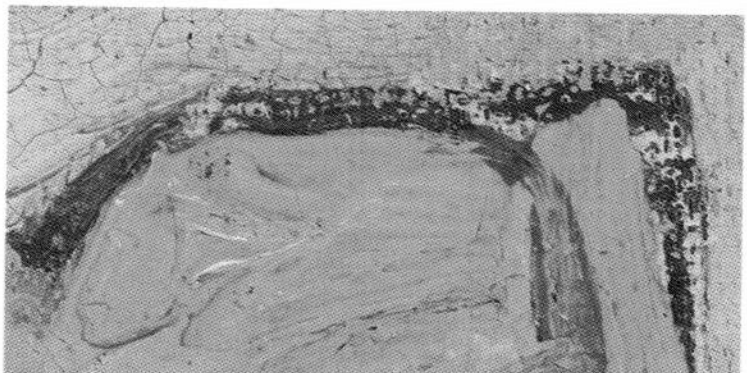

Painted sketch lines
■ Grayish brown

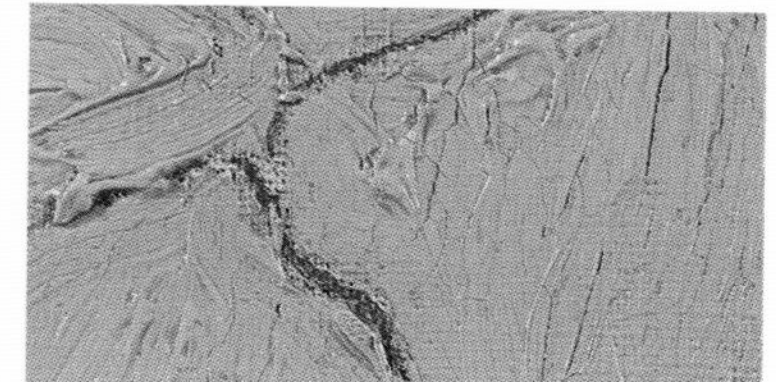

Painted sketch lines
■ Translucent red lake (retouched)

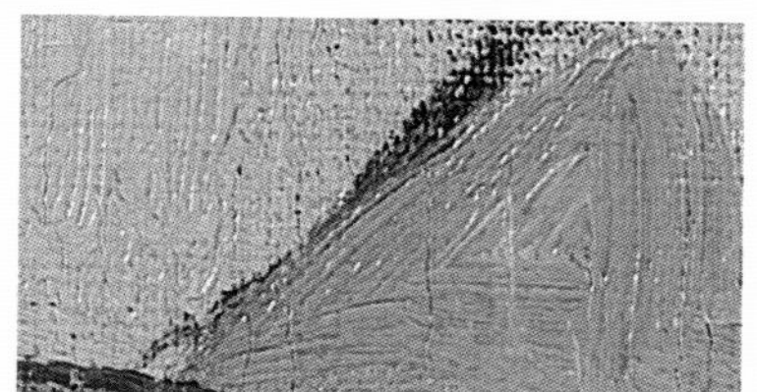

Painted sketch lines
■ Dark blue

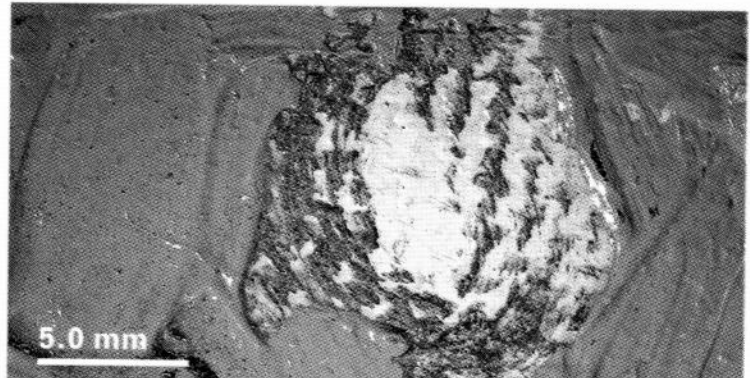

Painted sketch lines
■ Orange to orange-brown

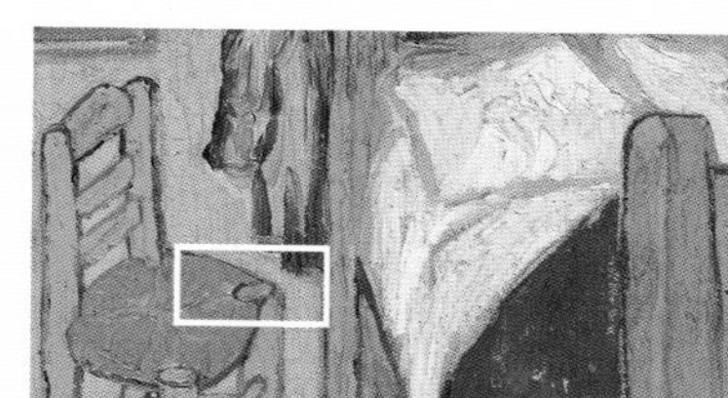
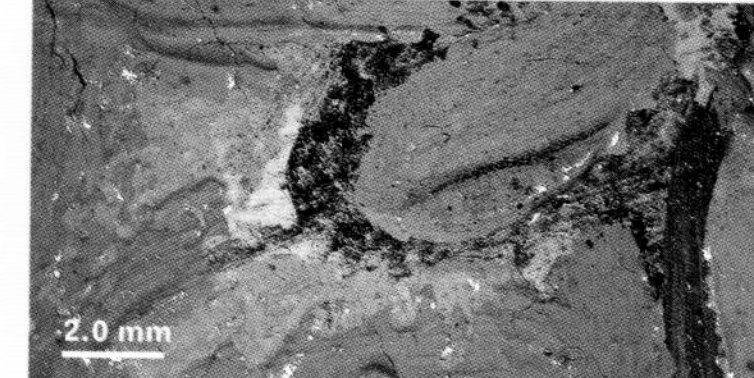

Painted sketch lines
■ Dark brownish black

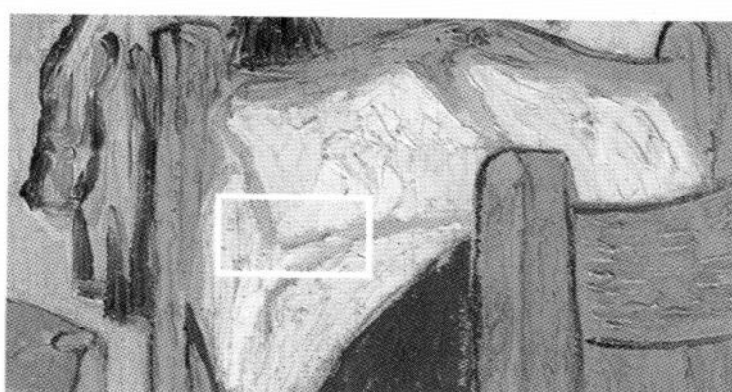

Painted sketch lines
■ Light grayish blue

Painted sketch lines
■ Blue

Fig. 6 X-ray images of the three *Bedroom* paintings highlight variations in brushwork between the three versions as well as show areas that the artist initially held in reserve (these appear darker in tone). In the Amsterdam painting, for example, the pictures on the wall on the right were painted on top of the blue (once violet) walls; therefore, they show up much lighter than the comparable areas in the Chicago and Paris versions, in which these features appear dark and more distinct.

6 Amsterdam

6 Chicago

6 Paris

multiple colors for the chair next to the bed (see fig. 4).[20] By using various hues for the painted sketching lines, the artist could have intended a loose indication of the often contrasting colors to be used for these components of the scene.

In the Chicago canvas, Van Gogh incorporated a wider range of colors for the preliminary painted sketch lines, such as a grayish blue for the contours of the doors, olive green for the left chair, a brownish green and greenish gray for the pillows and the bed frame, a grayish blue for the chair next to the bed and table, and a bluish green for the frame of the female portrait (see fig. 3). It is interesting to note that Van Gogh varied the colors of the painted outlines even for the same element.

In the smaller Paris version, Van Gogh utilized fewer colors for the preliminary painted sketch (see fig. 5). Examples include various shades of blue for the contours of the different walls, doors, and windows; light grayish blue to outline pillows and sheets; and an orange-to-orange-brown paint, rich in binding medium and varying in tint, to outline the furniture, clothes rack, and the landscape. Some preliminary dark-brownish-black outlines were also observed in certain areas of the bed and chairs.

After initially sketching out the various forms of the composition, Van Gogh then filled in the areas of the walls and doors while leaving other forms in reserve (see fig. 6). In the Amsterdam study, only some of the main elements of the composition were held in reserve, namely, the bed, the window, both chairs, and the table. Loosely defined areas were also left in reserve for the objects in the still life, such as the jug and the pitcher. The mirror, the pictures on the walls, the clothing, the hat, and the rack were painted over the already-finished walls in an additive process. In comparison, for the repetitions, Van Gogh left most of the elements in reserve while working on the walls. In a few cases, we noted variations on these main approaches: in the Chicago painting, the clothing, hat, and rack were painted at the same time as the first layer of paint was applied to the walls; and in the Paris version, some of the objects in the still life (such as the small bottles, jug, and pitcher) were added after the first layer of wall paint had already been applied.

Painting Technique and Compositional Changes

... the shadows and cast shadows are removed; it's coloured in flat, plain tints like Japanese prints.
Van Gogh to Theo, Arles, Oct. 16, 1888

X-radiography and raking-light imaging (figs. 6–7) highlight the variation in the types of brushwork between the three paintings.

The Amsterdam study is painted fairly thickly, with looser marks of the brush that vary in their shape and direction, but in a more uniform tone or color, particularly for the walls, doors, and floor. This execution fits Van Gogh's description of the picture as being similar to Japanese prints, an effect that is further reinforced by the use of final painted lines of contrasting colors to outline the main elements, such as the blue around the yellow chair on the left or the red in and around the bed frame. Other areas are coarsely textured, with strokes of fairly thick impasto, such as in the light-yellow side of the bed, the pillows and sheets, the orange table, and the sky in the landscape, illustrating Van Gogh's description of it being painted "in flat tints, but coarsely brushed in full impasto."[21]

Fig. 7 Raking-light images of the three *Bedroom* paintings. Lit at an oblique angle, these images show the variation and texture of Van Gogh's brushwork. The artist painted the Amsterdam version fairly thickly, with looser, more varied brushstrokes that were more uniform in tone. In comparison, the Chicago and Paris versions exhibit a more deliberate and tightly structured brushwork.

7 Amsterdam

7 Chicago

7 Paris

In comparison, both the Chicago and Paris versions have a more deliberate, controlled, rhythmic type of brushwork with a more precise depiction of details. For instance, in the Chicago repetition, areas of thick impasto were applied predominantly in the vertical direction for the walls and the floors, whereas longer, curved strokes define contours as well as the folds in the towels and the clothing. Shorter brushstrokes applied wet-in-wet in various directions were used for the pillows, the bed cover, and the chair seats. This type of expressive, pronounced brushwork found in the two repetitions, is characteristic of the distinctive style of painting—at times described as graphic due to its more linear quality—that Van Gogh developed later while in Saint-Rémy.

Walls and Doors *The walls are of a pale violet.... The doors lilac.*
Van Gogh to Theo, Arles, Oct. 16, 1888

Van Gogh's approach to painting the walls and doors was different in each version. In the Amsterdam *Bedroom* study, these areas appear to have been painted fairly quickly and in one single session, as indicated in a cross section that shows a single, fairly thick layer (fig. 8, top). Even though the paint was quite thickly applied, the overall effect is rather flat, despite variations of color in the brushwork. The darker-blue contour lines around the doorframe and the door panels, as well as the darker-blue lines delineating the walls, were all painted wet-in-wet in the lighter-colored paint. When sufficiently dry, the objects on the table, the pictures, and clothes rack were all painted on top of the existing wall paint (fig. 9, top).

In the two later versions, Van Gogh built up the composition in stages. In the Chicago picture, he first painted in the area of the walls and doors with a moderately thin, grayish-blue layer. This layer varies in tone with the admixture of different colored pigments. The upper layer of the wall, based on cobalt blue, appears to have been added last because, in

Fig. 8 A comparison of the paint cross sections taken from the walls and door of the three *Bedroom* paintings. In the Amsterdam version, the wall layer consists of a single, fairly thick layer of paint, whereas both later repetitions show two or more paint layers. In the Chicago painting, two applications of paint were identified: a fairly thin, grayish-blue underlayer, covered by a thicker, now mostly blue layer. In the Paris picture, three layers are visible in the cross sections from the wall and the door.

Blue (once violet) layer: zinc white, cobalt blue and some red lake (cochineal with an aluminum/calcium-based substrate [in lower part of the layer])

Ground layer

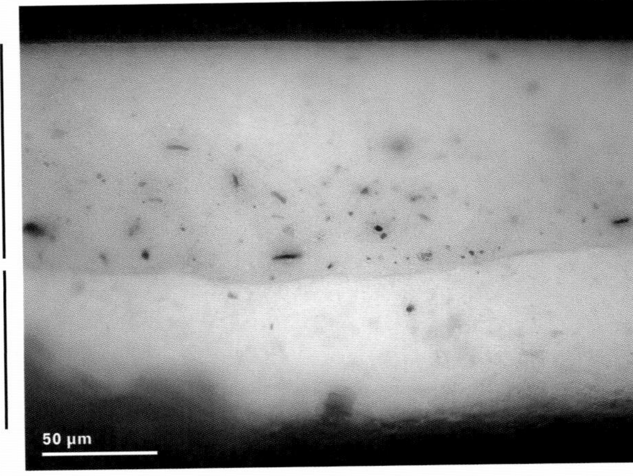

8 Amsterdam

Upper blue (once violet) layer: zinc white, cobalt blue, red lake (cochineal with an aluminum/calcium-based substrate [in lower part of the layer]), and a small amount of lead white

Grayish-blue underlayer: zinc white, ultramarine blue, vermilion, and a small amount of lead white

Ground layer

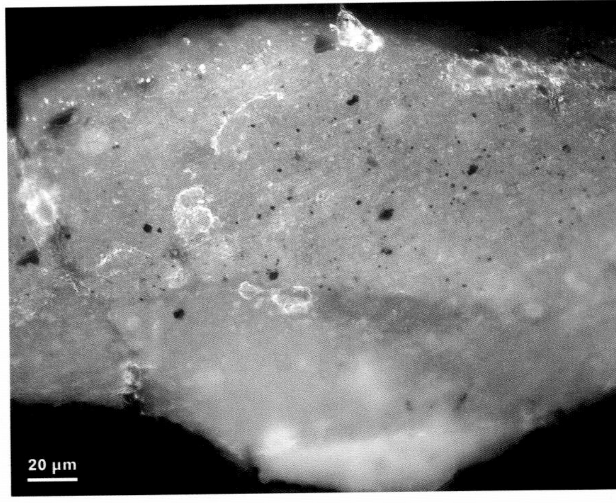

8 Chicago

Three colored layers based on zinc white, cobalt blue, and red lake (cochineal-based) (cross section of wall)

Ground layer

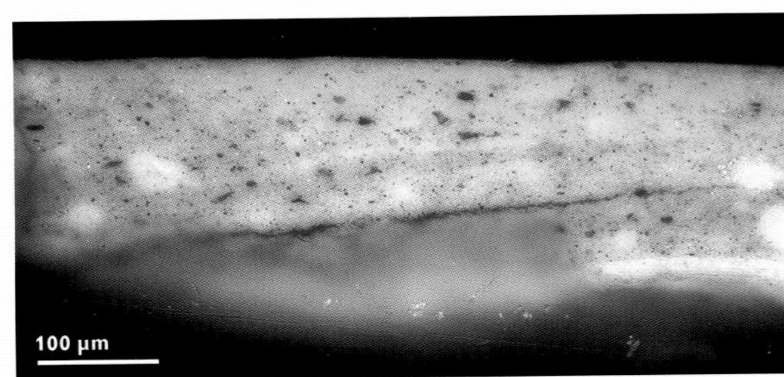

8 Paris

Three colored layers based on zinc white, cobalt blue, and red lake (cochineal-based) (cross section of left door)

Ground layer

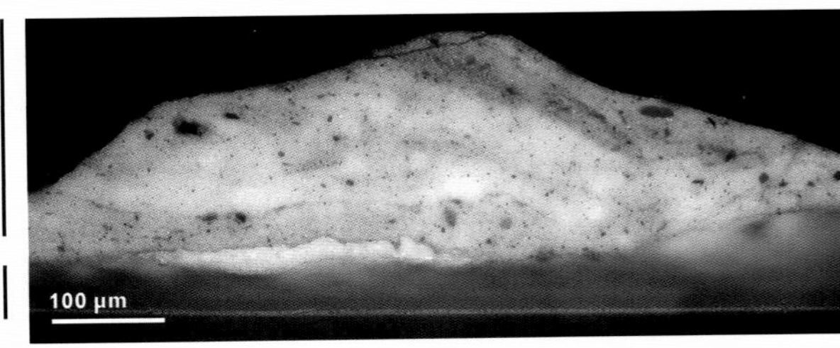

8 Paris

some cases, it comes up over outlines of compositional elements, such as the underside of the table. The bottom layer must have been sufficiently dry before the second layer was added, as there are two distinct layers in the paint cross sections (fig. 8, second from top). In the Paris version, the layering of paint in the walls and doors varied, and multiple layers are present. Careful observation of the cross sections taken from the wall (fig. 8, second from bottom) and door (fig. 8, bottom) as well as of the painting surface (fig. 10) suggests the presence of three layers, most likely painted wet-in-wet. The first paint layer on top of the ground is pale blue and is based on cobalt blue and zinc white with a small amount of cochineal lake. Above that layer is a lilac paint layer where a significant amount of red lake is present. This layer is also composed of zinc white, cobalt blue, and cochineal but in different proportions.[22] The top layer shows only a few particles of red lake, leading to the blue color perceived today.

In situ X-ray fluorescence (XRF) measurements on the walls and doors of all three paintings revealed that they are mainly cobalt blue mixed with zinc white.[23] Analysis of cross sections of paint from the walls and doors in all three paintings confirmed these results and also highlighted the addition of red lake particles, visible in the center area in each of the cross sections, which were identified as cochineal lake.[24] As will be discussed in a later section of this essay, the red lake particles can be understood as evidence of the original "pale violet" or "lilac" color, now faded, of the walls and doors, especially in the Amsterdam and Chicago pictures. In addition, in cross sections from the Chicago repetition, an array of differently colored pigment particles were observed in the lower grayish-blue paint layer, highlighting Van Gogh's use of complex mixtures of pigments, including zinc white, emerald green, vermilion, ultramarine blue, a little cobalt blue, and possibly some red lake, to create a range of diverse tones.

Floor *The floor—is of red tiles.*
Van Gogh to Theo, Arles, Oct. 16, 1888

The manner in which Van Gogh built up the floor of each version was complex and included multiple paint applications that vary across the floor area. However, Van Gogh's process remained rather similar for all three pictures, beginning with a fairly extensively applied initial layer: a buff-colored layer, which was originally pinker, in the Amsterdam picture; a light-pinkish-brown layer in the Chicago version; and a light-brownish layer in the Paris version.[25] This layer was completed by painted strokes to indicate perspective lines and to provide a first suggestion of the tiles. This stage of the work was followed by a second paint application that covers most

Fig. 9 In the Amsterdam version, the small landscape above the bed was painted directly on top of the blue (once violet) wall. In both the Chicago and Paris repetitions, Van Gogh initially left the landscape in reserve. Some of the off-white ground was left exposed, as can be seen in the photomicrograph from the Chicago painting.

9 Amsterdam

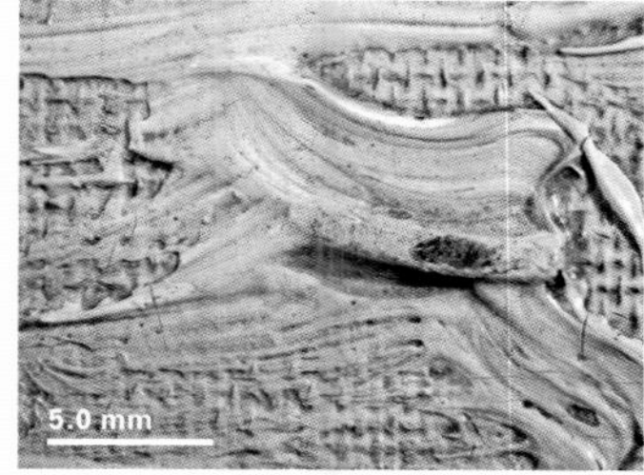

9 Chicago

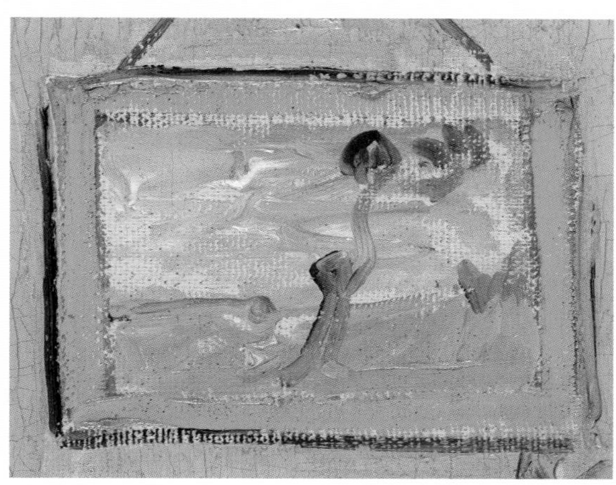

9 Paris

Fig. 10 A detail of the wall of the Paris *Bedroom* showing three different paint applications.

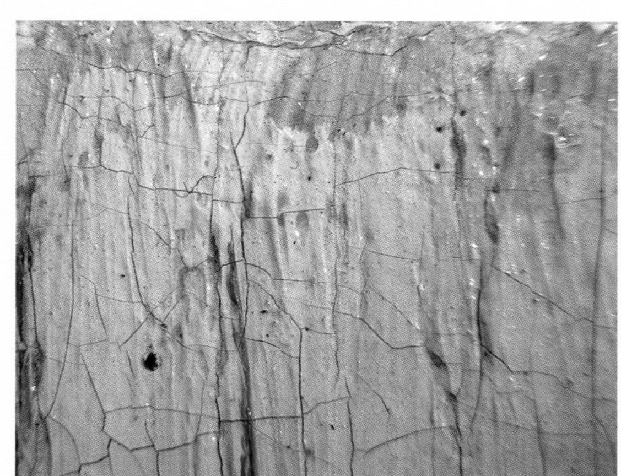

10 Paris

sections of the floor. The final step was to paint the outlines of the tiles (see fig. 11).

Scaffolded on this general scheme, the three versions show a number of significant variations. The second, salmon-pink layer of paint was more uniformly applied in the Amsterdam study, while in the two other versions it consisted of a discontinuous application of fairly broad brushstrokes (bright green in the case of Chicago, and brownish purple in the Paris version). The vertical brushstrokes in the two later versions follow the perspective lines and become less dense as they approach the foreground, where the earlier paint applications remain visible. This variation in paint application and color combination contributes to a very different final depiction of each of the floors: generally more even in the Amsterdam version (even taking into account some flattening of texture as a result of lining treatments), more textural, broken, and contrasting due to the hatched brushwork in the two later versions. This broken, hatched brushwork is reinforced in the Paris version, where the final outlines of the tiles are less prominent.

In terms of color, similar pigments—including zinc white, vermilion, emerald green, and red lake—were used in the floors in all three versions (see fig. 12), but in varying proportions, resulting in very different dominant color schemes in the floor, at least as it appears today. The floor of the Amsterdam painting is dominated by pinkish-to-purple colors with green outlines, while the exact opposite is true of the floor of the Chicago picture, which shows a bright-green color contrasting with the reddish-brown outlines of the tiles. Brownish purple is the predominant color of the floor in the Paris version, where emerald green in the paint mixture makes only a very limited contribution to the final tint. Geranium (eosin) lake was identified in the floor of all three paintings. In addition, a small amount of cochineal lake was found only in the Amsterdam and Paris versions.[26]

Table *The dressing table orange, the basin blue.* Van Gogh to Theo, Oct. 16, 1888

The buildup of the table and the still life resting on it followed a sequence that increased in complexity over the course of the three versions (see fig. 13), resulting in three-dimensional effects and a more detailed depiction of the objects in the two later versions. A major difference between the three paintings lies in the order in which the objects on the table were painted. In the Amsterdam study, only the pitcher and jug were partially left in reserve, together with the table. Most of the other objects were painted last, once the table was completed, by applying rough, thick impasto and thin contours wet-in-wet on top

11 Amsterdam

Intermediate blue painted lines

Green final outlines

Second main paint application, originally salmon pink, now discolored to purplish

First main buff-colored layer (originally pinker)

Intermediate thin orange painted lines

11 Chicago

First main light-pinkish-brown layer applied in thick, wet-in-wet brushstrokes of incompletely mixed colors of white, red, and green

Second main paint application made with bright-green impasto, including some blue mixed in some areas

Dark reddish-brown final outlines

A few intermediate dark-green painted lines

11 Paris

Second main paint application with brownish-purple paint

Intermediate light-grayish-blue painted lines

First main layer of a light-brownish color with a slightly green tint

Thin dark-brown final outlines

Intermediate pink painted lines

Fig. 11 Descriptive representation of the paint buildup for the floors of the three *Bedroom* paintings.

of the painted background wall and tabletop. Particularly remarkable in the Amsterdam version is the way in which Van Gogh depicted the soap and the three small bottles, which were summarily painted with only a few monochromatic brushstrokes. In contrast, in the two repetitions, the objects were painted at the same time as the table and the walls. In both cases, the still life was depicted more precisely, using a greater variety of paint applications and colors, following a more complex sequence of steps, which interacted with the painting of the table.[27]

As for the table on which the objects are placed, in the Amsterdam study Van Gogh used a very concise approach, rapidly filling in the table's entire volume with relatively thick, orange-colored impasto, adding wet-in-wet greenish paint to distinguish the drawer and tabletop, and then further outlining the table in contrasting dark blue (see fig. 13, top). Instead, in the two later versions, Van Gogh used more controlled paint applications in a variety of shades, thus providing dimensionality, shading, and richness of detail (see fig. 13, middle, bottom).

The Chair on the Left *The bedstead and the chairs are fresh butter yellow.* Van Gogh to Theo, Oct. 16, 1888

Van Gogh's resourcefulness as a painter is especially remarkable in his treatment of the chairs. He painted the chairs differently in each version, yet within each work, the two chairs are almost identical in style and color. Close observation reveals that the process used in painting the left chair, for example, followed a fairly similar general sequence in all three versions (see fig. 14). After initially sketching in the outlines of the chair with painted lines, the frame and seat were filled in with different colors.[28] In all three paintings, two distinct shades of yellow were used for the frame of the chair. The final contours of the chairs were reinforced using painted lines.

In the Amsterdam version, the chair was painted in predominantly flat tints, with the exception of the back of the chair, which was initially laid in with a light-green paint layer with contrasting bright-blue outlines. The wood portion of the chairs was also painted fairly uniformly in the other versions. The most dramatic variation is found in the depiction of the chair seats, which, in the Paris and Chicago pictures, are painted with far more textural brushwork, thicker impasto, and contrasting colors. There is also a marked difference in the directionality of the strokes, which in the two later versions follow the radiating pattern of the weave of the rush seats.

The artist's color choices were also unique in each version even as they relied on an underlying similarity of pigments. Zinc white and chrome yellow in different hues are the main pigments used for the frame and seat of the left chairs in all three works (see fig. 14). In addition, in the Chicago version, emerald

Fig. 12 The cross sections from the floors of the Amsterdam and Chicago *Bedrooms* show similarities in materials and paint stratigraphy. In the Amsterdam sample, there are two layers: the initial, buff-colored layer, which was originally much pinker (see fig. 18) and, above that, a second, salmon-pink paint layer that also has discolored toward purple. The cross section from the Chicago painting shows a light-pinkish-brown paint layer that appears much lighter toward the top of the layer, a possible indication of discoloration or fading in the paint layer.

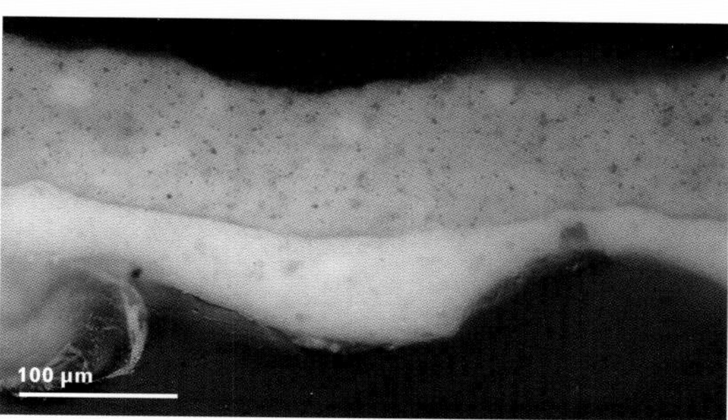

12 Amsterdam

Pinkish-to-purple layer (now discolored): mixture of zinc white and lead white, vermilion, eosin (geranium lake), and emerald green

Buff-colored layer (originally pinker): mixture of zinc white and lead white, vermilion, red lead, some emerald green, a few particles of cochineal red lake with low aluminum/calcium-based substrate, a little chrome yellow, and a trace of cobalt blue

Ground

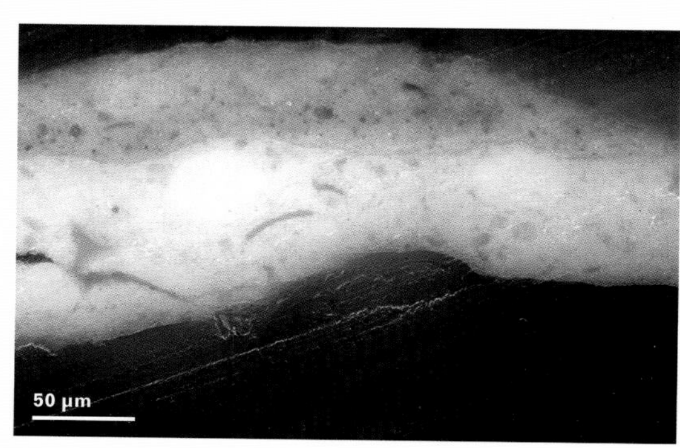

12 Chicago

Light-pinkish-brown (now discolored) layer: mixture of zinc white; vermilion; eosin (geranium lake); emerald green; and traces of calcium-based white, quartz, or other silicates; plus zinc clusters (possibly zinc soaps)

Ground

Fig. 13 Sequence of paint application for the table and still life on top of it for the three *Bedroom* paintings.

13 Amsterdam

13 Chicago

13 Paris

Detail of the small bottles, painted directly over the wall

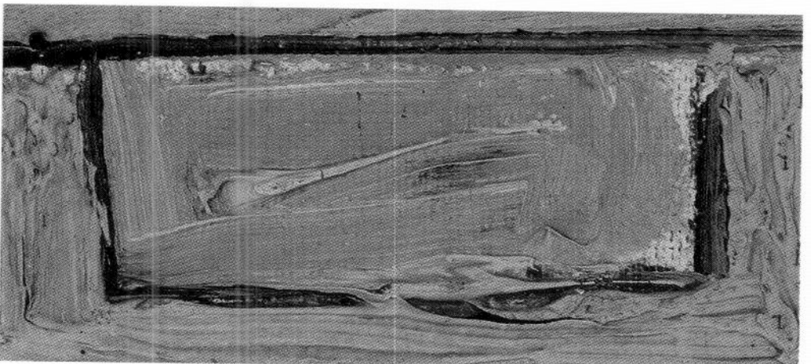

Detail of drawer showing wet-in-wet mixture of orange and green paint. Translucent red lake painted lines are reinforced by dark outlines around the drawer

Amsterdam

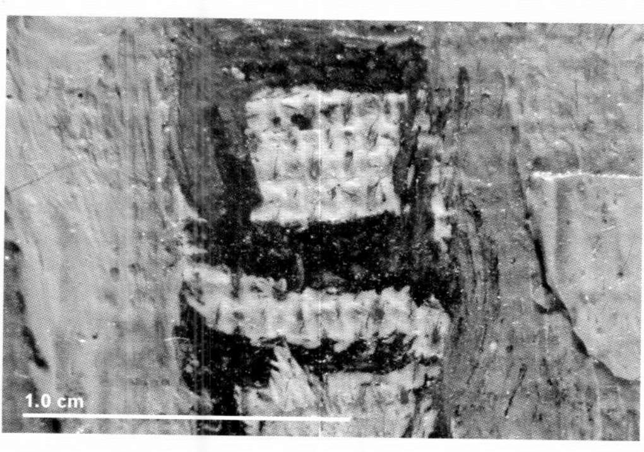

Photomicrograph of the top of the taller bottle with ground layer visible

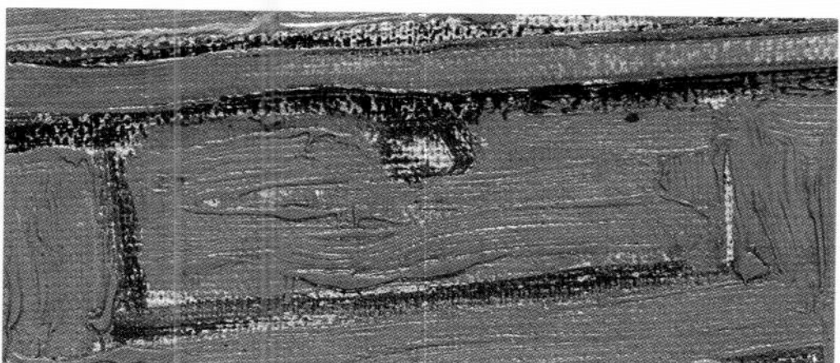

Detail of drawer showing the different colored contour lines

Chicago

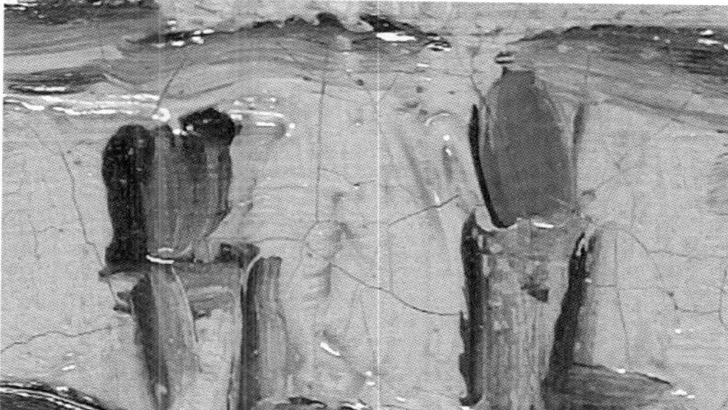

Detail of bottles showing very fluid brushwork and the brown strokes indicating the tops of the bottles that were painted over the first layer of wall paint

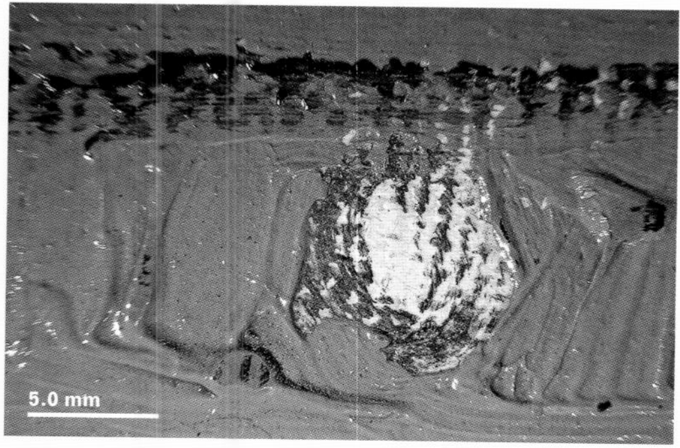

Photomicrograph of drawer knob with ground and initial yellow-brown outlining visible

Paris

green was added in varying proportion to the lighter-yellow paint mixture and viridian to the darker portion of the seat. In the Paris painting, only emerald green was added, resulting in a markedly different final color scheme for the seat. Red lakes were used for the painted outlines of the Amsterdam version: cochineal lake probably mixed with an iron-based pigment for the preliminary sketching and geranium lake mixed with a blue pigment for the final outlining.[29] The presence of iron-based pigments was also detected in the two later repetitions: in the Chicago painting, in the initial and final outlines of the chair, mixed with other pigments; and in the Paris version, in the highlights of the seat. Geranium lake was also found present in the reddish-brown outlines in the Chicago picture.[30]

Van Gogh's Painting Materials

I had wished to express utter repose *with all these very different tones, you see, among which the only white is the little note given by the mirror with a black frame (to cram in the fourth pair of complementaries as well).*
Van Gogh to Paul Gauguin, Oct. 17, 1888

We know from his letters that Van Gogh very much admired the artist Eugène Delacroix, whom he first came to know in depth through the writings of Charles Blanc, which he read in 1884.[31] Delacroix's use of complementary colors in his own paintings inspired and influenced Van Gogh's art making. He was also influenced by the application of color theories of the pointillist artists Georges Seurat and Paul Signac, hence the reference to the former in his letter to Gauguin (see fig. 2). As one can see, the color combinations that he used to paint the *Bedroom*s are all based on primary complementaries. With regard to the first *Bedroom*, Van Gogh wrote that "looking at the painting should *rest* the mind, or rather the imagination" and that "colour has to do the job here."[32] For instance, in both the Amsterdam and Chicago pictures, the floor is green and reddish brown, which are complementaries, although green is much more pronounced in the Chicago repetition. In the Paris picture, the floor presents little green, but this is compensated in part by the much more generous use of green in the chair seats. Likewise, the yellow bed, chairs, and the once "pale violet" walls and "lilac" doors in these pictures are complementaries, as are the orange table and the blue objects. Even within the landscape painting on the far wall, the pink of the sky and green foliage are complementaries. The towel also consists of complementary colors (an overall greenish tone with red stripes). An excerpt taken from Kate Newell Doggett's 1874 translation of Blanc's book provides an example of the concepts of complementary color theory and suggests the impact these ideas could have when used by painters: "If we combine two of the primary colors, yellow and blue, for

Fig. 14 Sequence of paint application for the three chairs on the left in the three *Bedroom* paintings.

Fill-in with three different shades of paint: light green, light yellow, and bright yellow

Fill-in of the seat with lead chromate–based light-green paint

Red preliminary painted outlines based on cochineal lake (*see cross section on opposite page*)

Final blue outlines containing eosin lake

14 Amsterdam

Olive-green preliminary painted outlines

Fill-in with two different shades of paints: bright yellow and orange-yellow

Dark-blue intermediate painted outlines

Blue intermediate outlines painted wet-in-wet

Fill-in with light-yellow-green paint

Brownish-yellow intermediate highlights on the seat

Final outlines in either dark green or reddish brown

14 Chicago

Fill-in with two different shades of paint: bright warm yellow-orange and light yellow

Red-brown intermediate painted outlines

Fill-in with bright-greenish-yellow paint

Greenish-brown intermediate painted outlines applied wet-in-wet

Orange-brown preliminary painted outlines

Bright-orange intermediate highlights

Heterogeneously mixed red/green intermediate painted outlines

Final red-brown outlines

Final dark-green outlines added selectively

14 Paris

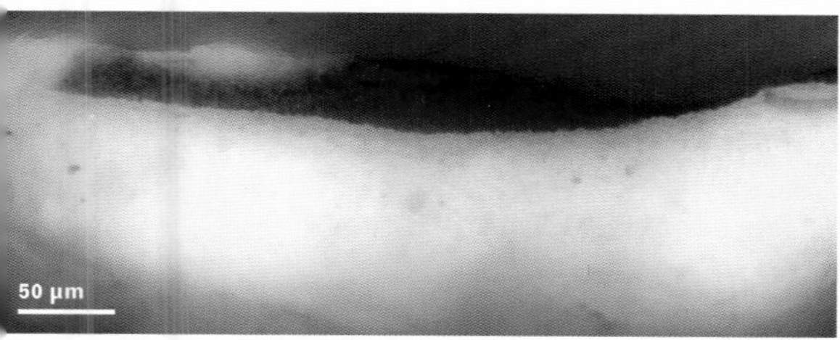

Cross section of the preliminary red outlines containing cochineal lake on an aluminum/calcium-based substrate (under UV-fluorescence illumination)

Ground layer

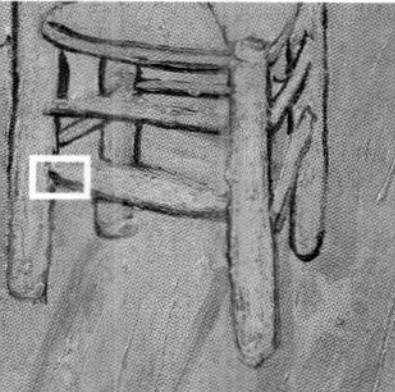

Amsterdam

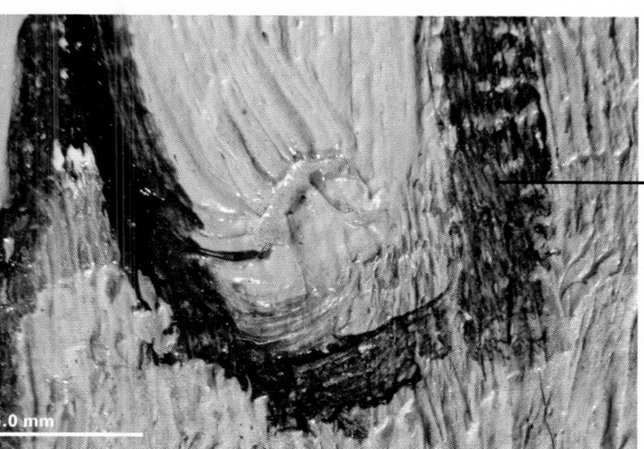

Photomicrograph showing final dark-green outlines

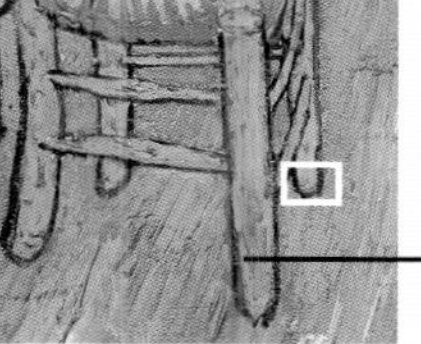

Final reddish-brown outlines

Chicago

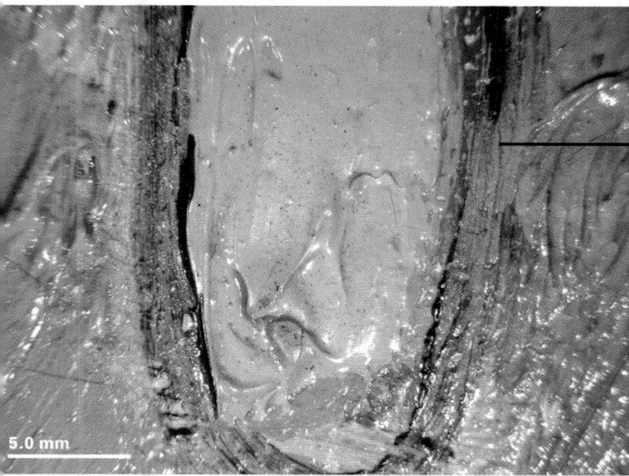

Photomicrograph showing final red-brown outlines

Paris

instance, to compose a secondary color, green, this secondary color will reach its maximum intensity if we place it near its complement, namely, red."[33] By carefully balancing the arrangement of colors in his *Bedroom* paintings, Van Gogh managed to exploit these bright complementary color contrasts while preserving the restful and harmonious effect that was so essential to the pictures' meaning.

Van Gogh began each work using a plain-weave linen canvas of ordinary quality that was commercially primed from the Paris firm Tasset et L'Hôte.[34] Indeed, unsatisfied by the primed canvases that were available locally in Arles, from July 1888 onward, the artist placed frequent orders through his brother Theo for this type of primed canvas, which was sold usually in rolls (2 × 10 m) or half rolls (2 × 5 m).[35] As he noted in a letter of August 21 or 22, 1888, to Theo, "Tasset ordinary canvas, which at 50 centimes was dearer than Bourgeois's, is very much to my liking and is very well prepared."[36] Van Gogh would then cut the canvas rolls into standard sizes, which he would attach onto a temporary stretcher to begin a new painting. Interestingly, a detailed evaluation of the physical attributes of the canvases, such as the thread density and weave matches, as well as the ground composition, has determined that the three versions of the *Bedroom* were produced from three different rolls of primed canvas.[37] It might appear especially surprising that the Chicago and Paris versions did not come from the same roll of canvas, since they were painted within a very short time of each other. This is likely because the artist used remnants of primed canvas from different rolls that were lying around in his studio at the time.

Relying mainly on Theo for his painting supplies, Van Gogh's letters often included lists of materials that he needed. Theo would order them from two different color merchants, Tasset et L'Hôte and Père Tanguy. On April 5, 1888, while living in Arles, Van Gogh requested the following paints:

20 Silver white large tubes	
10 ditto zinc white	
15 Veronese Green	*double tubes*
10 Lemon Chrome Yellow	*ditto*
10 (No. two) Chrome Yellow	*ditto*
3 Vermilion	*ditto*
3 No. three Chrome Yellow	*ditto*
6 Geranium lake small tubes	*freshly ground,*
12 ordinary [lake small tubes]	*if they're greasy I'll*
2 Carmine [lake small tubes]	*send them back.*
4 Prussian Blue	*small tubes*
4 very light cinnabar GREEN	*small tubes*
2 orange lead	*small tubes*
6 [viridian (Vert émeraude)][38]	*small tubes*

The pigments used for the three *Bedrooms* are all fairly similar and include many of those included in this list, as well as those reported in the literature.[39] Van Gogh used a very extensive

Fig. 15 *Top*, palette of Vincent van Gogh, Musée d'Orsay, Paris, gift of Paul Gachet, 1951. This is believed to be the palette Van Gogh used while he was living in Auvers-sur-Oise. *Bottom*, tube of Tasset et L'Hôte geranium lake oil paint, Musée d'Orsay, Paris, gift of Paul Gachet, 1951. This tube was probably used by the artist during this same period. Geranium lake is made from a synthetic dye, eosin, and it has a very brilliant red color. It is extremely fugitive—that is, it fades fairly quickly.

15

15

palette "to make simplicity with bright colours" (see fig. 15, top; see also pigment table, p. 87), as he explained in a letter on or about October 21, 1889, to his sister Willemien, referring to the third version of *The Bedroom*: "To make simplicity with bright colours isn't easy though, and I find that it can be useful to show that one can be simple with something other than grey, white, black and brown. That is the *raison d'être* for that study."[40]

For most of the colors, he did not rely on just a single colorant but rather used a variety of hues (such as three different shades of chrome yellow), thus increasing the number of colors and contributing to a brighter, more colorful palette in keeping with the brilliant southern French light that he was especially fond of. Two different white pigments, namely, zinc white and lead white (which is translated as "silver white"), have been identified. In all three paintings, zinc white was the main white, used either alone or in various mixtures; only very small amounts of lead white were used. Although zinc white has the disadvantage of drying more slowly than lead white, Van Gogh may have preferred it for its specific handling properties, which allowed him to apply the paint much more thickly, thereby creating higher impasto when compared to the more fluid lead white paints.[41]

Three types of blue pigments, used for different purposes, were identified. The primary blue for the walls and doors in all three *Bedrooms* was cobalt blue, mixed with zinc white and red lake. Ultramarine blue was also used in all three versions: extensively for the blue outlining and often mixed with other pigments to create different shades of blue. For example, as shown in the cross section (fig. 8, second from top), ultramarine blue was identified in the lower paint layers of the walls and doors in the Chicago version. Prussian blue, a very dark blue, which appears almost black, was applied selectively in all three works, mainly for accents and outlining (see fig. 16).

Van Gogh used at least two green pigments: emerald green and a chromium-based green. In the case of the Amsterdam version, the chromium-based green appears to be a mixture of Prussian blue and chrome yellow and may be the green noted in his paint orders as "cinnabar green." In the Chicago and Paris paintings, both emerald green and viridian were used.[42] Viridian is a transparent chromium oxide that has a very rich and dark hue in comparison to the bright, opaque, copper/arsenic-based emerald green.

In many of Van Gogh's letters, three different types of chrome yellow were often listed: a lighter, lemon yellow was designated as number 1, a medium yellow as number 2, and a deeper yellow or orange as number 3. These differ in hue and crystal structure.[43]

In the Amsterdam study, two varieties of chrome yellow were identified, and in the Chicago painting, all three types were present. Although chrome yellow was also found in the Paris version, the specific types were not identified; however, visually, it appears that at least two varieties were also employed in this third version.

Multiple red pigments were used, including vermilion, red lead, and several different red lakes, including geranium lake and cochineal lake.[44] In all three pictures, geranium lake (see fig. 15, bottom) was identified in the floor, and a cochineal lake, mixed with cobalt blue and zinc white, in the walls and doors.

Additional pigments used in both the Chicago and Paris repetitions but not in the Amsterdam study include yellow ocher and some red ocher. Small amounts of strontium yellow mixed with chrome yellow were identified in the lighter-yellow areas of the Chicago painting. The presence of ochers in the later repetitions may be due to the fact that, while in Saint-Rémy, Van Gogh's palette began changing in response to his desire to use more somber pigments similar to those he had used in the beginning of his career in the Netherlands. As he explained to Theo on August 22, 1889: "And it was precisely a more sober attempt, matt in colour without looking impressive, broken greens, reds and rusty ochre yellows, as I told you that from time to time I felt a desire to begin again with a palette like the one in the north."[45]

Color Change and Its Consequences in *The Bedroom*

Van Gogh was all too aware that paintings age and change in appearance over time. "Paintings fade like flowers," he wrote in April 1889, following a visit to the Musée Fabre in Montpellier, adding that even some works by Delacroix had suffered.[46] The artist's correspondence provides ample evidence that he was concerned about the durability of his painting materials, canvas, and tube paints. Remarks in his letters and paint orders show that he sought to balance affordability with quality in his purchases.[47] Although well aware of the fugitive nature of some of the colors he used, he was tempted to use them because of the "superb" effects they provided.[48] He hoped that applying his colors "boldly" and "too raw" would compensate for the fact that their brilliance would soften over time.[49] Unfortunately, this has turned out to be only partly true.

Technical studies have revealed that Van Gogh's *Bedroom* paintings were not spared the effects of color change; however, assessing the extent of this color change is a challenging task, and one that must take into account scientific findings as well as documentary evidence and art historical knowledge of the

Pigments identifed in the three *Bedroom* paintings

Pigment	Amsterdam	Chicaago	Paris
Whites			
Zinc white Zinc oxide	■	■	■
Lead white Basic lead carbonate	■	Minor to trace amount	Probably a little
Yellows			
Chrome yellow lemon Lead chromate sulfate		■	■
Chrome yellow medium Lead chromate	■	■	■†
Chrome yellow dark/orange Basic lead chromate	■	■	
Strontium yellow Strontium chromate		■	
Yellow ocher Hydrated iron oxide		■	Probably‡
Reds			
Vermilion Mercuric sulfide	■	■	■
Red lead Lead tetroxide	■	■	■
Geranium lake Eosin dye precipitated on an aluminum hydrate base	■	■	■
Cochineal lake Carminic acid dye on various substrates	■	■	■
Red ocher Iron oxide		Small amount	■‡
Blues			
Cobalt blue Cobalt aluminate	■	■	■
Ultramarine blue Sodium-aluminum sulfosilicate	■	■	■
Prussian blue Ferric ferrocyanide	■	■	■
Greens			
Emerald green Copper acetoarsenite	■	■	■
Viridian Hydrous chromium oxide		■	Possibly
Chrome green Mixture of chrome yellow and Prussian blue or chromium oxide	■		■

† For the Paris repetition, most of the pigment identification was carried out with XRF, which can only detect lead (Pb) and chromium (Cr) but not the specific type of lead chromate present. Only a few spots were analyzed with XRD in situ, detecting chrome yellow medium ($PbCrO_4$).

‡ For the ochers (iron-rich clays), only the chemical name of the coloring agents is indicated here (hematite for iron oxide and goethite for hydrated iron oxide).

artist's working practice. Examination of this evidence for the Amsterdam, Chicago, and Paris versions reveals that the interpretation of the colors is nuanced, as not all three versions were identically painted. Writing about the Amsterdam *Bedroom*, the artist told his brother that "the colour has to do the job here," but unfortunately some of those colors have lost their force since then, and the picture as it is today bears little resemblance to the original color scheme. Van Gogh gave detailed descriptions of the colors he used and their intended effect, but some of these have altered, departing from what the artist described.[50]

A major change affects the walls and doors, making them now appear blue rather than "pale violet" (or "pale lilac") and "lilac," respectively, to use the artist's own words.[51] In the Amsterdam study, only a trace of the violet color is still visible in small areas protected from the destructive exposure to light, such as the tail of a paint stroke that ends at the right edge of the painting where it was covered by the frame, and in the depths of paint cracks viewed under high magnification. Bright-red pigment particles survive in the lower part of a paint cross section mixed with zinc white and cobalt blue (see fig. 8, top), and were identified as cochineal lake (*Dactylopius coccus*) on a substrate containing aluminum and calcium. It is the fading of this pigment that accounts for the shift in color in the painting from lilac and violet toward blue.[52] The Chicago picture offers another glimpse of the original color through a sample of the top layer of paint from the bedroom's wall; when flipped over, this sample reveals the vibrancy of the violet color that originally covered this wall (fig. 17).

There is evidence that the colors of the "red" tiled or "broken and faded red" floor have changed as well. A brighter strip of color is preserved along the bottom edge of the Amsterdam painting that was formerly covered up by tape applied during the last restoration treatment in 1931 (the tape was later removed). Underneath the tape is a peachy pink that indicates what the color of the floor must have looked like in 1931 (see fig. 18). The adjacent, unprotected color is a much cooler grayish-pink, because exposure to light further aged the paint after this date. The green area in the floor by the left edge is also the result of damaging light exposure, rather than being true to the original. This change is illustrated by a strip of the painting that was folded over the left side of the stretcher during the 1931 treatment, where an orangey-pink (rather than green) color is preserved in the floor shielded from light (see fig. 19). This green patch now tends to read like a shadow under the chair, whereas Van Gogh wrote that he did not paint any shadows or cast shadows in the painting.[53] Sample analysis has confirmed that the color changes in the floor result from the fading of

Fig. 16 False-color infrared images of the Chicago *Bedroom* showing the distribution of pigments. Many materials absorb in the near-infrared range and therefore have what is called a spectral signature at a specific wavelength. Hyperspectral images can therefore help identify and map specific materials, such as pigments, based on this signature. They can also be combined in various ways to form false-color images. Here, Prussian blue has been identified in the outlining of the frame and the picture wire (red in these false-color images), cobalt blue (once violet) for the walls (here, purple), and a different iron-based pigment, a yellow ocher, for the clothing rack (here, pale yellow).

16 Chicago

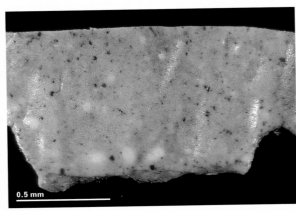

16 Chicago

Fig. 17 *Top*, the front of a paint fragment removed from the wall of the Chicago picture showing the faded blue top side. *Bottom*, the unfaded lilac on the underside of the fragment. When viewed from the side, this fragment resembles the upper layer of the cross section in figure 8, second from top.

17 Chicago

17 Chicago

geranium lake mixed with an elaborate range of pigments in the top paint layer.[54]

There is evidence in both the Amsterdam and Chicago pictures that other pink areas have lost color due to the fading of red lake pigment and consequently now look white. In the Amsterdam study, the impasto of the sky in the landscape painting was once pink but has shifted to white, in contrast to the pink skies of the repetitions (see fig. 9). The pink is very pale in the sky of the Chicago version, but this effect can likewise be explained by the use of a geranium lake pigment that has faded.[55] Van Gogh mentioned that "the only white is the little note given by the mirror with a black frame" and, in another letter, that the painting would look best in a white frame, "since there was no white in the picture."[56] Much later, after he had sent the painting to Theo, he advised him to give it a simple wooden frame, not a white one.[57] It is not known whether Theo did so, but photographs of exhibitions held in Cologne and Antwerp in 1912 and 1914 show that *The Bedroom* then had a broad, white frame.[58]

Later on, when writing to Theo from the asylum in Saint-Rémy, Van Gogh explained that what he found so successful in *The Bedroom* painting was that "the thing depicted is stylistically absolutely in agreement and at one with the manner of depiction," and he concluded, "Isn't that what creates the quality of a piece of art?"[59] The color changes have caused a shift in the relationship between the picture's subject and its means of expression, which raises the question, what remains of the original quality of the work of art? More specifically, to what extent do the colors of *The Bedroom*, as we see them today, still convey the feeling of "unshakeable repose" that Van Gogh intended?[60] And how does color change affect the relationship between the first *Bedroom* study and the repetitions made after it?

To tackle these complex questions, in 2010 an interdisciplinary team composed of art historians, conservators, conservation scientists, imaging specialists, a color scientist, and a practicing artist set out to create a digital recolorized visualization of the original color scheme of the Amsterdam *Bedroom* study (fig. 20). In 2015, this was followed up with a digital recolorized visualization of the unfaded colors in the Chicago picture (fig. 21), using the Amsterdam reconstruction as a reference point. While these visualizations synthesize a broad array of technical and analytical data in conjunction with documentary and visual evidence, they can give only the broadest sense of the original color schemes, not the refined modeling of details and subtle color nuances. Despite the limitations of any digital recolorized visualization, they allow us to approximate the effects and relationships intended by Van Gogh.[61]

Fig. 18 Detail of the floor area in the Amsterdam painting (original magnification 6×), showing the pinker color along the bottom, which was formerly covered by tape and thus protected from light.

In the Paris version, the walls and doors are painted in a more cobalt blue (see fig. 8, second to bottom and bottom). The presence of a few red lake particles within the upper layer suggests only a slight purplish tone to the overall color. Because the middle layer has an abundance of red lake particles, perhaps the purple hue of the wall is rather the effect of transparency and juxtaposition of the three layers (see fig. 10).

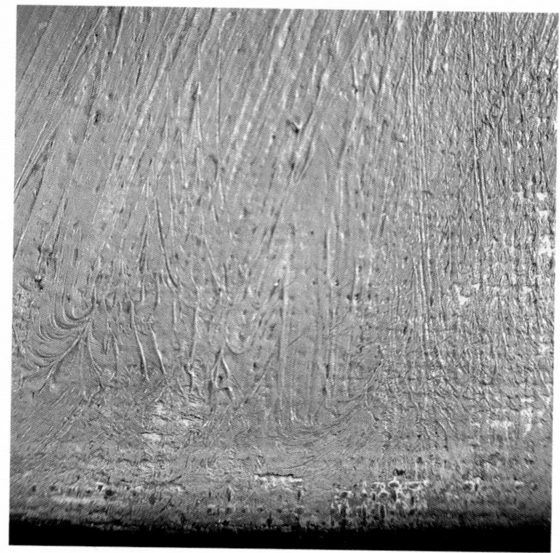

18 Amsterdam

Evaluating the Consequences of Color Change

Beginning with the Amsterdam *Bedroom*, the most striking difference in the painting now is the total absence of the violet walls and lilac doors mentioned so markedly by Van Gogh in his letters to Theo and Gauguin. This change has many consequences for the way we see the bedroom, some of which are described here.

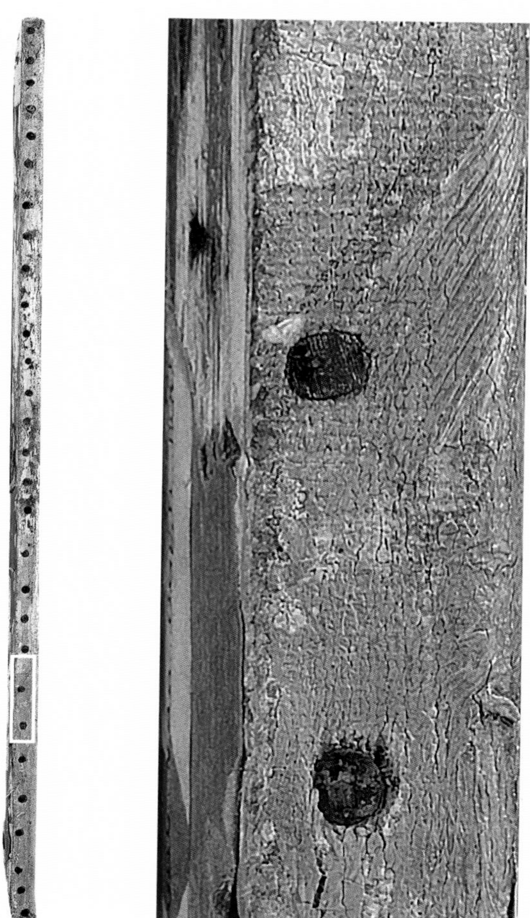

19 Amsterdam

Fig. 19 *Left,* side view of the Amsterdam painting that shows the portion of the painted canvas folded over the left edge of the stretcher during the 1931 restoration. *Right,* a detail of the side view showing the folded-over floor area, which retains the original orangey pink, compared to the front, which has discolored to green from light exposure.

First, the current light-blue background acts like the sky of a landscape to give a false sense of spaciousness. Replaced by violet in the visualization, the result is a flatter effect that conveys the cramped space of the bedroom interior more effectively, which is suggestive of the Japanese prints that Van Gogh mentions in his letters.[62] Even more importantly, the dominant violet hue in the digital recolorized visualization conveys far better the restful, shaded atmosphere in the room, with most of the light excluded by the closed shutters. The presence of violet and lilac creates a convincing impression of subdued light in a warm space, whereas the present blue variant looks light, bright, and cool. The vivid slash of yellow along the right side of the window stands out against the violet back wall, as if one could feel the blistering sunlight outside. This effect loses its force when contrasted with the present blue wall.

There are consequences also for specific components of the scene. For example, Van Gogh gave the bed linen and the prints a yellowish-green cast that creates a vibrant contrast with the violet of the adjacent walls. The present pale blue tends to make them look dull and dirty. The blues of the jackets on the clothing rack and the objects on the table were easier to make out against the violet background. The complementary contrast between the small orange table and the blue water jug, washbowl, glass, carafe, and bottles stood out more, whereas today the now-dominant blue overpowers and destroys this color effect.

In his letter to Gauguin, Van Gogh wrote, "It amused me enormously doing this bare interior. With a simplicity à la *Seurat.*"[63] That remark becomes more understandable if one looks at the original color scheme. On the morning that he left for Arles, Van Gogh and Theo had paid a visit to Seurat's studio.[64]

The latter's *A Sunday on La Grande Jatte—1884* (1884–86; Art Institute of Chicago) took up a whole wall, and Seurat was already working on another large canvas, *Models (Poseuses)* (1886–88; Barnes Foundation, Philadelphia). Van Gogh was fascinated and deeply impressed by Seurat's striking color contrasts and harmonies. Purple tints predominate in Seurat's paintings, and the color contrasts in Van Gogh's violet bedroom must have seemed to him an echo of this aspect of Seurat's work.

Further evidence that he had Seurat on his mind comes in a letter that he wrote to Theo a day before he began work on *The Bedroom*. "But tell me what Seurat's doing. If you see him, tell him on my behalf that I have in progress a decoration which at present amounts to 15 square no. 30 canvases, and which, to make an ensemble, will take at least 15 more, and that in this work on a broader scale it's often the memory of his personality and of the visit that we made to his studio to see his beautiful big canvases that gives me courage in this task."[65] He had said earlier that he regarded Seurat as the leader of the painters of the Petit Boulevard—the new generation of innovative artists, among them not only Seurat but also Signac, Gauguin, Émile Bernard, Louis Anquetin, Henri de Toulouse-Lautrec, and himself.[66] In the first version of *The Bedroom*, Van Gogh hoped to achieve, in his own painterly style, the kind of effect that Seurat championed with his pointillism: "unshakeable repose" with the aid of "all these very different tones."[67]

Importantly, the more accurate complementary scheme recovered in *The Bedroom* visualization seems to be more faithful to Van Gogh's intention that the painting should be soothingly suggestive "*of rest* or *of sleep*" in general. It is now more understandable why he felt that *The Bedroom* painting would provide a "contrast" to his *Night Café* (p. 39, fig. 2), which was meant to evoke "a place where you can ruin yourself, go mad, commit crimes."[68] Originally the contrasting subject and mood of the two paintings was conveyed through their color schemes based on opposite complementary pairs: yellow and violet in the *Bedroom* and red and green in *The Night Café*, respectively (fig. 22, top). The paintings are illustrated here alongside two skeins of wool contained in a small Chinese lacquerware chest that was once owned by Van Gogh (fig. 22, middle). It is believed that he used these samples of wool to try out different color combinations for his paintings, and indeed, this pair strikingly echoes the color schemes of these pictures.

Comparison of the digital recolorized visualizations of the Amsterdam and Chicago *Bedrooms* (figs. 20–21) suggests that the two paintings probably looked more similar at first than they do now that their colors have changed. This is hardly surprising, given

Figs. 20–21 Digital recolorized visualizations of the Amsterdam and Chicago paintings before the red lakes faded in the floors, walls, and doors. This suggests that the paintings originally looked far more similar than they do now. These images also show how Van Gogh applied Charles Blanc's color theory in his work. Adding back the red lakes in the visualizations has restored the intended complementary contrast between the violet walls and lilac doors, on the one hand, and the different shades of yellow in the chairs and the bed, on the other. The contrast is heightened with other features painted in complementary colors (such as the orange table with the blue items on it, and the red blanket and green window panes), producing a more forceful yet balanced effect.

20 Amsterdam

that the Chicago *Bedroom* was based directly on the Amsterdam example. However, some differences persist, due to variations in the way that Van Gogh originally mixed and applied his colors in each work, as already mentioned. One example of this is in the floor. Adding back geranium lake in the digital colorized visualization has pulled together the green and the pink shades in the floor of the Chicago picture for a more coherent effect that is closer to the Amsterdam one. Yet the result in the Chicago repetition is still less uniform than in the Amsterdam picture. The hatched application of paint with variable color mixtures, in which green plays a much larger role, differs markedly from the even areas with "no stippling, no hatching" of the Amsterdam version.[69] Similarly, vertical pink stripes (now white) appear on the right wall of the Chicago picture, which are absent on the plain walls of the Amsterdam picture. Differences too between the two pictures are noticeable in the narrow painted outlines: the red outlines of the left chair are only found in the Amsterdam picture, and the dark Prussian blue outlines of the right wall and door are likewise unique to the Chicago painting. These details become more apparent in the digital recolorized visualization. The simulations of the original color schemes indeed help us to identify and appreciate the many variations between the two works.

The Conservation History of the Three *Bedroom* Paintings

It is not only Van Gogh's inventive variations in the use of materials and techniques and the subsequent, unintended effects of color change that help to explain the varied appearance of the three *Bedroom* paintings today. Differences in past handling and restoration treatment of the paintings have also left their mark and contribute to the distinctive look of each work. Examining the paintings in forensic detail reveals fascinating clues to what has happened to them over time. The clues include: flattened passages of impasto sometimes combined with an impression of the canvas weave made in the paint when fresh; telltale signs of newspaper stuck onto the paint surfaces; early paint loss that may be traced back to the period before the pictures left Van Gogh's studio; and suppliers' stamps on the bars of the stretchers on which the canvases are mounted. Such isolated details may seem inconsequential at first, but when pieced together with other forms of evidence, notably Van Gogh's own account in his letters, they yield a plausible reconstruction of the physical history of each work and lay to rest any remaining doubts about the order in which the three pictures were painted.

21 Chicago

22

22

Fig. 22 *Left*, the digital recolorized visualization of the Amsterdam painting. *Right*, Van Gogh's *Night Café* (p. 39, fig. 2). Yale University Art Gallery, New Haven, Connecticut. The more balanced complementary scheme recovered in the Amsterdam *Bedroom* visualization seems in keeping with Van Gogh's intention to convey "*rest . . .* or *sleep*" in this picture, which he wished to contrast with his *Night Café* and its view of the dark side of life.

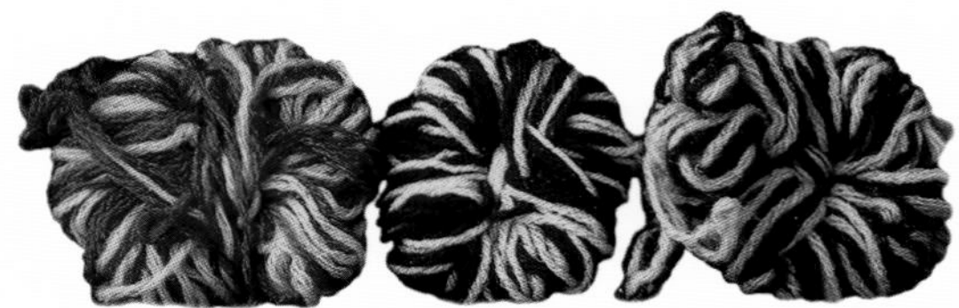

Colored wool samples. Van Gogh Museum, Amsterdam.

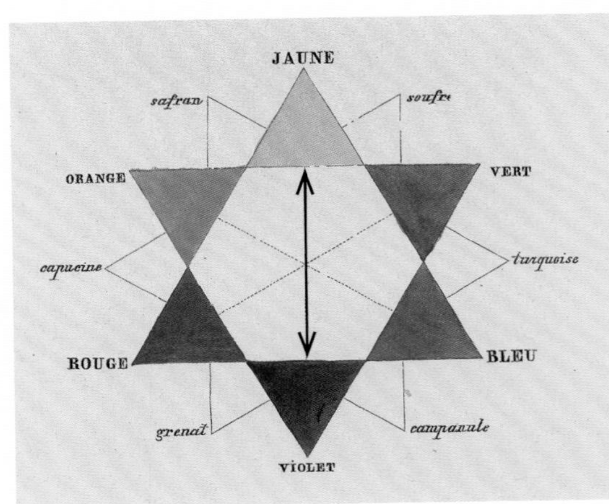

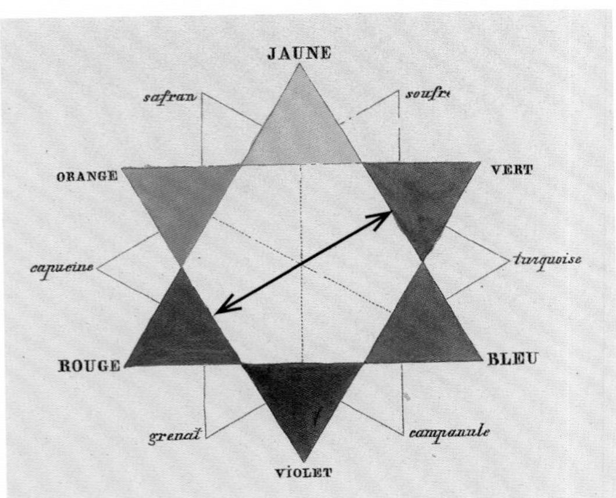

Color chart showing complementary colors. From Charles Blanc, *Grammaire des arts du dessin: Architecture, sculpture, peinture* (Paris, 1867), between pp. 598 and 599.

The First Study (The Amsterdam *Bedroom*)

Damp in the Studio *Today I'm packing up a crate of paintings and studies.*

There's one which is flaking, onto which I've stuck newspapers—it's one of the best and I think that when you look at it you'll see more clearly what my studio, now foundered, could have been. This study, as well as a few others, was spoiled by damp during my illness.

The water from a flood rose up to a few feet from the house and, more importantly, when I came back water and saltpetre were oozing from the walls because the house had been without a fire during my absence.
Van Gogh to Theo, Apr. 30, 1889

It is now universally accepted, on both art historical and technical grounds, that the first *Bedroom* study is the Amsterdam picture.[70] As discussed earlier, this sequence has become evident from the manner in which Van Gogh painted this picture, including the fact that areas were not left in reserve because he was still deciding the details of this first version. In addition, as explained below, this is the picture that displays the closest accord between its physical properties and the information contained in the letter that Van Gogh wrote to Theo on April 30, 1889, quoted above. In it he mentions that one of his "best" studies and a few other paintings had suffered damage from damp in his studio while he had been away in the hospital in Arles. Floodwater from the Rhône had passed within a few feet of the Yellow House, and the artist describes how water and saltpeter oozed from the walls of his studio, which had remained unheated during his absence.[71] He explains that he had stuck newspapers onto the "study" with flaking paint, identified in a following letter as the first *Bedroom* painting.[72]

Flaking Paint The repeated cycles of damp and heating in Van Gogh's studio in the Yellow House must have created an unhealthy environment for paintings, especially freshly made ones like *The Bedroom* that would have been particularly vulnerable to the effects of fluctuating relative humidity and temperature. The various layers of a painting (canvas, glue layer or "size," ground, and paint layers) will respond to such fluctuating conditions by expanding and contracting in different ways, creating mechanical stresses in the paint, with cracking and flaking as a result.[73]

When *The Bedroom* in Amsterdam was cleaned and restored in 2010, the full extent of damage related to the episode of damp described by Van Gogh was revealed.[74] This damage included numerous stress cracks in the paint, with sharp-edged losses of paint and ground that had flaked off down to the level of the bare canvas, especially in thickly applied regions of paint containing zinc white, including the floor, walls, and doors (see fig. 23). The flaking damage was consistent with what one would expect from exposing a painting to high levels of relative humidity: the canvas shrinks, while the coating of glue with which it is prepared (known as "size") swells to a jelly-like consistency, releasing the inelastic paint layers on top.[75]

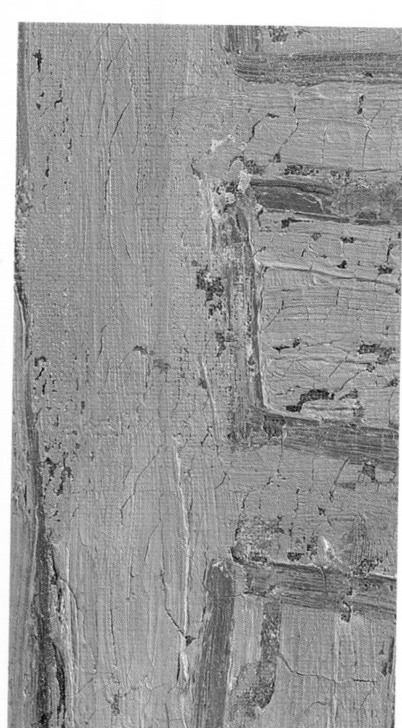

23 Amsterdam

Fig. 23 Detail of the Amsterdam *Bedroom* during its 2010 restoration, showing the extensive paint and ground losses in the right door.

Newspaper Besides cracking and paint loss, another physical clue links the Amsterdam study to the episode of damage described in Van Gogh's studio, and thus confirms its chronological identity as the first in the series. Tiny black stains are spread across the raised parts of the paint surface, which turn out to be newsprint letters when viewed under magnification, although the existing letters are too few to be able to spell out any text (see fig. 24). The letters are accompanied by the fibrous imprint of newspaper that continues into the crevices of the paint. The fact that the newspaper intimately followed the topography of the paint surface indicates that it was softened by wetting with water or the glue used to adhere it. However, no residues of the actual paper or glue survive. At some later point, the newspaper covering must have been soaked and thoroughly removed.

That we are dealing with traces from the newspaper that Van Gogh describes having stuck onto the painting in the studio, some six months after the picture was made, is supported by the fact that remaining newsprint letters and imprinted texture of the paper now form an inseparable part of the skin of the paint, indicating that the newspaper was intimately bonded to its surface.[76] Especially in the damp climate of the studio in the Yellow House, the slower-drying thick passages of paint would not yet have had the chance to dry properly, making them receptive to the impression of newspaper firmly pressed and stuck onto their surface.

In the same April 30 letter, Van Gogh recounted that he subsequently took the damaged canvas off its stretching frame and rolled it up to send in a crate as part of a large consignment of works for Theo, presumably leaving the newspaper on to hold the loose paint. Van Gogh added in this letter that he considered *The Bedroom* one of the enclosed works worthy of being mounted on a stretching frame and that he would add some stretching frames in the crate "if there's room," supporting the idea that *The Bedroom* canvas was sent rolled rather than stretched.

Lining At first sight the idea of Van Gogh sticking newspaper onto *The Bedroom* painting to fix loose paint may seem somewhat odd, yet it resembles a tried and tested method used at the time by professional liners. In January 1889, several months before Van Gogh wrote to Theo regarding damage, Gauguin had shared with Van Gogh a detailed description of the method. It entailed sticking newspaper onto the front of a canvas with flour paste, then placing it on a smooth board and pressing it with very hot irons to flatten and secure flaking paint. In that way, "All the breaks in your colour will remain but will be flattened down and you'll have a very fine surface." Gauguin added, "That's largely the whole secret of relining."[77]

When Van Gogh sent off the damaged *Bedroom* to Theo with newspaper on its surface, he must have had in mind that the painting would undergo treatment of this kind. Three weeks later, on May 23, he wrote to Theo suggesting that Gauguin would be able to provide him with the address of a liner for *The Bedroom* who would not be too expensive, adding that if it cost more than five francs, which he thought was the most that Gauguin usually paid, he should not have it done.[78] On June 9, he wrote to Theo that since his mind had grown calmer, he now thought that he could redo *The Bedroom* painting after all, asking him to send back the painting rolled up when he sent other canvas.[79] Theo replied on June 16 that he would send back *The Bedroom* but that Van Gogh should not retouch the painting since it could be repaired. Instead, he should make a copy and send that one back to Theo so that he could have it lined.[80] Prompted by second thoughts about the risk entailed in having Theo send him the damaged *Bedroom* canvas, Van Gogh in turn replied, "If you can get the Bedroom lined it's better to have it done *before* sending it to me."[81]

After this letter written on or about June 18, 1889, there was an interlude of roughly eleven weeks before Van Gogh suddenly announced in a letter of September 5–6, 1889, that he has "redone the canvas of the Bedroom."[82] This is understood to be the version now in Chicago, establishing it as the second in the series. The most likely reason for this long

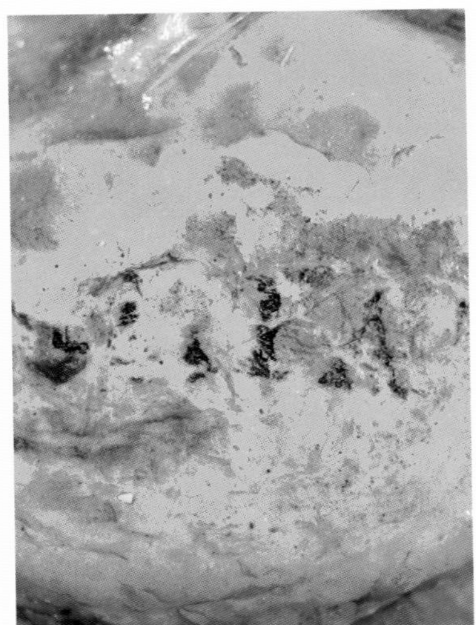

24 Amsterdam

Fig. 24 Microscopic evidence showing newspaper pressed into the surface of the Amsterdam *Bedroom* (original magnification 25×).

interval—between Theo announcing his intention to send back the original painting and Van Gogh redoing it—is that Theo had indeed followed his brother's instructions and had the painting lined before returning it. The lined painting probably arrived shortly before Van Gogh made the repetition, even though he did not mention it. In his letter, he goes on from a discussion of *The Bedroom* to comment that Theo had "taken some excellent stretching frames," suggesting that this time the painting was on a stretcher when he received it, rather than sent back to him rolled up.

No traces of the first lining remain after it was removed in 1931–32 by the restorer J. C. Traas when he relined the painting in the Netherlands. Traas complained about the awfully bad quality of the old lining and that the paint layer had been terribly messed with.[83] Indeed, the surface conditions of the Amsterdam *Bedroom* picture today—with its flattened hills of impasto and open cracks in the ground and paint that have been neatly "flattened down," to use Gauguin's words—all bear witness to the effect of a treatment like the one Gauguin described. While modern-day conservators may shudder at the thought of such a heavy-handed intervention, it is worth remembering that, in fact, artists like Gauguin appreciated the "fine," compact surface that such treatment provided.[84]

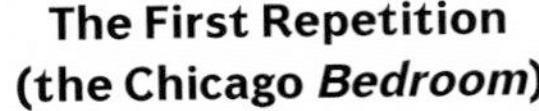

The First Repetition (the Chicago *Bedroom*)

Flaking paint *Thus I've redone the canvas of the Bedroom. That study is certainly one of the best—sooner or later it will definitely have to be lined. It was painted so quickly and dried in such a way that, as the thinner evaporated immediately, the painting doesn't adhere at all firmly to the canvas. This will also be the case with other studies of mine that were painted very quickly and with a thick impasto. Besides, this thin canvas perishes after a while and can't take a lot of impasto.*

You've taken some excellent stretching frames, damn it, if I had some like that here to work on that would be better than these strips of wood from here that warp in the sun.
Van Gogh to Theo, Sept. 5–6, 1889

In early September 1889, Van Gogh announced to Theo that he had redone the canvas of *The Bedroom*, commenting that it was "certainly one of the best." Apparently switching mid-sentence from discussing the first *Bedroom* study, he went on to describe a phenomenon of flaking paint in the version now in Chicago, which was the result of a faulty technique of paint application rather than water damage. The preciseness of his description also suggests a phenomenon he has recently dealt with rather than a past incident described from memory. He explained, "It was painted so quickly and dried in such a way that, as the thinner evaporated immediately, the painting doesn't adhere at all firmly to the canvas," going on to add, "This will also be the case with other studies of mine that were painted very quickly and with a thick impasto."

The Chicago *Bedroom* does exhibit substantial areas of paint loss that accord with what Van Gogh described. In the past, poor adhesion has caused the thick strokes of light-blue (originally pale-violet) paint in the walls and doors to cleave from the grayish-lilac layer underneath (see fig. 25, top). One cross section of the paint shows tiny air pockets at the interface between the two layers, apparently voids that formed as the final, fast strokes of impasto skipped across the dry surface of the grayish-lilac paint without properly taking to it (fig. 25, bottom). In the right door of the Paris *Bedroom*, similar, though much smaller, passages of interlayer cleavage occur where thick blue strokes have flaked off the grayish-blue underlayer, confirming Van Gogh's prediction that other "studies" with fast strokes of impasto could be similarly affected.

The flaking losses in the first *Bedroom* repetition were documented when the picture was acquired by the Art Institute of Chicago in 1926, at which time its condition was reported to be stable, and the paint losses old. Recent technical studies have provided new evidence—albeit on a very small scale—to suggest that at least some of the flaking may already have occurred at the time the painting was made, as Van Gogh's letter would lead us to suppose. Detailed examination under magnification shows that some of the dark-blue strokes depicting the picture wire run over flaking losses, distinguished from surrounding paint by their grayer appearance and lower level, which must therefore already have existed when the strokes were applied (see fig. 26).[85] Like the outlines of the frame, the picture wire is depicted by a series of short touches with the brush that are entirely coherent in terms of their rhythm of application, blue color, and material composition.[86] Consequently, there is no reason to think that any of the strokes are later retouches added by another hand rather than belonging to Van Gogh's own paint application.

Lining Van Gogh considered it inevitable that *The Bedroom* painting in Chicago, and other studies of his that were painted very quickly and with a thick impasto, would sooner or later need to be lined. He added another reason, namely, that the thin canvas he used "perishes after a while and can't take a lot of impasto."[87] The Chicago *Bedroom* does retain an early lining that was carried out in France using the traditional glue-paste method. The lining has a messy character, with broad smears of adhesive and drip stains evident on the reverse of the finely woven lining canvas (see fig. 27, top). The edges of the original canvas were cut off before lining, and toothed marks with ripple distortions at intervals along the edges of the lining canvas reveal that stretching pliers (*pince dentelée*) were used to mount the canvas on its stretcher after lining. As yet it has not proved possible to identify the liner based on these characteristic features, and there is no documentation going back further than 1926, when the picture was already noted to be lined as it entered the collection of the Art Institute.[88] However, the stretcher on which the canvas is mounted provides further clues.

The stretcher is from the French company Bourgeois Aîné, bearing the firm's lozenge-shaped brand mark on the crossbar, as well as a stamp with its trademark and the stretcher dimensions (see fig. 27a–c). The particular design of the stretcher, with a crossbar and half-bridle joints with keys, was available in the time that Van Gogh worked, and for several decades thereafter the details of its assembly remained unchanged.[89] A more exact date is offered by the marks on the stretcher. So far, the specific combination of a brand mark and stamp has only been found on Bourgeois Aîné stretchers from paintings dated between 1910 and 1915, making it likely that the stretcher (and lining) dates from this approximate period.[90] Combining this evidence of the stretcher with the known provenance of the painting makes it likely that it was first lined shortly before 1909 (almost twenty years after Van Gogh wrote that this would be needed), by which time we know that the painting had left France.[91]

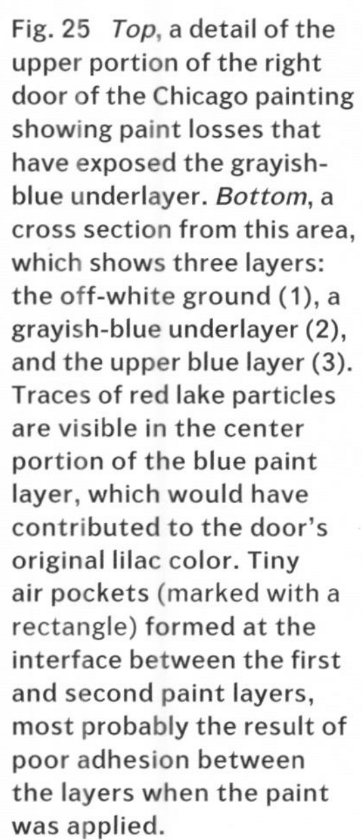
Fig. 25 *Top*, a detail of the upper portion of the right door of the Chicago painting showing paint losses that have exposed the grayish-blue underlayer. *Bottom*, a cross section from this area, which shows three layers: the off-white ground (1), a grayish-blue underlayer (2), and the upper blue layer (3). Traces of red lake particles are visible in the center portion of the blue paint layer, which would have contributed to the door's original lilac color. Tiny air pockets (marked with a rectangle) formed at the interface between the first and second paint layers, most probably the result of poor adhesion between the layers when the paint was applied.

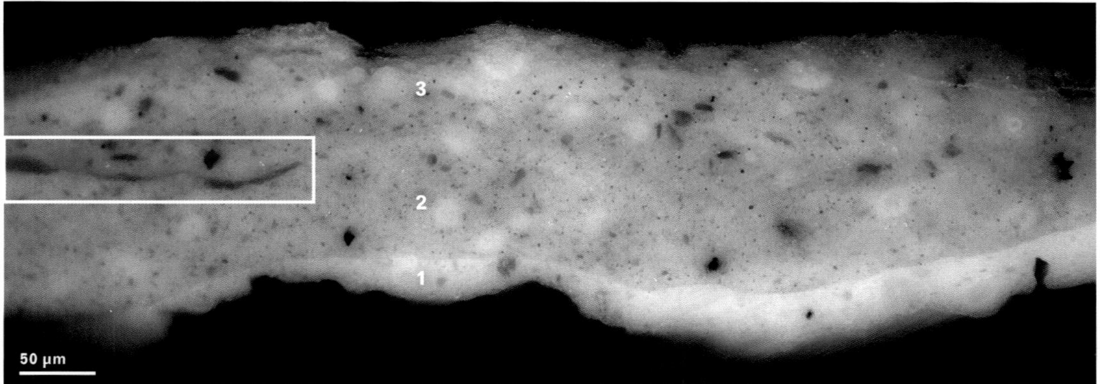

25 Chicago

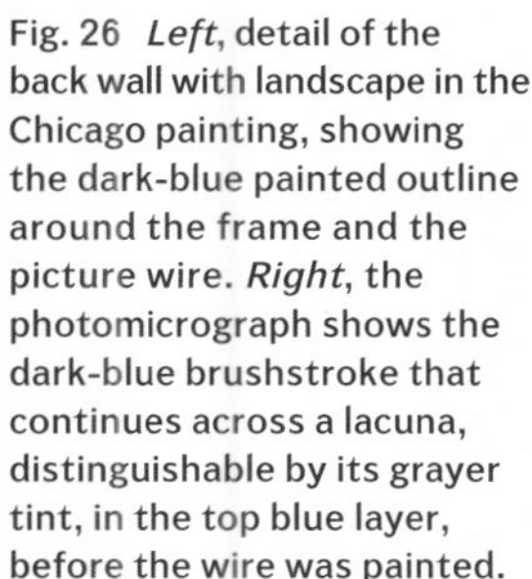
Fig. 26 *Left*, detail of the back wall with landscape in the Chicago painting, showing the dark-blue painted outline around the frame and the picture wire. *Right*, the photomicrograph shows the dark-blue brushstroke that continues across a lacuna, distinguishable by its grayer tint, in the top blue layer, before the wire was painted.

26 Chicago

Fig. 27 Back of the Chicago painting.

27 Chicago

A Marks from toothed stretching pliers.

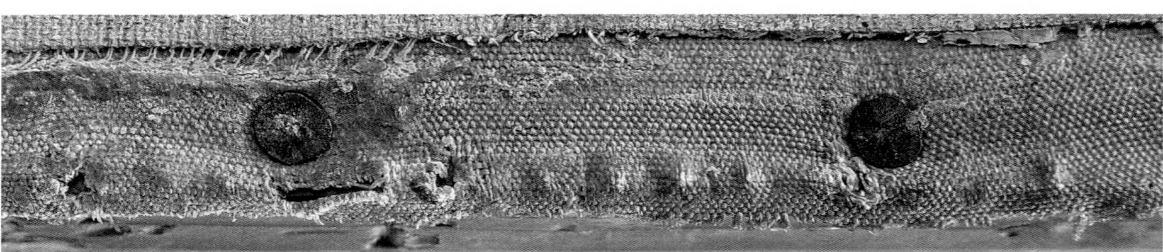

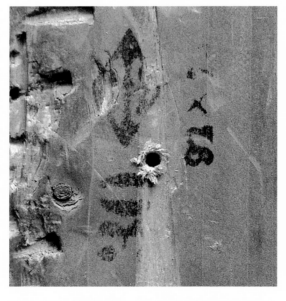

B Stamp with the Bourgeois Aîné trademark and the no. 30 portrait standard-size stretcher dimensions, "30F/ 92 × 7[3]."

C Lozenge-shaped iron brand mark with Bourgeois Aîné trademark, "MODÈLE DÉPOSÉ."

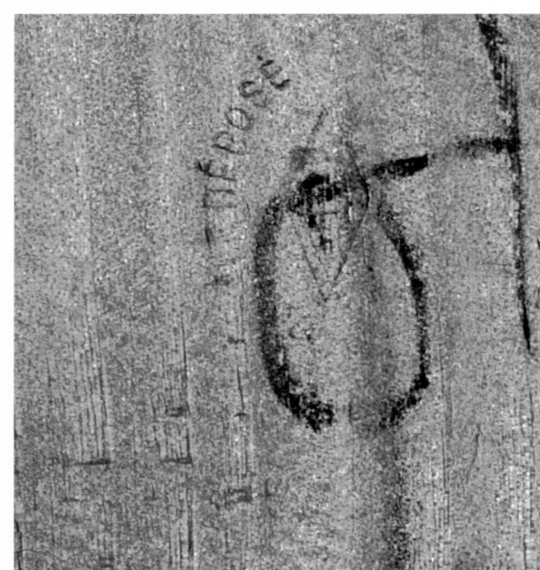

Illustration of caduceus mark registered on May 24, 1867, by François Alexandre Joseph Bourgeois, founder of Maison Bourgeois Aîné, Paris.

The Final Shipment

From Van Gogh's correspondence we learn that the Paris reduction was painted by September 28, 1889, and was still drying at that time, thus establishing its chronological place as the third work in the *Bedroom* series.[92] On December 6, 1889, he sent this work by parcel post to Theo, together with other works destined for his mother and sister.[93] Soon afterward, the other *Bedroom* paintings followed. On December 19, 1889, Van Gogh announced to Theo, "You'll receive the Bedroom," and three days later, on December 22, Theo confirmed, "I've safely received your consignment of the *Wheatfield* and the two *Bedrooms*," now referring to the original study (the Amsterdam picture) and the first repetition of the *Bedroom* (the Chicago picture).[94]

Telltale signs of a canvas weave pattern pressed into the flattened surface of slower drying areas of thick paint in the two *Bedroom* repetitions must have resulted from the canvases being removed from their stretcher and sent rolled before the paint had properly hardened (see fig. 28). Only the first *Bedroom* study lacks this particular feature, confirming that this was the first damaged study sent to Theo with newspaper protecting its surface, and that when Theo sent the painting back after lining for the purpose of making a copy, it was mounted on a stretcher instead. When the first painting was finally removed from its stretcher and rolled once again to send back to Theo more than a year after it was made, the paint must have been sufficiently hard to resist any damage.

In the Paris repetition it is striking that, besides the weave pattern imprinted in the fresh paint of the bed frame, small remnants of newspaper survive on the left part of the painting: on the drawer and legs of the table and on the frame of the left chair (see fig. 29). The pieces of newspaper are held neatly on the paint surface rather than having been pressed into it, as in the Amsterdam study discussed earlier, thus reflecting a more gentle approach. A record from when the Paris picture was lined for the first time in 1958 notes that the "incrustations of newspaper in the impasto" were already present prior to treatment, and links them to the fact that Van Gogh had rolled his canvas when the paint was still fresh.[95] At first sight the idea that Van Gogh rolled the painting with newspaper to protect its surface would seem at odds with the presence of canvas weave imprinted in the fresh paint of the bed frame. However, taking into account the distribution of newspaper residues versus weave imprint, one possible explanation is that newspaper only covered the left part of the painting when it was rolled, perhaps since this part was to be wound more tightly on the inside.[96]

Close examination of the paint surfaces, in conjunction with a careful reading of Van Gogh's letters, has demonstrated that the absence or presence of newsprint (which may have been applied for a variety of reasons)

Fig. 28 Microscopic details of canvas weave imprinted in the paint surface of the Chicago and Paris *Bedroom* paintings.

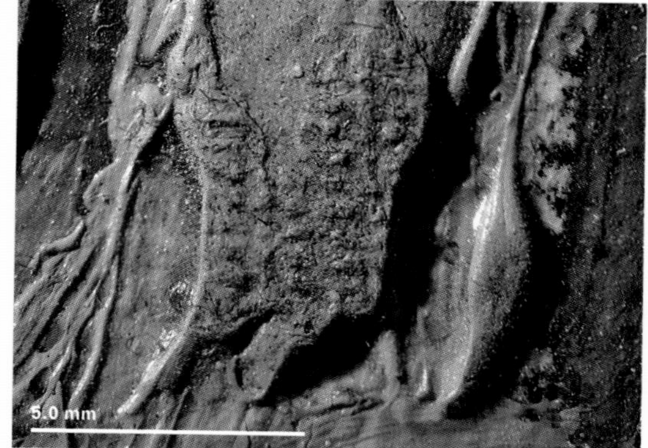

28 Chicago

28 Paris

Fig. 29 Microscopic details of the Paris *Bedroom* showing newspaper residue on the left chair frame and the leg of the table.

29 Paris

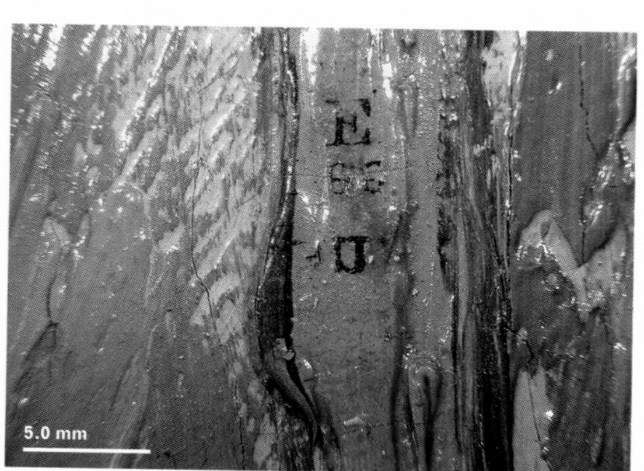

29 Paris

and weave imprint on the *Bedroom* paintings is another useful feature to help confirm the sequence in which the canvases were painted and shipped.

—

In closing, the detailed observations and scientific analyses that was carried out in collaboration by an international team of experts have shed new light on the making and evolution of the three versions of *The Bedroom*. These new insights echo Van Gogh's own words in describing a composition that he believed to be one of his best works. After the pictures' dispersal, which led to their current locations across the world, these three versions of a theme that was so dear to Van Gogh can now be admired together again. We hope that our investigation of the working process documented in this sequence of pictures will illuminate the multifaceted aspects of Van Gogh's creative journey and lead to a greater appreciation of the complexity that underlies the artist's treatment of this seemingly simple, yet iconic subject.

Acknowledgments We are grateful for the contributions of many of our colleagues. At the Art Institute of Chicago, we would like to thank Gloria Groom for initiating the project and for her enthusiastic support for conservation research. Our thanks go to Francesca Casadio and Frank Zuccari for a critical reading of this essay and for many useful discussions. Francesca also carried out scanning macro-XRF of the Chicago painting and Raman spectroscopy analysis of the chrome yellows. We are grateful to Kimberley Muir for her detailed examination and photomicrography of the Art Institute's painting, to Kelly Keegan for creating masks for the digital recolorized visualization of the unfaded version of the Chicago picture, to Federica Pozzi for conducting SERS analysis on the red lakes, and to Kenneth Sutherland for performing media analysis. We would also like to thank Faye Wrubel, who carried out the outstanding conservation treatment of the Chicago painting, and Kristin Hoermann Lister for sharing her knowledge of Van Gogh's working methods and past conservation treatments of paintings by Paul Gauguin. In addition, we would like to thank Allison Perelman in the Department of European Painting and Sculpture; the staff in Publishing, especially Sarah E. Guernsey, Maia M. Rigas, Joseph Mohan, and Katie Levi; freelance editor Margherita Andreotti; and in the Department of Imaging, Chris Gallagher, Robert Liftson, and Louis Meluso.

SEM/EDX analysis of samples from the Chicago painting was carried out at Northwestern University's EPIC facility (NUANCE Center), which has received support from the MRSEC program (NSF DMR-1121262) at the Materials Research Center; the International Institute for Nanotechnology (IIN); and the State of Illinois, through the IIN. In particular we would like to thank Benjamin Myers and Professor Vinayak Dravid.

We are also indebted to Professor Roy S. Berns, Munsell Color Science Laboratory, Rochester Institute of Technology, for spectral reflectance measurements and for scientific guidance for the digital recolorized visualization of both the Amsterdam and Chicago pictures, and Brittany Cox, graduate student in Color Science Appearance and Technology, in the same lab, for the computer graphics rendering of the recolorized visualization of the Chicago painting; John Delaney, Senior Imaging Scientist and Kathryn A. Dooley, Research Fellow, both at the National Gallery of Art, Washington, D.C., for hyperspectral and FORS for both the Amsterdam and Chicago pictures, and Professors C. Richard Johnson Jr. (Cornell University), Don H. Johnson (Rice University) and Robert Erdmann (Rijksmuseum and Universiteit van Amsterdam) for the automated thread count analysis that was conducted on all three *Bedroom* paintings. Special thanks are due to Marcia Steele, Senior Conservator of Paintings, Cleveland Museum of Art; Elizabeth Steele, Head of Conservation, the Phillips Collection; and H. Travers Newton, Independent Fine Arts Conservator; for their helpful discussions and observations on the three paintings. We also thank Professor Joris Dik (Antoni van Leeuwenhoek Chair, Materials in Art and Archaeology, Laboratory of Materials Science, Technische Universiteit Delft); Professor Koen Janssens (AXES Research Group: Department of Chemistry—Universiteit Antwerpen); Michael Haschke (formerly of Bruker AXS, Inc.) and his colleague Ken Romalino (Field Engineer-Microanalysis, Bruker AXS, Inc.) for their assistance and support in getting a Bruker M6 Macro-scanning XRF on loan to the Art Institute of Chicago. The macro-XRF research was enabled by the Nederlandse Organisatie voor Wetenschappelijk Onderzoek through a VIDI research grant for Joris Dik.

In Amsterdam, we would especially like to thank Muriel Geldof from the Rijksdienst voor het Cultureel Erfgoed (RCE) for her cross-sectional analysis and pigment identification and Luc Megens (RCE) for XRF measurements on the painting, as well as Maarten van Bommel, formerly at RCE, now Professor of Conservation Science, Universiteit van Amsterdam, who conducted HPLC analysis of the red lake samples from the Amsterdam, Chicago, and Paris paintings. SEM/EDX analysis was performed by Kees Mensch, courtesy of Shell as sponsoring "Partner in Science" to the Van Gogh Museum. We are grateful to the following colleagues who traveled to Amsterdam to perform in situ analysis of the painting: Jacques Castaing, formerly of the Centre de Recherche et de Restauration des Musées de France for XRF/XRD; and Geert Van der Snickt from the Department of Chemistry, Universiteit Antwerpen, for scanning macro-XRF. Thanks also to Pascal Labreuche, Paintings Conservator in Paris, for information on the sources of artists' materials in nineteenth-century France. We are indebted to our colleagues at the Van Gogh Museum, including Imaging Specialist Maurice Tromp for his help towards the digital recolorized visualization of the unfaded painting, as well as Sjraar van Heugten, former Head of Collections, and Leo Jansen, former Curator of Paintings, for their invaluable support during the 2009–10 conservation treatment and accompanying research. Translations from the Dutch are by Michael Hoyle.

In Paris, we would like to acknowledge the contributions from our colleagues at the Centre de Recherche et de Restauration des Musées de France (C2RMF). We are especially grateful to Elisabeth Ravaud for acquisition of X-ray images; to Myriam Eveno, along with Jacques Castaing, for XRF-XRD analysis; to Myriam Eveno, Eric Laval, and Laurence de Viguerie for XRF analysis; and Sandrine Pagès-Camagna for micro Raman analysis. Myriam Eveno carried out the sampling and analysis of the samples from the wall and door of the Paris painting. Both she and Elisabeth Ravaud were responsible for the examination of the painting and the interpretation of the analytical results that were obtained on the Paris picture. We would also like to thank Witold Nowik for HPLC analysis; Elsa Lambert for the imaging of the Paris painting, which included color photography and raking-light, infrared, and UV imaging; and Ruven Pillay for acquisition of mosaic images. At the Museé d'Orsay, a very special thanks is due to Guy Cogeval, President; to Anne Roquebert, curator; to Laurence Madeline, former curator; and to Isabelle Cahn, chief curator of paintings, who gave us the opportunity to conduct in-depth investigations, including limited sampling of the Paris *Bedroom* through the C2RMF.

1. The considerable amount of published and unpublished research on the artist's technique and materials, including that for the three *Bedroom* paintings, constitutes the foundation for this work. All three paintings underwent extensive technical study, which included X-radiography; infrared reflectography; ultraviolet-light, transmitted-light, and transmitted-infrared-light examination; and photomicrography to document Van Gogh's painting technique. High-resolution X-ray films were composited and analyzed using Thread Count Automation Project (TCAP) software that provided information on weave density and thread-angle maps. In addition, noninvasive X-ray fluorescence (XRF) was conducted on all three works to get an overall idea of the palette. Select sampling and analysis were also performed, which included pigment identification by polarized light microscopy (PLM) (specifically for Chicago's picture) and scanning electron microscopy coupled with energy-dispersive X-ray spectroscopy (SEM/EDX) analysis on paint cross sections to provide information on the paint stratigraphy and mixtures within the paint layers. In situ Raman spectroscopy was conducted on Paris's painting, as well as in situ X-ray diffraction (XRD) on both the Amsterdam and Paris pictures. High-performance liquid chromatography (HPLC) was also conducted on samples from the floors of Amsterdam and Chicago paintings. Spectral reflectance color measurements were taken on Amsterdam's picture, and a digital recolorized visualization of the unfaded colors was produced. See Hendriks et al., "Comparative Study of Vincent van Gogh's *Bedroom* Series," pp. 237–43; Vellekoop et al., *Van Gogh's Studio Practice*; Vellekoop, *Van Gogh at Work*; Rathbone et al., *Van Gogh Repetitions.*

2. A coordinated international effort of research included conducting scanning macro-X-ray fluorescence spectroscopy (macro-XRF) and hyperspectral imaging on both the Amsterdam and Chicago paintings. Additional research was also conducted on the fading of some of the organic red lake pigments that were used in both the Chicago and Paris versions to compare them to what has been found in the first *Bedroom* study. HPLC and surface-enhanced Raman spectroscopy (SERS) were performed on samples from the walls and doors to determine the identification of the red lakes present in the Chicago painting. Spectral reflectance color measurements were also made on Chicago's picture to aid us with the digital recolorized visualization of the unfaded colors for comparison with the artist's first version. Further sampling and sample analysis by HPLC was also performed on the Paris version to investigate the presence of organic red lakes in the walls and floor.

3. A digital recolorized visualization of the Paris picture was not created, because, as is common in any serious study of this kind, unanimity of opinion did not exist in this case as it did among the technical experts in Amsterdam and Chicago about the works in their collections. The Paris conservation team prefers to entertain the possibility that their picture does not exhibit fading in the bedroom walls and doors and that the presence of a few red lake particles in the Paris repetition only gave the slightest purplish tinge to the top light-blue layer.

4. For Van Gogh's letters establishing the dates of the three works, see Van Gogh to Theo, Oct. 16, 1888; Van Gogh to Gauguin, Oct. 17, 1888; Van Gogh to Theo, Sept. 5–6, 1889; and Van Gogh to Theo, Sept. 28, 1889, *Letters*, 705, 706, 800, and 806, respectively.

5. See Hendriks et al., "Comparative Study," for a more detailed history of opinion regarding the pictures' chronology. When it was purchased in 1926, the Chicago picture was thought to be the first version, a belief argued by Brettell, "Van Gogh's Bedrooms at Arles," and then effectively rebutted by Hulsker, "Bedroom Problems." While the latter view is now generally accepted, confusion still appears in the literature regarding which of these two pictures is the first. For example, see Zimmer, "Saint-Rémy: From Triptych to Polyptych," p. 110.

6. For a discussion of these terms, see Robinson, "On the Origins and Evolution of Van Gogh's Repetitions."

7. For a discussion of Van Gogh's own terminology regarding his oeuvre, see Van Tilborgh and Van Uitert, "Ten-Year Career."

8. Van Gogh to Theo, Sept. 9, 1888, *Letters*, 677. The "sower" refers to the sketch *Sower with Setting Sun* (begun c. June 17, 1888; Kröller-Müller Museum, Otterlo [F422, JH1470]); the "night café" refers to *The Night Café* (p. 39, fig. 2).

9. This is true in the case of the étude *Wheat Field with Reaper and Sun* (June 1889; Kröller-Müller Museum, Otterlo [F617, JH1753]) and the attempted tableau *Enclosed Field with Reaper at Sunrise* from September 1889 (Van Gogh Museum [F618, JH1773]), which he initially preferred, but about which he later noted in a letter to Émile Bernard, "the effect is weaker." On or about Nov. 26, 1889, *Letters*, 822.

10. Before starting on the sketch he marked out the position of the main objects in the room with dotted lines. Technical examination has revealed that no details in the Amsterdam picture were overpainted or concealed in any way, that is, the artist did not change his mind while he was painting. The position of the objects in the sketch thus clearly predates any attempt to paint them.

11. A small part of the left-hand wall was originally visible in the Amsterdam painting, but during past restoration treatment the canvas was stretched onto a smaller stretcher so that this section is now folded around the stretcher. See Hendriks et al., "Comparative Study," pp. 237–43.

12. The rear wall of the bedroom was at an angle of approximately 115° to the left-hand wall. The room measured roughly 12.5 m^2, while Gauguin had some 8 m^2 in his adjoining room. The dimensions are based on a blueprint of the rooms in the Yellow House that was made in the 1920s and is now in the Van Gogh Museum. Coquiot Archive, inv. no. b3317/V1966.

13. The stretch of wall from the door to the corner is 2.85 m long, which is enough for a bed despite the angled rear wall.

14. By then Van Gogh felt more confident in approaching his subject directly, without the help of an intermediary instrument. The last painting on which the lines of a perspective frame were discovered beneath the paint layers is *The Drawbridge* from May 1888 (Wallraf-Richartz Museum, Cologne [F570, JH1421]). During this same month, Van Gogh started drawing around Montmajour without his frame, and he made no use of it in Saintes-Maries-de-la-Mer, as he explained to Theo. There is no evidence that he ever went back to it, although he made small sketches of such a frame in Saint-Rémy and Auvers-sur-Oise. But these probably do not refer to his using such a device; the sketches were in all likelihood meant to explain to some other party how such a frame looked and functioned. Why else bother to draw them? For Van Gogh's use of the perspective frame, see Hendriks, "Underdrawing and Use of the 'Perspective Frame'"; and Meedendorp, "Perspective Frame."

15. For a discussion and diagrams showing the contours of one image superimposed on the other, see Rathbone et al., *Van Gogh Repetitions*, p. 89, fig. 41; 171, fig. 87. In this same publication, see also Steele and Steele, "Methods for Making Repetitions," and the section on *The Bedroom* (pp. 83–89), on Van Gogh's repetitions.

16. See Steele and Steele, "Methods for Making Repetitions."

17. The black particles were identified as charcoal by PLM based on particle morphology and comparison to reference material. Microscopically, the particles are brown to dark brown, almost black in color, semiopaque to opaque, and very angular in shape, sometimes appearing quite splintery.

18. It should be noted, however, that dark particles, possibly charcoal, were identified in one cross section from the Amsterdam picture, suggesting that perhaps some preliminary charcoal underdrawing may also be present in some areas of this painting. Ashok Roy has reported finding charcoal particles on top of the ground layer in several samples in the National Gallery's Van Gogh painting, *A Wheatfield, with Cypresses* (F615, JH1755), painted in September 1889. See Roy, " Materials of Van Gogh's *A Cornfield, with Cypresses*," p. 50. At some point after the publication of this paper, the painting was renamed.

All paint cross sections from the Amsterdam picture were prepared and examined with the light microscope by Muriel Geldof, Rijksdienst voor het Cultureel Erfgoed (formerly ICN), report dated Jan. 2009 and revised Jan. 2015. SEM/EDX analysis of samples was performed by Kees Mensch, courtesy of Shell, sponsoring "Partner in Science" to the Van Gogh Museum.

19. In the Chicago repetition, it was observed, however, that in one area—the chair on the left side—the artist made minor modifications by slightly extending two of the legs over the floor. Also, in some places, no charcoal underdrawing was seen in association with the painted outlines (e.g., in the headboard). It is difficult to determine whether such examples indicate a divergence from the charcoal underdrawing, whether they represent additional compositional planning carried out in this initial stage of paint application, or whether the charcoal simply skipped an area.

20. The presence of a visible underlying grayish-blue wash, exposed along the edges of the final blue contour delineating the corner of the ceiling, suggests it might also belong to a first painted sketch for the walls, although it was not observed in any other areas of the walls and doors.

21. Van Gogh to Gauguin, Oct. 17, 1888, *Letters*, 706.

22. The layering also shows a very distinct thin band of red lake.

23. This was also confirmed with fiber-optical reflectance spectroscopy (FORS) and SEM/EDX conducted on paint cross sections.

24. HPLC identified cochineal lake in samples from the walls in all three paintings. SERS was also performed on samples from the wall in Chicago's painting and confirmed the presence of carminic acid. Cochineal lake is a natural organic dyestuff made from the dried bodies of the female insect *Dactylopius coccus* (also known as *Coccus cacti*). The coloring matter of cochineal extract is carminic acid. HPLC was conducted by Maarten van Bommel (Amsterdam) and Witold Nowik (Paris). SERS was conducted by Federica Pozzi (Chicago). For more information on SERS, see Pozzi et al., "Systematic Analysis of Red Lake Pigments."

25. In the Amsterdam version, Van Gogh did not seem to have applied the initial buff-colored layer in the left part of the floor under the chair but instead used a different paint mixture. This now has a greenish shade but seems originally to have been an orange-pink that remains clearly visible along and over the bottom left side of the painting. A second paint layer, which originally had a warmer pink tone, was applied over most of the floor, except again in the left area. In the Chicago painting, a thin, dilute, dull-green underpaint was observed present in a few areas (i.e., below the left chair and the bed). It does not appear to have been an underlayer that was applied to the entire surface of the floor, but rather underpainting related to the initial laying in of the composition. In addition, a thin brown layer is present in some areas, mostly at the bottom left corner and could also be related to the initial laying in of the color. In the application of the second paint layer of the floor in the Paris version, distinct tints are observed between the far back (a more deep brownish purple) and the front part of the floor (a lighter shade of the same color).

26. The results are based on HPLC analysis conducted by Maarten van Bommel (Amsterdam), revealing a mixture of eosin (geranium lake) and carminic acid (cochineal lake) for Amsterdam and Paris, and only eosin (geranium lake) for Chicago. Light microscopy and SEM/EDX analysis of cross sections from the Amsterdam picture suggests that the cochineal lake is present in the first paint layer of the floor, and geranium lake in the one on top. Geranium lake is made from the synthetic organic red pigment eosin, which is a crystalline red powder derived from fluorescein by bromination. See Geldof et al., "Van Gogh's Geranium Lake," 268–89. Noninvasive XRF analysis conducted in areas of the floor of the Paris picture found a paint mixture similar to that used in the Amsterdam and Chicago versions. An additional unidentified tin-containing lake was detected in the Paris version in the final outlines of the tiles based on visual examination and XRF analysis where a significant amount of tin was detected.

27. However, some differences were noted even between the two later versions: for instance, in the Paris painting, some of the objects, such as the small bottles, jug, and pitcher, were not left in reserve, but were painted directly over the first grayish-blue layer of the wall.

28. This was done after reinforcing the initial charcoal underdrawing in the Chicago version.

29. A sample that included the initial painted red lines was taken from the left chair. A combination of HPLC and SEM/EDX analysis showed that the red paint is cochineal lake on an aluminum/calcium-based substrate. The presence of geranium lake in the final blue outlines is supported by the detection of bromine in these areas by macro-XRF mapping.

30. Macro-XRF analysis determined that bromine is present in the reddish-brown outlines of the chair, suggesting that Van Gogh mixed in some geranium lake, a pigment that contains bromine.

31. See Van Gogh to Theo, on or about June 6, 1884; and Van Gogh to Anthon van Rappard, Sept. 21, 1884, *Letters*, 449 and 459, respectively. We know that Van Gogh first read Charles Blanc's text, *Les artistes de mon temps*, in 1884, based on letters in which he described an essay on Delacroix's use of color. He subsequently ordered Charles Blanc's other book, *Grammaire des arts du dessin: Architecture, sculpture, peinture.* Blanc's writings are based on Michel-Eugène Chevreul's theories on color in his book *De la loi du contraste simultané des couleurs, et de l'assortiment des objets colorés*, which was first published in Paris in 1839. See also Van Dijk, "Van Gogh and the Laws of Color."

32. Van Gogh to Theo, Oct. 16, 1888, *Letters*, 705.

33. Blanc, *Grammar of Painting and Engraving.*

34. Ravaud, "Use of X-Radiography to Study Paintings by Cézanne and Van Gogh in the Gachet Collection," pp. 65–70; Hoermann Lister, Peres, and Fiedler, "Tracing an Interaction," pp. 354–69; Hendriks and Van Tilborgh, "Van Gogh's 'Garden of the Asylum,'" p. 151; Hendriks et al., "Comparative Study."

35. On his dissatisfaction with available primed canvases, see Van Gogh to Theo, on or about Feb. 24, 1888; Van Gogh to Theo, Mar. 9, 1888; and Van Gogh to Theo, on or about Apr. 5, 1888, *Letters*, 578, 583, and 593, respectively. On ordering from Tasset et L'Hôte, see Van Gogh to Theo, on or about Apr. 5, 1888; Van Gogh to Theo, Aug. 21 or 22, 1888; and Van Gogh to Theo, Apr. 29, 1890, *Letters*, 593, 666, and 863, respectively.

36. Van Gogh to Theo, Aug. 21 or 22, 1888, *Letters*, 666.

37. The formats for both the Amsterdam and Chicago paintings are similar, a no. 30 portrait (*figure*) standard-size (92 × 73 cm) primed canvas. The smaller Paris painting measures 57.5 × 74 cm and, although not standard, is close to a no. 20 landscape (*paysage*) canvas (56.7 × 73 cm). The automated thread-count analysis done on all three works (average thread counts [threads/cm] [warp × weft]: Amsterdam 11.4 × 16.1; Chicago, 11.5 × 18.1; Paris: 11.4 × 17.0) found no thread density matches between the three canvases. For more specifics, see Johnson, Johnson, and Hendriks, "Automated Thread Counting"; Hendriks et al., "Automated Thread Counting and the Studio Practice Project." Analysis of the ground reveals dissimilar priming, indicating that the three canvases originated from distinct rolls. Amsterdam's ground consists of one layer (approximately 30–70 μm in thickness) with a mixture of lead white, calcium carbonate, a little barite, probably a little zinc white, traces of an orange ocher, and blue particles; Chicago's ground also consists of one layer (approximately 50–80 μm in thickness) containing a mixture of lead white, calcium carbonate (chalk; some whole coccoliths were identified by PLM), and traces of iron oxide yellow with associated silicate minerals, carbon black, and possibly barite (one barite particle was detected by SEM/EDX in a cross section of ground and canvas). Paris's ground consists of two layers with a combined thickness of about 160 μm (and is more typical of the types of grounds used later in Saint-Rémy), with the first layer consisting of lead white, a little calcium carbonate, lithopone, and traces of silica. The top layer is similar to the lower layer but contains more lead white with traces of yellow and blue particles. See Inge Fiedler, "1926_417_Van_Gogh_ *Bedroom*_Analytical_Report," Feb. 2, 2015, on file in the Conservation Department, Art Institute of Chicago. For more details on the research conducted on the different Tasset et L'Hôte ground types identified in Van Gogh's paintings from 1888 to 1890, see Salvant et al., "Investigation of the Grounds of Tasset et L'Hôte Commercially Primed Canvas."

38. *Vert émeraude* (a hydrated chromium oxide green pigment, also known as viridian) is mistakenly translated as "emerald green," which is the English term for a copper acetoarsenite green. Van Gogh to Theo, Arles, on or about Apr. 5, 1888, *Letters*, 593.

39. Geldof, Megens, and Salvant, "Van Gogh's Palette in Arles, Saint-Rémy and Auvers-Sur-Oise"; Bang, "Van Gogh's Palette"; Farrell and Newman, "Van Gogh's Painting Materials," pp. 28–38; and Leighton et al., "Vincent Van Gogh's *A Cornfield, with Cypresses*," pp. 42–59.

40. Van Gogh to Willemien van Gogh, on or about Oct. 21, 1889, *Letters*, 812.

41. Rheology is the study of the deformation and flow behavior of materials under applied force. See Salvant Plisson et al., "Rheology of White Paints." Van Gogh also considered zinc white to have advantages when used in mixtures with other pigments, including Prussian blue. See Van Gogh to Theo, on or about June 25, 1888; Van Gogh to Theo, Sept. 25, 1888, *Letters*, 631 and 687, respectively.

42. The Paris painting was examined by in situ XRF, XRD, and Raman spectroscopy. While XRF only detects chromium, which can be attributed to several pigments, the poor crystallinity of viridian renders its identification with in situ XRD and Raman problematic, so that only the presence of Cr_2O_3 could be unambiguously confirmed.

43. Additional research that was conducted on the chrome yellows in the Amsterdam painting found a monoclinic crystal structure of the lead chromate used for the bed frame, see Monico et al., "Degradation Process of Lead Chromate in Paintings by Vincent van Gogh Studied by Means of Spectromicroscopic Methods. 3." In the Chicago picture, three different types of chrome yellow were identified using Raman spectroscopy: a lemon yellow with a monoclinic crystal structure but containing some sulfate; a lead chromate (crocoite) with a monoclinic crystal structure; and a darker variety, possibly chrome orange, containing a mixture of crocoite and phoenicochroite. See Monico et al., "Degradation Process of Lead Chromate in Paintings by Vincent van Gogh Studied by Means of Synchrotron X-ray Spectromicroscopy and Related

Methods. 2"; and Monico et al., "Degradation Process of Lead Chromate in Paintings by Vincent van Gogh Studied by Means of Spectromicroscopic Methods. 3." See also Kühn and Curran, "Chrome Yellow and Other Chromate Pigments."

44. For the Amsterdam and Chicago paintings, the cochineal red lakes in the wall area were shown to have an aluminum/calcium-based substrate, whereas the cochineal lake used for the lines in the floor of the Paris picture has a tin-based substrate. In Van Gogh's list of pigments he often also includes a "laque ordinaire," which is believed to be a type of cochineal lake extended by the manufacturer with redwood, a cheaper but particularly unstable variety of red lake pigment. See Geldof et al., "Van Gogh's Palette in Arles, Saint-Rémy and Auvers-sur-Oise," pp. 248–49. See also Van Bommel, Geldof, and Hendriks, "Investigation of Organic Red Pigments Used in Paintings by Vincent van Gogh"; and Rioux, "Discoloration of Pinks and Purples in Van Gogh's Paintings from Auvers."

45. Van Gogh to Theo, Aug. 22, 1889, *Letters*, 797.

46. Van Gogh to Theo, Apr. 30, 1889, *Letters*, 765.

47. On the price and quality of his colors, see Van Gogh to Theo, Sept. 25–29, 1885; Van Gogh to Theo, Nov. 3 or 4, 1885; Van Gogh to Theo, Dec. 19, 1885; Van Gogh to Theo, Dec. 28, 1885; Van Gogh to Theo, on or about Apr. 13, 1888; Van Gogh to Theo, Aug. 23 or 24, 1888; Van Gogh to Theo, Sept. 25, 1885; and Van Gogh to Theo, Apr. 29, 1890, *Letters*, 532, 538, 549, 550, 597, 668, 687, and 863, respectively.

48. Van Gogh to Theo, on or about Apr. 11, 1888, *Letters*, 595, in which he justifies his use of the unstable colors Prussian blue and lemon yellow (pale chrome yellow) by giving the example of Delacroix who was able to create "superb" effects with them.

49. Van Gogh to Theo, on or about Apr. 11, 1888, *Letters*, 595.

50. Van Gogh to Theo, Oct. 16, 1888; Van Gogh to Gauguin, Oct. 17, 1888; and Van Gogh to Theo, Oct. 17, 1888, *Letters*, 705, 706, and 707, respectively.

51. Van Gogh used "pale violet" to describe the walls and "lilac" for the doors. Van Gogh to Theo, Oct. 16, 1888, *Letters*, 705. The following day he described the color of the walls instead as "pale lilac." Van Gogh to Gauguin, Oct. 17, 1888, *Letters*, 706. This suggests that the color of walls and doors was closely related. For the purpose of internal consistency, we use the term "violet" for the walls and "lilac" for the doors throughout this essay.

52. As exposure to light has caused the red lake to fade, the pink color has disappeared from the pink particles starting from the top of the paint layer. This is why the pink particles are visible today only in the bottom part of the cross section.

53. Van Gogh to Theo, Arles, Oct. 16, 1888, *Letters*, 705. The green patch under the chair is not yet visible in early twentieth-century black-and-white reproductions of the painting, including a photograph by Eugène Druet of 1908, and is only faintly visible in a color reproduction published in 1928. See Druet no. 7224, *Chambre à coucher de l'artiste* in Galerie E. Druet, *Tableaux modernes*, exh. cat. (n.p., n.d.); and Fels, *Van Gogh*, respectively. A later, partial copy of the Amsterdam *Bedroom* painting made by Isaac Israël, who was able to borrow the picture and included it in his painting, *Two Women in the Studio* (c. 1920; Gemeentemuseum, The Hague), shows the floor in this region to be a warm pink color.

54. HPLC analysis identified a small amount of cochineal, presumably the particles of red lake on an aluminum/calcium-based substrate seen in the first layer of the floor. A trace of indigo (*Indigofera tinctoria L.*) was also found, probably a manufacturer's ingredient added to the cochineal lake. This mixture of cochineal with a little indigo has been found more often in samples from Van Gogh's Paris period paintings.

55. XRF identified the presence of bromine, which is characteristic for geranium lake.

56. Van Gogh to Gauguin, Oct. 17, 1888; and Van Gogh to Theo, Oct. 16, 1888, *Letters*, 706 and 705, respectively.

57. Van Gogh to Theo, on or about May 23, 1889, *Letters*, 776. Van Gogh had sent his sunflowers framed that way, saying: "You see that this framing of simple laths does quite well, and a frame like that costs only very little. It would be perhaps good to frame the green and red vineyards, the sower and the furrows and the interior of the bedroom with them too."

58. See Blühm, "Displaying Van Gogh, 1886–1999," pp. 62–83, esp. pp. 71, 73.

59. Van Gogh to Theo, June 9, 1889, *Letters*, 779.

60. Van Gogh to Theo, Oct. 16, 1888, *Letters*, 705.

61. The term "visualization" has been chosen to make clear that the images are not exact replicas of how the paintings looked before their colors changed, which we can no longer precisely know. Roy S. Berns of the Munsell Color Science Laboratory, Rochester Institute of Technology, Rochester, New York, used Kubelka-Munk turbid medium theory to calculate levels of red lake color that could be fed back into faded paint areas. For an explanation of this approach, see Berns and Mohammadi, "Evaluating Single- and Two-Constant Kubelka-Munk Turbid Media Theory for Instrumental-based Inpainting." We were able to use spectral reflectance data derived from measurements on actual paintings by Van Gogh, as well as on historically informed reconstructions of Van Gogh's red lake paints that had been made and artificially aged. See Burnstock et al., "Comparison of the Fading and Surface Deterioration of Red Lake Pigments in Six Paintings by Vincent van Gogh with Artificially Aged Paint Reconstructions"; Van den Berg et al., "Fading of Red Lake Paints after Vincent van Gogh." Fine-tuning of the visualizations was guided by the reconstruction team, sometimes involving subjective choices based on informed judgment.

62. Van Gogh to Theo, Oct. 16, 1888, *Letters*, 705.

63. Van Gogh to Gauguin, Oct. 17, 1888, *Letters*, 706. In his previous letter to Theo he had described the painting as forming a contrast with two works he had made shortly before, *The Night Café* (p. 39, fig. 2) and *Tarascon Diligence* (p. 63, fig. 12); see page 70 and the essays by David J. Getsy and Louis van Tilborgh in this catalogue.

64. After Seurat's death, Gustave Kahn published a description of his studio: it was painted completely white, with drawings and paintings by himself and others (Armand Guillaumin, Jean-Louis Forain, Constantin Guys) as patches of color on the walls. There was a red divan, a couple of chairs, a small table, and one wall was filled with *La Grande Jatte*; see Kahn, "Seurat."

65. Van Gogh to Theo, Oct. 15, 1888, *Letters*, 704.

66. Van Gogh to Theo, on or about June 5, 1888, *Letters*, 620.

67. Van Gogh to Theo, Oct. 16, 1888; and Van Gogh to Gauguin, Oct. 17, 1888, *Letters*, 705 and 706, respectively.

68. Van Gogh to Theo, Oct. 16, 1888; and Van Gogh to Theo, Sept. 9, 1888, *Letters*, 705 and 677, respectively.

69. Van Gogh to Theo, Oct. 17, 1888, *Letters*, 707.

70. See note 5 above for a summary of the previous debates about the pictures' chronology.

71. Saltpeter is a collective term for several nitrogen-containing compounds, including hygroscopic potassium nitrate salts, which can absorb moisture from the air, especially at relative humidity above 75 percent. In a room that is sometimes unoccupied, with fluctuating relative humidity levels, this can result in the regular appearance of salt blooms on the surface, giving the appearance of rising damp.

72. Van Gogh to Theo, June 9, 1889, *Letters*, 779.

73. On this topic, see, for example, Mecklenburg and Tumosa, "Mechanical Behaviour of Paintings Subjected to Changes in Temperature and Relative Humidity."

74. Prior to this treatment it had been hard to properly assess the condition of the painting obscured by old fillings and retouches. A condition report compiled in June 1984 by Ernst van der Wetering and Monique Behrends had noted that the X-ray gave cause to question the extent of damage and adhesion of paint in the floor, recommending that a full treatment be considered at some future date following a highly critical investigation of the painting. Conservation archives, Van Gogh Museum, Amsterdam.

75. Paint cross sections confirm that the canvas was sized with a layer of glue, approximately 15 µm thick.

76. This differs from what we see in the Paris version of *The Bedroom*, where small remnants of newspaper with yellowed adhesive lie under the current varnish, held neatly on the paint surface rather than pressed into it, showing a more gentle approach. These fragments of a former newspaper covering (a so-called facing) may presumably be associated with the glue-paste lining applied by M. Rostain in 1958; see report kept at the archives of the Centre de Recherche et de Restauration des Musées de France (C2RMF), Paris.

77. "The grape harvests are totally covered in scales as a result of the *white* which has separated. I've stuck all of it back down using a process shown to me by the reliner. If I tell you about it it's because the thing is easy to do and can be very good for those of your canvases that need retouching—you stick newspapers on your canvas with *flour paste*. Once dry, you put your canvas on a smooth board and with very hot irons you press down *hard* on it. All the breaks in your colour will remain but will be flattened down and you'll have a *very fine* surface. Afterwards you soak your paper covering well and take off all the paper. That's largely the whole secret of relining." Paul Gauguin to Van Gogh, between Jan. 8 and 16, 1889, *Letters*, 734.

78. Van Gogh to Theo, on or about May 23, 1889, *Letters*, 776. The identity of the liner mentioned is not known, but it could be Contet (who in 1886 had taken over the business of Mrs. Latouche) since it is known that Gauguin had had canvases relined there in 1883.

79. Van Gogh to Theo, June 9, 1889, *Letters*, 779.

80. Theo to Van Gogh, June 16, 1889, *Letters*, 781.

81. Van Gogh to Theo, on or about June 18, 1889, *Letters*, 782.

82. Van Gogh to Theo, Sept. 5–6, 1889, *Letters*, 800.

83. Invoice b 4200 v/1962, Van Gogh Museum (Vincent van Gogh Foundation), Amsterdam, Dec. 1931–Jan. 1932. In his complaint, however, Traas makes no distinction between damage as a prior consequence of damp in the artist's studio and as a result of the lining treatment itself.

84. On this topic, see Van der Wetering, "Autonomy of Restoration," p. 195.

85. Not all of the gaps in the touches of dark-blue paint are due to paint loss. Some are the result of rapid paint application, whereby the brush strokes skipped across the surface of the canvas, only catching onto it in places. Under the microscope a careful distinction can be made between the two, since spots of cleavage loss are characterized by sharp edges formed when the paint fractured and broke off. We are grateful to Kimberley Muir, Assistant Research Conservator at the Art Institute at Chicago, for making these observations and sharing them with us.

86. This was determined with false-color infrared imaging performed by John K. Delaney, Senior Imaging Scientist and Kathryn A. Dooley, Research Fellow at the National Gallery of Art, Washington, D.C. The instrument used is a Surface Optics modified near-infrared hyperspectral camera (which collects 3.4 nm spectral-band images [1000–1680 nm]). This analytical imaging confirmed that the blue brushstrokes running over the lacunae not only look the same color as the rest in normal light, but that they also contain the same mixture of pigments and therefore appear identical in the false-color infrared image as well.

87. Van Gogh to Theo, Sept. 5–6, 1889, *Letters*, 800.

88. In view of Van Gogh's suggestion to have the first *Bedroom* study lined in Paris by the liner used by Paul Gauguin, the features of the lining of the Chicago *Bedroom* were compared with those of five pictures by Paul Gauguin in the collection of the Art Institute at Chicago that still bear old French glue-paste linings. However, Kristin Hoermann Lister, Conservator of Paintings at the Art Institute, kindly informed us that none of these paintings have inscriptions, labels, brand marks, or stamps that can be ascribed to a particular liner or art supplier. Furthermore, though still on old stretchers, none of them are mounted on a Bourgeois Aîné stretcher, as is the case for the Chicago *Bedroom*. Hoermann Lister's research has shown that some of Gauguin's paintings have aqueous linings that contain chalk in the adhesive mixture, including *The Grape Harvest at Arles (Human Misery)* (1888; Ordrupgaard, Copenhagen), a painting that Gauguin is known to have consolidated according to reliner's instructions. Whether this is the case for the glue-paste lining of the Chicago *Bedroom* painting has not yet been investigated.

89. Labreuche, *Paris, capitale de la toile à peindre*, p. 308.

90. For this information we are indebted to Pascal Labreuche, Paintings Conservator in Paris, who generously shared his expertise on this topic, as well as examples from his online database of artist suppliers. For examples of Bourgeois Aîné stretchers with both a brand mark and stamp resembling those on the Chicago *Bedroom* painting, see http://www.labreuche-fournisseurs-artistes-paris.fr/maison/bourgeois-aine. Based on known examples, it appears that the combination of a brand mark on the crossbar and a trade stamp with dimensions appears on Bourgeois Aîné stretchers from paintings dated around 1910–15. Stretchers with both a brand mark and a label (rather than stamp) with trademark and dimensions are documented on paintings dated from around 1908 to at least 1927. So far, documented examples of stretchers from before 1900 never bear both a brand mark and a stamp or label.

91. It is documented that the Chicago painting was in possession of the Paris dealer Jos Hessel in 1901 and that Carl Reininghaus in Vienna owned the painting in 1909, although the exact date of transfer from one to the other gallery is not known. From the Thannhauser archives it appears that Reininghaus had purchased the painting, presumably from Hessel or Bernheim Jeune (for whom the latter also worked) before 1909, probably around 1905, when he is known to have acquired three of the four other Van Gogh paintings that he owned. See curatorial file, Department of European Painting and Sculpture, Art Institute of Chicago.

92. Van Gogh to Theo, Sept. 28, 1889, *Letters*, 806.

93. Van Gogh to Theo, Dec. 7, 1889, *Letters*, 824.

94. Van Gogh to Theo, on or about Dec. 19, 1889; and Theo to Van Gogh, Dec. 22, 1889, *Letters*, 829 and 830, respectively.

95. All conservation records for the painting, including those of the first 1958 glue-paste lining by M. Rostain, are kept at the C2RMF archives.

96. Neither the Paris painting nor the other two *Bedroom* pictures bear further signs to indicate precisely how they were rolled. There are no series of parallel cracks in the paint formed perpendicular to the direction of rolling, for example, nor any concentration of cracking and paint loss on the side of the canvas that was rolled more tightly.

WORKS BY VAN GOGH

1

Plate 1 Vincent van Gogh (Dutch, 1853–1890). *The Parsonage at Nuenen at Dusk*, 1885. Oil on canvas; 41 × 54.5 cm (16 1/8 × 21 7/16 in.). Het Noordbrabants Museum, 's-Hertogenbosch, the Netherlands, on loan from a private collection. F183, JH952

In December 1883, debt and a lack of other options forced Van Gogh to move to Nuenen to live with his parents, whom he had not seen since Christmas 1881 when a terrible fight ended with the artist storming out. Two years later, tensions were still high, with Van Gogh provoking his father into daily arguments. As a child, Van Gogh was known by villagers as the pastor's antisocial son, whose face was recognized peeking out from his bedroom window, and he developed the same reputation as an adult artist living with his parents for two fretful years.

Van Gogh's one refuge was the outbuilding behind the parsonage, seen here to the right of the main house, which he converted into a studio. In the house, he found that there were too many interruptions and prying eyes, so the artist preferred to work in this shedlike structure, despite its shortcomings (Van Gogh explained in a letter to Theo that it was next to the coal pit, sewer, and privy). In this studio, he painted his first iconic work, *The Potato Eaters* (1885; Kröller-Müller Museum, Otterlo [p. 53, fig. 2]).

Plate 2 Vincent van Gogh (Dutch, 1853–1890). *A Peasant Woman Digging in front of Her Cottage*, c. 1885. Oil on canvas; 31.3 × 42 cm (12 5/16 × 16 1/2 in.). The Art Institute of Chicago, bequest of Dr. John J. Ireland, 1968.92. F142, JH807

In the second half of 1885, Van Gogh began painting two interconnected series: cottages and birds' nests. Van Gogh had long been taken with the paintings of cottages by Charles-François Daubigny and Georges Michel. As Van Gogh wandered among the cottages near his parents' home in Nuenen, the mossy thatched roofs reminded him of the work of a different sort of artist: the wren, who he claimed could "truly be counted among the artists" (Aug. 8–15, 1885, *Letters*, 526). He described this series to his brother Theo, reflecting, "I feel for *the brood and the nests*—particularly those *human* nests, those cottages on the heath and their inhabitants" (Oct. 4, 1885, *Letters*, 533). The artist used an almost monochromatic palette of browns, greens, and grays not only for the cottage, trees, and earth, but also for the woman digging out front. In doing so, Van Gogh stressed that she belongs to this place and it to her.

Plate 3 Vincent van Gogh (Dutch, 1853–1890). *Birds' Nests*, 1885. Oil on canvas; 39.3 × 46.5 cm (15 1/2 × 18 5/16 in.). Van Gogh Museum, Amsterdam (Vincent van Gogh Foundation). F111, JH939

One of Van Gogh's sisters, Elisabeth du Quesne van Gogh ("Lies"), fondly recalled how he spent his youth wandering the woods that surrounded their family home in Groot-Zundert, the Netherlands, carefully studying the wildlife and their habitats. He would take home abandoned birds' nests and display his specimens in the attic bedroom he shared with Theo. As an adult, again living in his parents' home, he employed local children to find nests for him, paying 10 cents each—though rarer or more intricate nests, like the two wrens' nests seen here at top and right, could fetch a higher reward. Visitors to Van Gogh's studio at Nuenen later recalled his collection of at least thirty different nests among the clutter in his studio. In one corner of the room, he had planted a felled branch in a box filled with soil and balanced several of his birds' nests on it.

2

3

Plate 4 Vincent van Gogh (Dutch, 1853–1890). *Terrace and Observation Deck at the Moulin de Blute-Fin, Montmartre*, 1887. Oil on canvas, mounted on hardboard; 43.6 × 33 cm (17 1/8 × 13 in.). The Art Institute of Chicago, Helen Birch Bartlett Memorial Collection, 1926.202. F272, JH1183

This painting dates to early 1887, roughly a year after Van Gogh arrived in Paris. It is one of a group of landscapes featuring the Butte Montmartre, which rises high above the city's northern edge and was only a short climb from Van Gogh and Theo's apartment on the rue Lepic. Here, the artist depicted the observation deck at the Moulin de Blute-Fin—one of three surviving windmills in the neighborhood—which he kept out of the frame to keep the focus off the picturesque and on the newer elements, such as the gaslights and observation deck, of this rapidly changing neighborhood. He positioned himself as one among several tourists taking in the sights of Paris, suggesting that he still thought of himself as an outsider—even after having lived there for a while. Though Van Gogh ultimately found himself unsuited for Parisian life, his time there was a watershed in his artistic career, and the experience forever changed him: "Paris is Paris, there is but one Paris ... however hard living may be here" (Sept. or Oct. 1886, *Letters*, 569).

5

6

Plate 5 Vincent van Gogh (Dutch, 1853–1890). *A Pair of Shoes, One Shoe Upside Down*, 1887. Oil on canvas; 37.5 × 45.5 cm (14 3/4 × 17 15/16 in.). Private collection, courtesy of Eykyn Maclean, L.P. F332a, JH1233

Friend and fellow artist François Gauzi recalled that Van Gogh visited a Paris flea market where he bought a pair of peddler's shoes, old but in good condition. Nevertheless, he painted the shoes to appear worn and scuffed from excessive use. His choice of subject matter confused his fellow artists, including Gauzi, who "couldn't imagine that, in a dining room, a plate of apples could hang as a pendant to a pair of clodhoppers" (quoted in Stein, *Van Gogh: A Retrospective*, p. 72). Yet his choice was not without precedent; this painting of shoes echoed the works of Van Gogh's artistic hero, Jean-François Millet, who had drawn *sabots* (clogs), using this mundane subject to express transcendence. His nearly monochromatic still life of shoes belongs to the artist's ongoing exploration of the humble. For Van Gogh, this well-worn, banal, convincingly real footwear served as a metaphor of the artist who has traveled a long way—often on foot. The shoes embody the artist's need for domesticity, even as he continually left or was asked to leave the many homes he inhabited.

Plate 6 Vincent van Gogh (Dutch, 1853–1890). *A Pair of Boots*, 1887. Oil on canvas; 32.7 × 41.3 cm (12 7/8 × 16 1/4 in.). The Baltimore Museum of Art, The Cone Collection, formed by Dr. Claribel Cone and Miss Etta Cone of Baltimore, Maryland, BMA 1950.302. F333, JH1236

Painted only months after *A Pair of Shoes, One Shoe Upside Down*, this painting of boots reveals the enormous transformation in Van Gogh's palette during his time in Paris. Though the artist always worked in a bold, unique aesthetic—characterized by pronounced brushwork and impasto—he had been painting in a descriptive style and using local, earth-tone colors. While living in Antwerp in 1885, Van Gogh had dismissed Theo's written praise of the Impressionists, yet he could not help but fall under their spell when he finally saw their paintings in person for the first time in Paris. *A Pair of Boots* reflects the artist's highly personal assimilation of these influences, as he began using ornamental lines and bright colors. Though his details are less refined compared to the earlier painting, he was no less careful in his depiction: sinuous lines of alternating orange and brown define the shoelaces, and an array of white dots suggests the hobnails on the visible sole. His use of complementary colors, orange and blue, presages the work he would do as he became more familiar with the work of his Neo-Impressionist colleagues.

Plate 7 Vincent van Gogh (Dutch, 1853–1890). *View from Theo's Apartment*, 1887. Oil on board; 45.8 × 38 cm (18 × 15 in.). Private collection, courtesy of Galerie Bruno Bischofberger, Switzerland. F341a, JH1243

Van Gogh arrived in Paris in mid-March 1886 with no warning to Theo other than a hand-delivered note asking his brother to meet him at the Musée du Louvre that afternoon. The two Van Goghs lived for three months in a cramped apartment in Montmartre on the rue de Laval, which did not even have enough room for an easel. Finally in June, they moved to a larger three-bedroom apartment nearby at 54, rue Lepic. Van Gogh claimed the smallest bedroom for himself and the largest bedroom for his studio.

Even before he had any intention of being an artist, Van Gogh had often sketched the views from his windows when he moved into a new home. Here, he painted the view of the Paris skyline from the rue Lepic apartment, which the brothers considered the most "remarkable thing about our flat" (*Letters*, 569, n. 9). In this painting, the artist experimented with the pure, unmixed colors and stippled brushstrokes of the Neo-Impressionists, but the flattened composition draws from the Japanese prints he was seriously collecting at this time. Van Gogh's friend, neighbor, and fellow artist Henri de Toulouse-Lautrec greatly admired his collection of Japanese prints and would visit the apartment to study them. Lautrec was given *View from Theo's Apartment* as a gift and possibly in exchange for his portrait of Van Gogh (p. 21, bottom row, middle).

7

Plate 8 Vincent van Gogh (Dutch, 1853–1890). *Self-Portrait*, 1887. Oil on cardboard with pebble-textured priming, mounted on cradled wood panel; 41 × 32.5 cm (16 1/8 × 12 13/16 in.). The Art Institute of Chicago, Joseph Winterbotham Collection, 1954.326. F345, JH1249

Van Gogh's earliest surviving self-portrait dates to March 1886, just after arriving in Paris, and he painted at least three dozen more over the course of his career. Each self-portrait is not a mere representation of the artist's face but a symbolic expression of his current goals, social position, and state of mind. Over his lifetime, he portrayed himself as a well-dressed gentleman in a suit, a peasant in a smock and straw hat, an artist at his easel, and even a Japanese monk. In this self-portrait from 1887, Van Gogh depicted himself as an avant-garde artist, a Neo-Impressionist; for this painting he adhered closely to the pointillist brushstroke and use of complementary colors red and green, blue and orange. However, he was never as theoretically rigorous or painstakingly meticulous as the founder of Neo-Impressionism, Georges Seurat, or its strongest advocate, Paul Signac, both of whom he was acquainted with. Instead, after experimenting with their techniques here, he would appropriate only the elements he found personally useful and assimilate them into his own idiosyncratic, assertive style.

9

Plate 9 Vincent van Gogh (Dutch, 1853–1890). *Parisian Novels*, 1887. Oil on canvas; 73 × 93 cm (28 3/4 × 36 5/8 in.). Private collection. F359, JH1332

Van Gogh was a voracious reader his entire life, claiming to have an "irresistible passion for books" in three languages (Dutch, French, and English; June 22–24, 1880, *Letters*, 155). As he wrote to Theo, "I'd wish that everyone had what I'm gradually beginning to acquire, the ability to read a book easily and quickly and to retain a strong impression of it. Reading books is like looking at paintings: without doubting, without hesitating, with self-assurance, one must find beautiful that which is beautiful" (Aug. 5, 1881, *Letters*, 170). Van Gogh did not draw a distinction between the goals of modern artists and modern authors, but rather thought that while the former painted with pigments, the latter painted with words. When he discovered the French Realist authors, such as Gustave Flaubert and Émile Zola, he felt an affinity that was as strong as his connection to his favorite painters. The characteristic yellow covers of Realist books are prominently scattered throughout *Parisian Novels*. This painting is a manifesto, unequivocally articulating the artist's ambition to make paintings that would equal in significance and stature the literature he so admired.

10

Plate 10 Vincent van Gogh (Dutch, 1853–1890). *Grapes, Lemons, Pears, and Apples*, 1887. Oil on canvas; 46.5 × 55.2 cm (18 5/16 × 21 3/4 in.). The Art Institute of Chicago, gift of Kate L. Brewster, 1949.215. F382, JH1337

Van Gogh had always insisted on working directly from life, whether he was trudging out to the fields with his easel or paying for costly models with what he could scrape together from the allowance provided by Theo. During inclement weather and when his means were limited, Van Gogh could always paint still lifes in his studio; therefore, it is not surprising that this type of painting was a vehicle throughout his career for so much of his aesthetic evolution. *Grapes, Lemons, Pears, and Apples* belongs to a series of related canvases Van Gogh painted in the fall of 1887, when he was experimenting with a thicker, broader paint application in more vibrant colors. Van Gogh was exploring color complementaries, especially pairing yellows with purples and reds with greens. The chromatic intensity is further heightened by the radiating strokes of blue, purple, and pink. The resulting halo effect would have been even more prominent in the original composition, which included only lemons and grapes, before Van Gogh returned to the canvas to add the apples, pears, and leaves.

Plate 11 Vincent van Gogh (Dutch, 1853–1890). *The Park and Pond in front of the Yellow House*, 1888. Pencil, pen, reed pen, and brown ink, on paper; 32 × 50.1 cm (12 5/8 × 19 3/4 in.). Van Gogh Museum, Amsterdam (Vincent van Gogh Foundation). F1513, JH1412

Van Gogh sketched this "hasty croquis" just before May 1, 1888, the day he signed the lease on the Yellow House. It was included in a batch of about a dozen pen drawings he sent to Theo, along with a letter sharing the news of his soon-to-be new home. The Yellow House can be identified in the background of the landscape as the right portion of a larger structure, though a small tree obscures all but the second-story windows and gabled roof. The sketch is one of his earliest views of the small, "unremarkable" park situated along the place Lamartine on the north edge of Arles. This quick drawing is Van Gogh's only representation of the public garden in its urban setting; soon he would transform it into a timeless pastoral in his *Poet's Garden* series (see plate 15). With this more contextualized landscape, the artist gives us a glimpse (though seen from the opposite perspective) of the view from his and Paul Gauguin's bedroom windows.

Plate 12 Vincent van Gogh (Dutch, 1853–1890). *Landscape at Arles*, 1888. Pen and brown ink over graphite on cream wove paper; 25.4 × 34.3 cm (10 × 13 1/2 in.). The Art Institute of Chicago, anonymous loan, 12.9.1989. F1518, JH1493

When the winter snows began to thaw in Arles, Van Gogh was determined to produce an "enormous amount of drawings" of nature. Inspired by the albums of Japanese prints he had collected with his brother in Paris, the artist hoped to group these drawings together into albums to give to Paul Gauguin and Émile Bernard as gifts. He purposely drew quickly and with little refinement in an emulation of how he imagined Japanese artists worked: "The Japanese draws quickly, very quickly, like a flash of lightning, because his nerves are finer, his feeling simpler" (on or about June 5, 1888, *Letters*, 620). To produce these loosely styled sketches, such as *Landscape at Arles*, the artist began using a reed pen, a delicate tool for which he showed great aptitude despite little experience. Van Gogh used the reed pen to create the dynamic and painterly lines of the trees and leaves, but he employed a finer pen for the details in the background.

11

12

Plate 13 Vincent van Gogh (Dutch, 1853–1890). *Eugène Boch*, 1888. Oil on canvas; 60.3 × 45.4 cm (23 3/4 × 17 15/16 in.). Musée d'Orsay, Paris, legacy of Mr. Eugène Boch, 1941. F462, JH1574

Filled with enthusiasm for his plans to decorate his Yellow House, Van Gogh envisioned a group of portraits for the walls of his own bedroom. The first was of Eugène Boch, a Belgian Impressionist painter living in Arles. He intended this portrait to be an almost allegorical depiction of his "friend who dreams great dreams" as a poet and possibly also a surrogate representation of Paul Gauguin (Aug. 18, 1888, *Letters*, 663). Writing to Theo, Van Gogh chronicled his process of imbuing his portrayal with a deeper symbolism. After painting a faithful representation, he returned to the canvas to exaggerate the palette, rendering Boch's pale face and blond hair in shades of lemon, chrome yellow, orange, and ocher. Behind him, Van Gogh omitted the mundane wall of his studio and instead painted "the infinite"—a dark midnight sky filled with twinkling stars. In doing so, the artist hoped to create the effect of Boch's head as another star in the heavens. The stark contrast between complementary colors also speaks to Van Gogh's experimentation with his palette just before he first painted *The Bedroom* (plate 20), in which this portrait is depicted hanging over his bed.

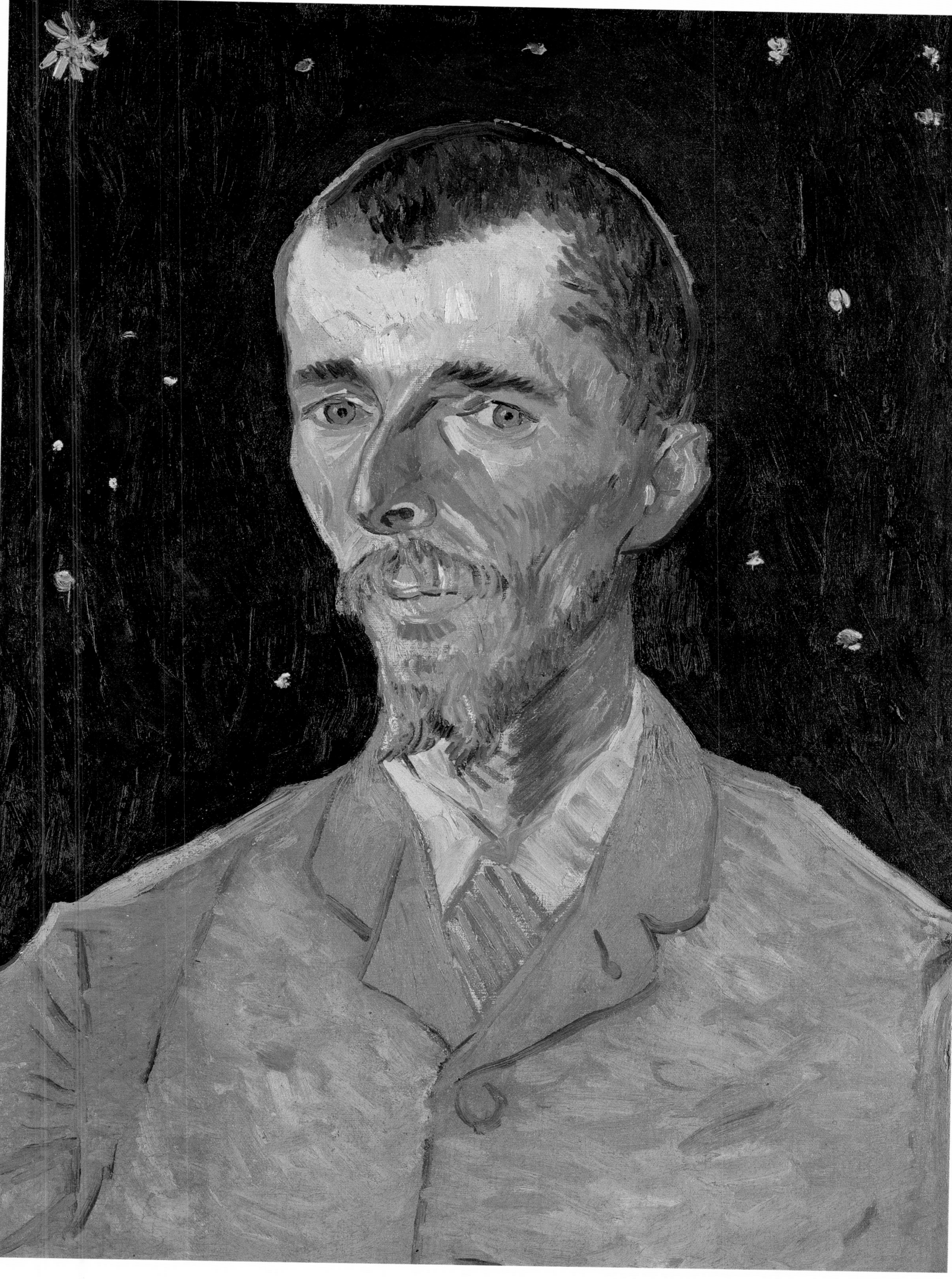

Plate 14 Vincent van Gogh (Dutch, 1853–1890). *The Lover (Portrait of Lieutenant Milliet)*, late September–early October 1888. Oil on canvas; 60.3 × 49.5 cm (23 3/4 × 19 1/2 in.). Kröller-Müller Museum, Otterlo, the Netherlands. F473, JH1588

After completing Eugène Boch's portrait, Van Gogh looked for a subject whose personality as well as countenance could serve as a pendant. The artist chose to paint his friend Lieutenant Paul-Eugène Milliet, a member of the Zouaves—French soldiers serving in North Africa. Milliet's boisterous, easygoing attitude contrasted with Boch's sensitive introversion. Van Gogh and Milliet bonded over a shared interest in art, and the former would take the latter along on some of his walks to give him drawing lessons. This portrait is another study in complementary colors, which Van Gogh deployed in depicting several of the sitter's personal details: "I have his portrait now, with the red képi against an emerald background, and in this background the emblem of his regiment, the crescent and 5-pointed star" (on or about Sept. 29, 1888, *Letters*, 691). Though this emblem and his uniform identify the sitter as a soldier, Van Gogh gave this painting the title *The Lover*, designating Milliet as an embodiment of a masculine ideal.

15

Plate 15 Vincent van Gogh (Dutch, 1853–1890). *The Poet's Garden*, 1888. Oil on canvas; 73 × 92.1 cm (28 3/4 × 36 1/4 in.). The Art Institute of Chicago, Mr. and Mrs. Lewis Larned Coburn Memorial Collection, 1933.433. F468, JH1578

Van Gogh produced eight paintings and twelve drawings and sketches of the public garden across the street from his Yellow House in Arles, but he only considered four paintings to belong to the group *The Poet's Garden*. These four landscapes, as well as at least two still lifes of sunflowers, were installed as the decoration in the second bedroom, where Paul Gauguin would live. Gauguin's bedroom was the smaller of the two, with a diagonal back wall, a door, and two windows. The six paintings in their frames would likely have taken up almost half the available wall space in the room. Van Gogh purposely cluttered the walls, following what he believed to be a Japanese approach to decoration: "I want to stuff at least 6 very large canvases into this tiny little room, the way the Japanese do.... You know that the Japanese instinctively look for contrasts.... Following the same system you should probably only put very small paintings in a large room, but in a very small room you'll put a lot of big ones" (Sept. 9 and about 14, 1888, *Letters*, 678).

16

Plate 16 Vincent van Gogh (Dutch, 1853–1890). *Entrance to the Public Gardens in Arles*, 1888. Oil on canvas; 72.39 × 90.805 cm (28 1/2 × 35 3/4 in.). The Phillips Collection, Washington, D.C. F566, JH1585

In mid-October 1888, Van Gogh received a letter from Paul Gauguin in which he again postponed his arrival in Arles, claiming illness. Frustrated by the older artist's dithering, Van Gogh threw himself into his work and returned to the public garden in front of the Yellow House. This painting depicts the northern entrance to the park, almost directly across the street from his front door. The gentle diagonal of the sulfurous path leads the viewer's gaze into the lush scene up to where the trail forks around a pond. The dense foliage takes up nearly half of the canvas and casts the only shadows in this otherwise sunlit landscape. Van Gogh populated the space with townspeople, but—in contrast to his previous paintings of the garden—there are no couples. Each of the figures stands, sits, or strolls alone with his or her thoughts, which perhaps alludes to the artist's fear that his housemate would never arrive. *Entrance to the Public Gardens in Arles* belongs to the final group of paintings Van Gogh completed before collapsing in his bed from exhaustion; roused from two days of uninterrupted rest, the artist was inspired to paint *The Bedroom* (plate 20).

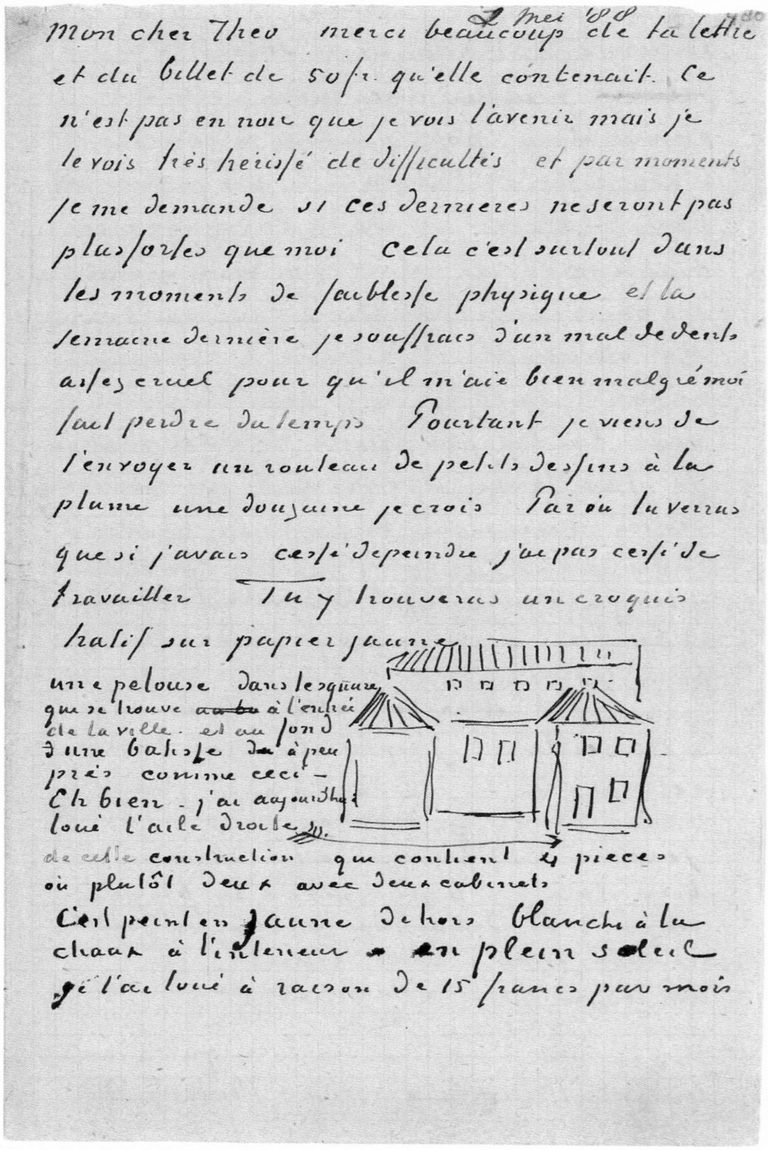

17

Plate 17 Vincent van Gogh (Dutch, 1853–1890). *Letter to Theo van Gogh with the Sketch "The Yellow House,"* May 1, 1888. Pen and black ink on cream, machine-made wove paper; 27 × 21 cm (10 5/8 × 8 1/4 in.). Van Gogh Museum, Amsterdam (Vincent van Gogh Foundation). JH1413

18

Plate 18 Vincent van Gogh (Dutch, 1853–1890). *Letter to Theo van Gogh with the Sketch "The Public Garden with Couple Strolling (The Poet's Garden),"* Oct. 13, 1888. Black ink on cream, machine-made wove paper; 20.7 × 13.5 cm (8 1/8 × 5 5/16 in.). Van Gogh Museum, Amsterdam (Vincent van Gogh Foundation). JH1602

19

Plate 19 Vincent van Gogh (Dutch, 1853–1890). *Letter to Theo van Gogh with the Sketch "The Bedroom,"* Oct. 16, 1888. Pen and black ink on cream, machine-made wove paper; 13 × 21 cm (5 1/8 × 8 1/4 in.). Van Gogh Museum, Amsterdam (Vincent van Gogh Foundation). JH1609

Long before becoming an artist, Van Gogh would include sketches of his latest neighborhood and surroundings in his letters to his family. When he wrote to Theo from Arles announcing that he had rented a little yellow house, this news was accompanied by a quick sketch of the building. Once Van Gogh moved in and began to focus on decorating his home, he continued to share his plans and ideas with his brother. In half a dozen letters, he refers to *The Poet's Garden* series, the decorative suite for Paul Gauguin's bedroom that Van Gogh hoped would lure the older artist to Arles. These letter sketches sometimes offer the best traces of Van Gogh's artistic process. When he wrote to Theo on October 16, 1888, with a new idea to make a painting of his bedroom, he included a full-page drawing. The compositional differences between this sketch and the painting he completed the following day (plate 20)—such as the painting behind the bed and the basin under the washstand—reveal Van Gogh's changing mind.

20

Plate 20 Vincent van Gogh (Dutch, 1853–1890). *The Bedroom*, Oct. 16–17, 1888. Oil on canvas; 72.4 × 91.3 cm (28 1/2 × 35 15/16 in.). Van Gogh Museum, Amsterdam (Vincent van Gogh Foundation). F482, JH1608

Plate 21 Vincent van Gogh (Dutch, 1853–1890). *The Bedroom*, by Sept. 5, 1889. Oil on canvas; 73.6 × 92.3 cm (29 × 36 5/16 in.). The Art Institute of Chicago, Helen Birch Bartlett Memorial Collection, 1926.417. F484, JH1771

Plate 22 Vincent van Gogh (Dutch, 1853–1890). *The Bedroom*, by Sept. 28, 1889. Oil on canvas; 57.5 × 74 cm (22 5/8 × 29 1/8 in.). Musée d'Orsay, Paris, sold to national museums under the Treaty of Peace with Japan, 1959. F483, JH1793

21

Facing page

Plate 23 Vincent van Gogh (Dutch, 1853–1890). *Van Gogh's Chair*, 1888. Oil on canvas; 91.8 × 73 cm (36 1/8 × 28 3/4 in.). The National Gallery, London. Bought, Courtauld Fund, 1924. F498, JH1635

A week before moving into the Yellow House, Van Gogh bought twelve deal pine chairs, suggesting his almost blind optimism about how many artists he hoped would join his Studio of the South. In this painting, one of those chairs acts as a stand-in for the artist. Van Gogh chose to represent himself with just a simple chair, his pipe, a pouch of tobacco, and a crate of onions on which he signed his name. This work continues the theme of humble objects in his oeuvre; it also speaks to the simplicity Van Gogh was seeking not just in his life but in his art as well. Six months after arriving in Arles, he wrote to Theo that what he had learned from the Parisian avant-garde had faded. Instead, Van Gogh was pursuing a new aesthetic that would be at once both deeply personal and universal: "I'm beginning more and more to look for a simple technique that perhaps isn't Impressionist. I'd like to paint in such a way that if it comes to it, everyone who has eyes could understand it" (Aug. 21 or 22, 1888, *Letters*, 666).

Following pages

Plate 24 Vincent van Gogh (Dutch, 1853–1890). *Gauguin's Chair*, 1888. Oil on canvas; 90.5 × 72.7 cm (35 5/8 × 28 5/8 in.). Van Gogh Museum, Amsterdam (Vincent van Gogh Foundation). F499, JH1636

Van Gogh painted the chair from Paul Gauguin's bedroom around November 19, what would ultimately be the halfway mark in their cohabitation in Arles. At the time, he considered this study of an empty chair "rather funny." However, after Gauguin's departure and Van Gogh's hospitalization, the discouraged artist reinterpreted its meaning. Describing the painting to art critic Albert Aurier, he wrote: "Gauguin, that curious artist, that stranger . . . I tried to paint 'his empty place.' It is a study of his armchair of dark, red-brown wood, the seat of greenish straw, and in the absent person's place a lighted candlestick and some modern novels" (Feb. 9 or 10, 1890, *Letters*, 853). What had once symbolized Gauguin's role as the head of the Studio of the South now symbolized the emptiness of Van Gogh's dreams: Gauguin alone had been given a carved walnut chair by Van Gogh, instead of a far more ordinary rush-bottomed one, in a gesture that was meant to set his friend apart from his disciples. Van Gogh's mental breakdown and his subsequent hospitalizations altered his understanding of many of his works from Arles. The revisions he made in the process of painting the second and third versions of *The Bedroom* (plates 21–22) captured Van Gogh's changing state of mind.

Plate 25 Vincent van Gogh (Dutch, 1853–1890). *Madame Roulin Rocking the Cradle* (*La berceuse*), 1889. Oil on canvas; 92.7 × 73.8 cm (36 1/2 × 29 in.). The Art Institute of Chicago, Helen Birch Bartlett Memorial Collection, 1926.200. F506, JH1670

Van Gogh considered Joseph Roulin—a postman from Arles—his wife Augustine, and their three children to be a living ideal of love and family life. Here he depicted Augustine sitting beside a cradle, outside the picture's frame, which she is rocking by pulling on a rope. He gave the painting the title *La berceuse*, meaning lullaby. This portrait, of which Van Gogh painted five distinct repetitions, was laden with personal meaning and associations for the artist. He painted this version in late January 1889, soon after returning to the Yellow House following Paul Gauguin's departure. Van Gogh sat Madame Roulin in Gauguin's chair, which in the older artist's absence became a vain attempt to fill the empty space, and transformed her image into a soothing "lullaby in colours." In May 1889, Van Gogh gave the Art Institute's version of *Madame Roulin* as a gift to Gauguin in a gesture of friendship with the explicit instructions that it should be hung between two paintings of sunflowers to form a triptych.

23

25

Plate 26 Vincent van Gogh (Dutch, 1853–1890). *Self-Portrait*, 1889. Oil on canvas; 57.79 × 44.5 cm (22 3/4 × 17 1/2 in.). National Gallery of Art, Washington, D.C., Collection of Mr. and Mrs. John Hay Whitney, 1998.74.5. F626, JH1770

After becoming an artist in 1880, Van Gogh drew and painted countless portraits in an ongoing attempt to simultaneously capture the truth of his subjects' likenesses and the timelessness of their stations in life. In Saint-Rémy-de-Provence, he could not convince the other patients to sit for him, so he was forced to paint self-portraits, though he found himself a difficult model: "People say—and I'm quite willing to believe it—that it's difficult to know oneself —but it's not easy to paint oneself either" (Sept. 5 and 6, 1889, *Letters*, 800). In this self-portrait, Van Gogh depicted himself as an artist with his palette, brushes, and blue smock. He chose to portray his right side to hide his disfigured left ear. This canvas was still drying in his studio when Van Gogh returned to *The Bedroom* to paint a second version (plate 21). It bears a very close resemblance to the small self-portrait on the wall of the Art Institute's *Bedroom*, and indeed may have served as the direct model for it.

27

Previous pages

Plate 27 Vincent van Gogh (Dutch, 1853–1890). *Weeping Tree*, 1889. Reed pen and black-brown ink, with black chalk, on off-white wove paper; 49.8 × 61.3 cm (19 5/8 × 24 1/8 in.). The Art Institute of Chicago, gift of Tiffany and Margaret Day Blake, 1945.31. F1468, JH1498

A year after making *Landscape at Arles* (plate 12), Van Gogh returned to the medium of the reed pen after an extended break. By this time, his circumstances had changed considerably: no longer an optimistic newcomer, the artist had been in and out of the Arles hospital three times over the course of four months, his last stay lasting longer than a month. The somber, darker *Weeping Tree* reveals the change in his state of mind. He described the work as being "very dark and quite melancholic for springtime" (May 3, 1889, *Letters*, 768). He oddly also described *Weeping Tree* as being "more coloured" than most of his drawings, although no color is visible nor is there any trace of faded pigments on the paper. The artist was likely referring to the rich gradations between black and white that he accomplished, which give this large-scale drawing as striking a presence as his painted oils. Van Gogh tacked this work to the wall of his hospital bedroom alongside Japanese prints and a lithograph after Eugène Delacroix.

Plate 28 Vincent van Gogh (Dutch, 1853–1890). *Cypresses*, 1889. Pen and reed pen and brown inks, with graphite, on buff wove paper, laid down on card; 62.5 × 46.4 cm (24 5/8 × 18 1/4 in.). The Art Institute of Chicago, gift of Robert Allerton, 1927.543. F1524, JH1749

Living in the Saint-Paul-de-Mausole asylum in Saint-Rémy-de-Provence, Van Gogh painted and drew a series of cypress trees, which he considered a symbol of Provence. Though he was intimidated by their sinuous forms and monumental proportions—which he likened to those of an Egyptian obelisk—he felt compelled to paint them because no other artist had ever "yet done them as I see them" (June 25, 1889, *Letters*, 783). Van Gogh became obsessed with trying to capture what he saw in these trees but found that his attempts fell short. Out in nature among the cypresses, he was overwhelmed by their intense presence almost to the point of fainting. In this drawing, Van Gogh depicted the leaves and branches as clusters of curling lines that are almost flame-like as they stretch upward. Behind them, a cottage is dwarfed in comparison. The artist was determined to master these trees before leaving the South of France: "Before leaving here, I am planning to return to the fray to attack the cypresses" (Feb. 9 or 10, 1890, *Letters*, 853).

Facing page

Plate 29 Vincent van Gogh (Dutch, 1853–1890). *Corridor in the Asylum*, 1889. Oil color and essence over black chalk on pink laid ("Ingres") paper; 65.1 × 49.1 cm (25 5/8 × 19 5/16 in.). The Metropolitan Museum of Art, New York, bequest of Abby Aldrich Rockefeller, 1948. F1529, JH1808

Van Gogh rarely depicted the interior of the asylum and never the bedroom to which he was intermittently confined during extended bouts of illness. One of only three interior studies, this view of the corridor reflects the desolate state of the asylum during his stay there. According to his letters to Theo, more than thirty rooms stood empty. When Van Gogh arrived at the asylum, he was relieved to find that the other patients did not mock his strange behavior while working or the resulting paintings; nevertheless, he did not develop any friendships with the patients there and kept mostly to himself. Given that his supervision by the hospital staff was minimal while he was lucid, his days in Saint-Rémy-de-Provence must have been among his most isolated. Van Gogh depicted the corridor as unpopulated save for one small figure who is moving away from the artist. The deep perspective, rendered in a telescopic fashion, denies the viewer any indication of how many rooms and closed doors might line this long, funnel-shaped hallway, while suggesting an almost endless sequence of such spaces.

29

Previous pages

Plate 30 Vincent van Gogh (Dutch, 1853–1890). *Hospital at Saint-Rémy*, 1889. Oil on canvas; 92.2 × 73.4 cm (36 5/16 × 28 7/8 in.). Hammer Museum, Los Angeles, The Armand Hammer Collection, gift of the Armand Hammer Foundation.
F643, JH1799

This is one of two large landscapes Van Gogh painted in early October 1889 of the trees in the garden and the asylum facade behind them. He described them in a letter to Theo: "I also have two views of the park and the asylum in which this place appears most agreeable. I tried to reconstruct the thing as it may have been by simplifying and accentuating the proud, unchanging nature of the pines and the cedar bushes against the blue" (on or about Oct. 8, 1889, *Letters*, 810). In trying to make the asylum look more "agreeable," the artist took several liberties in his representation, especially with the colors. Although the former monastery was mostly made of stone with faded shutters, Van Gogh painted a bright-yellow building with brilliant green shutters and an orange-red roof. Consciously or not, he repeated the palette he used to paint his Yellow House in Arles (p. 23, middle row, right), perhaps in an attempt to make himself feel more at home. In his letters, he rarely refers to the building as the "hospital" or "asylum"; instead, he preferred to call it "the house."

Plate 31 Vincent van Gogh (Dutch, 1853–1890). *View of the Asylum with a Pine Tree*, 1889. Oil on canvas; 63.4 × 49 cm (24 15/16 × 19 5/16 in.). Musée d'Orsay, Paris, gift of Max and Rosy Kaganovitch, 1973.
F653, JH1840

In the foreground, a man stands with his hands in his pockets beside a tree, and another has just walked through the open door; neither their dress nor stance indicate whether they are patients or hospital staff. Van Gogh populated his views in and around the asylum with figures that seem to have more in common with those found in his *Poet's Garden* series than in contemporary images of invalids. In these portrayals, he seems to be following the philosophy of the hospital, which referred to its patients as "boarders."

The window to the left of the doorway belongs to the large room the artist was given as a studio. Taking over the space for his own purposes, he would lean his fresh canvases along the wall in the hallway just outside his studio to dry. This landscape was painted as a gift for Dr. Théophile Peyron, a retired ophthalmologist and navy doctor who served as director of the Saint-Paul-de-Mausole asylum despite a lack of medical experience with mental illness. While Van Gogh was under his care, Dr. Peyron supported the artist by giving him permission to paint and space for a studio.

Facing page

Plate 32 Vincent van Gogh (Dutch, 1853–1890). *A Corner of the Asylum and the Garden with a Heavy, Sawed-Off Tree*, 1889. Oil on canvas; 75 × 93.5 cm (29 1/2 × 36 13/16 in.). Museum Folkwang, Essen.
F660, JH1849

In front of the asylum stood a large tree that, after being struck by lightning, had been partially sawed down. Van Gogh described it as having the character of a proud man brought low, which he contrasted to the fading rose blossoms peacefully surrendering to the end of the season. The foreground is dominated by the contrast of reds and greens, which Van Gogh intentionally emphasized for its emotional impact, as he explained in a letter to Émile Bernard: "You'll understand that this combination of red ochre, of green saddened with grey, of black lines that define the outlines, this gives rise a little to the feeling of anxiety from which some of my companions in misfortune often suffer, and which is called 'seeing red'" (on or about Nov. 26, 1889, *Letters*, 822). Since Van Gogh's death, scholars have been tempted to read mental illness in his paintings, but his written accounts confirm that such references to mental states were included deliberately. The artist only painted during his periods of lucidity, when he had full command of his talent.

32

33

Plate 33 Vincent van Gogh (Dutch, 1853–1890). *Portrait of Dr. Gachet*, 1890. Etching on tan wove paper; 18.2 × 14.8 cm (7 3/16 × 5 13/16 in.) (image/plate); 20.5 × 17.2 cm (8 × 6 3/4 in.) (sheet). The Art Institute of Chicago, Clarence Buckingham Collection, 1962.83. F1664, JH2028

Van Gogh only moved to Auvers-sur-Oise because of the presence there of Dr. Paul Gachet, a well-known physician who was admired among the artists' community. Dr. Gachet was acquainted with such notable men as Gustave Courbet, Victor Hugo, Paul Cézanne, and Camille Pissarro, who recommended the doctor to Theo. His willingness to supervise Van Gogh's health gave his doctors in Saint-Rémy-de-Provence the reassurance they required to release the artist and Theo the confidence to finance yet another home. At first Van Gogh was disappointed with Dr. Gachet, who struck him as being as "ill and confused" as he was; however, the neurotic physician soon won him over, and the two became fast friends. The artist painted the doctor twice, and he also made this portrait—his first etching. Dr. Gachet owned a printing press and taught him the process. Never less than ambitious, Van Gogh wrote to his brother about his hope of creating a series of six prints as well as of recruiting other artists, such as Paul Gauguin, to do the same. Ultimately this was the only etching he ever produced.

34

Plate 34 Vincent van Gogh (Dutch, 1853–1890). *Cottages with a Woman Working in the Middle Ground*, 1890. Charcoal, reed pen and black ink, blue pastel, and white chalk on bluish-gray laid paper with blue fibers (discolored to gray); 47 × 62 cm (18 1/2 × 24 7/16 in.). The Art Institute of Chicago, bequest of Kate L. Brewster, 1949.382. F1642, JH1994

Van Gogh was a remarkably prolific artist, especially considering that he only pursued art as a career for the last decade of his life. However, he rarely worked in the medium of pastel. He encouraged Theo to collect pastels by other artists, and in a letter to his brother he stated his hope that he might learn this technique: "Pastel is a process I'd really like to know" (on or about Nov. 7, 1885, *Letters*, 539). In this painting-sized drawing, Van Gogh used alternating bands of blue pastel and white chalk, with some additions in charcoal, to suggest the hazy sky over Auvers-sur-Oise. The bottom half of the paper is filled by a carefully delineated landscape with cottages in pen and ink. The sinuous lines of the bushes and trees, as well as the short hatch marks for the fields, mimic his characteristic brushstrokes. The artist incorporated the color of the paper into his image, and the varying amount of exposed ground recalls the texture of his impastoed surfaces.

35

Plate 35 Vincent van Gogh (Dutch, 1853–1890). *Houses at Auvers*, 1890. Oil on canvas; 60 × 73 cm (23 5/8 × 28 3/4 in.). Lent by the Toledo Museum of Art, purchased with funds from the Libbey Endowment, gift of Edward Drummond Libbey, 1935.5. F759, JH1988

The picturesque town of Auvers-sur-Oise had been a popular destination for artists since Charles-François Daubigny—the Barbizon painter and one of Van Gogh's idols—moved there in 1860. He was followed by the likes of Jean-Baptiste-Camille Corot, Paul Cézanne, and Camille Pissarro, the last of whom recommended the village to the Van Gogh brothers. Upon his arrival, Van Gogh was immediately taken with the long, winding roads that skirted cottages, farms, vineyards, marketplaces, and contemporary suburban homes. The homes charmed the artist despite his noted preference for more rustic architecture: "I find the modern villas and the middle-class country houses almost as pretty as the old thatched cottages that are falling into ruin" (on or about May 21, 1890, *Letters*, 874). In *Houses at Auvers*, Van Gogh depicted both structures side by side. The diagonal brushstrokes of the thatched roof contrast with those depicting the horizontal tiles of the modern roof, but the two houses are both in harmony with the landscape.

36

Plate 36 Vincent van Gogh (Dutch, 1853–1890). *Thatched-Roofed Cottages of Jorgus*, 1890. Oil on canvas; 33 × 40.5 cm (13 × 16 in.). Private collection. F758, JH2016

Just as Van Gogh felt he had found Japan in Arles, in Auvers-sur-Oise he felt he had returned to the Netherlands. Although he produced what he considered some of his best work in the South of France, the year and a half he spent in and out of hospitals convinced him that his temperament was not suited to Provence. He looked to Auvers as a sanctuary where he could cure his "malady of the South." There, he returned to the theme of "human nests," the idyllic peasant cottages that conveyed to him a sense of refuge ever since he first painted them in Nuenen (see plate 2). The bright palette and stylized brushwork in these later canvases reveal the influence on his art of his stays in Arles and Saint-Rémy-de-Provence. Van Gogh did not regret the time he spent in Provence but rather considered it a meaningful detour: "Now I have a study of old thatched roofs . . . and I perceive already that it did me good to go into the south the better to see the north" (on or about May 21, 1890, *Letters*, 874).

Van Gogh bought his first Japanese prints in 1885 while living in Antwerp, where he could purchase them directly from sailors returning from voyages to the Far East. He began collecting in earnest after moving to Paris a few months later. He and his brother had a combined collection of more than 350 sheets in their apartment. Many were *ukiyo-e* ("visions of the floating world"), colorful wood-block prints that often depicted landscapes, flora and fauna, figural studies, and interiors. This selection of prints reflects the subjects and artists Van Gogh collected, and he in fact owned copies of the four prints by Hiroshige and Hiroshige II. His palette became more vivid, which he attributed to the influence of these Japanese prints: "With a more Japanese eye, you feel colour differently" (on or about June 5, 1888, *Letters*, 620). Furthermore, his canvases were more heavily impastoed with oil paint in an attempt to mimic the crinkled texture of crepe paper. Noting the common reverence for Japanese art among the Impressionists, Van Gogh felt that the future of art would be found in the South of France, which, in his mind, would be as sunny, simple, and close to nature as his imagined Japan.

Japanese Prints

Utagawa Hiroshige (Japanese, 1797–1858). *Plum Garden at Kameido* (*Kameido Umeyashiki*), from the series *One Hundred Famous Views of Edo* (*Meisho Edo hyakkei*), 1857.
Color wood-block print, *ōban*; 36 × 24.1 cm (14 3/16 × 9 1/2 in.). The Art Institute of Chicago, Clarence Buckingham Collection, 1925.3752.

Utagawa Hiroshige (Japanese, 1797–1858). *Maple Trees at Mama, Tekona Shrine and Tsugi Bridge* (*Mama no momiji, Tekona no yashiro, Tsugihashi*), from the series *One Hundred Famous Views of Edo* (*Meisho Edo hyakkei*), 1857.
Color wood-block print; *ōban*, 36.1 × 24.4 cm (14 3/16 × 9 5/8 in.). The Art Institute of Chicago, Clarence Buckingham Collection, 1925.3735.

Utagawa Hiroshige II (Japanese, 1826–1869). *Night Rain at the Paulownia Grove at Akasaka* (*Akasaka Kiribatake uchū yūkei*), from the series *One Hundred Famous Views of Edo* (*Meisho Edo hyakkei*), 1859.
Color wood-block print; *ōban*; 35.1 × 24.5 cm (13 13/16 × 9 5/8 in.). The Art Institute of Chicago, gift of Chester W. Wright, 1961.159.

Utagawa Toyokuni I (Japanese, 1769–1825). *The Parlor of a Brothel*, 1789/95.
Color wood-block print, right sheet of an *ōban* triptych; 38.7 × 26.7 cm (15 1/4 × 10 1/2 in.). The Art Institute of Chicago, gift of Mr. and Mrs. Gaylord Donnelley, 1971.498.

Utagawa Kunisada I (Toyokuni III) (Japanese, 1786–1864). *Brothel-Ledger Courtesan's Tale of Spring Passions* (*Shunjō gidan mizuage chō*), 1836.
Wood-block-printed books (three volumes); each book, 22.2 × 16 cm (8 3/4 × 6 5/16 in.); spread, 22.1 × 28.3 cm (8 11/16 × 11 1/8 in.). The Art Institute of Chicago, gift of Dorothy Braude Edinburg to the Harry B. and Bessie K. Braude Memorial Collection, 2013.337.1 and 2013.337.3.

Utagawa Hiroshige (Japanese, 1797–1858). *Ishibe Station*, no. 52 from the series *Fifty-three Stations of the Tōkaidō* (*Tōkaidō gojūsan-tsugi*), 1855.
Color wood-block print; 36.5 × 24.7 cm (14 3/8 × 9 3/4 in.). The Art Institute of Chicago, Bruce Goff Archive, gift of Shin'enkan, Inc., 1990.607.153.

Van Gogh counted Honoré Daumier among his favorite artists, referring to him as a "pioneer," a "genius," and "the master" (he even claimed that Daumier's works could cure tooth pain). By 1882, Van Gogh was tearing Daumier lithographs out of illustrated journals, similar to those included here, and decorating his walls with them. He identified with the older artist's social consciousness and financial struggles. Preoccupied with portraits and figure studies throughout his entire career, Van Gogh admired the aspect of caricature in Daumier's figures, which was "essentially modern" because it valued character over accuracy. Following this example, Van Gogh used physiognomy, gesture, and facial expressions to convey the inner spirit of his models. Daumier's lithographs brought to life the different types of modern-day France and the oppositions among them: artist versus bourgeois, country versus city, secure bourgeoisie versus lonely masses. These images were never more potent for Van Gogh than when he was living in Paris and feeling torn by the same dichotomies.

Daumier Prints

Honoré Daumier (French, 1808–1879). *"—Well, are you finally finished?... after all it's tiring to relax for such a long time,"* plate 1 from *Les artistes à la campagne*, 1865.
Lithograph in black on ivory wove paper; 23 × 20 cm (9 × 7 7/8 in.) (image); 36.2 × 27.3 cm (14 1/4 × 10 3/4 in.) (sheet). The Art Institute of Chicago, William McCallin McKee Memorial Endowment, 1953.602.

Honoré Daumier (French, 1808–1879). *Black and White*, plate 23 from *Émotions parisiennes*, 1840.
Lithograph in black on off-white wove paper; 25.3 × 19.6 cm (9 15/16 × 7 3/4 in.) (image); 34.3 × 26.2 cm (13 1/2 × 10 5/16 in.) (sheet). The Art Institute of Chicago, Mr. and Mrs. Carter H. Harrison Collection, 1935.209.

Honoré Daumier (French, 1808–1879). *Worker and Bourgeois*, from *Les Parisiens en 1848*, 1848.
Lithograph in black on off-white wove paper; 26.6 × 21.3 cm (10 1/2 × 8 3/8 in.) (image); 34.9 × 26.5 cm (13 3/4 × 10 7/16 in.) (sheet). The Art Institute of Chicago, Sidney A. Kent Fund, gift of Martin A. Ryerson and the Print and Drawing Club, 1923.67.

Honoré Daumier (French, 1808–1879). *"You tramp! I would like to see you drown in your beer! Leaving me alone like that with my three children, he gives me twelve sous, and when he comes back in the evening, he asks for his change!,"* plate 48 from *Moeurs conjugales*, 1842.
Lithograph in black on off-white wove paper; 24.7 × 21 cm (9 3/4 × 8 1/4 in.) (image); 34.2 × 26.6 cm (13 7/16 × 10 1/2 in.) (sheet). The Art Institute of Chicago, gift of Mr. and Mrs. Carter H. Harrison, 1952.27.

Honoré Daumier (French, 1808–1879). *This Is What a Bourgeois Considers a Small Distraction*, plate 14 from *Les bons bourgeois*, 1846.
Lithograph in black on white wove paper; 25.7 × 21.7 cm (10 1/8 × 8 9/16 in.) (image); 33.8 × 25.9 cm (13 5/16 × 10 3/16 in.) (sheet). The Art Institute of Chicago, Print Sales Miscellaneous Fund, 1947.635.

Honoré Daumier (French, 1808–1879). *This Is What Nowadays Is Called a Light Work: "—My God, what's this!... an encyclopaedia?" "—No, sir... it is the novel 'the mysteries of Paris' that Madame bought at the bookshop of our Master. We will bring you the rest of the oeuvre as soon as it appears...,"* plate 13 from *Revue caricaturale*, 1843.
Lithograph in black on ivory wove paper; 24.4 × 20 cm (9 5/8 × 7 7/8 in.) (image); 33.5 × 20 cm (13 3/16 × 7 7/8 in.) (sheet). The Art Institute of Chicago, Mr. and Mrs. Carter H. Harrison Collection, 1935.211.

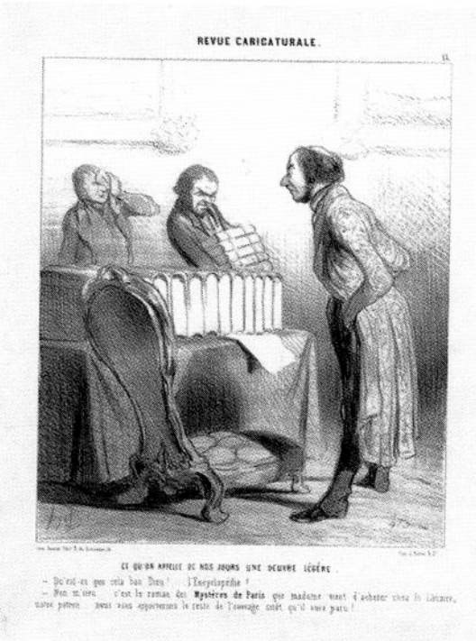

Throughout his many letters, Van Gogh referred reverently to only one artist as "father": Jean-François Millet. He began collecting prints by Millet as a young man working as an art dealer. When he decided to become an artist, Van Gogh was inspired by the example of Millet's life, embracing the popular notion of him as the painter among the peasants. Early in his career, Van Gogh developed an earth-colored palette because he felt that Millet painted as if using the soil from the fields. However, at this point he had never seen a Millet painting in person and was only familiar with them through reproductions and written descriptions. In 1880, he purchased the print series *The Labors of the Fields*, Jacques Adrien Lavieille's wood engravings after Millet's drawings, and immediately sketched copies of them. In the Saint-Rémy-de-Provence asylum ten years later, transformed artistically, physically, and mentally, Van Gogh returned to *The Labors of the Fields*. He hung his prints (now at the Van Gogh Museum) on the wall of his hospital bedroom and again made copies from them. His paintings after Millet were not mere reproductions, however, but unique and personal creations that embraced the brilliant palette and vigorous brushwork he had developed in France.

Millet Prints

Jacques-Adrien Lavieille (French, 1818–1862), after Jean-François Millet (French, 1814–1875). *Reaper*, from *The Labors of the Fields*, 1853.
Wood engraving in black on gray China paper, laid down on ivory wove paper (chine collé); 13.5 × 7.4 cm (5 5/16 × 2 15/16 in.) (image); 18.2 × 13.2 cm (7 3/16 × 5 3/16 in.) (primary support); 29.1 × 23.5 cm (11 7/16 × 9 1/4 in.) (secondary support). The Art Institute of Chicago, gift of Alice H. Brown in memory of Cyrus Hall McCormick, 1944.80.

Jacques-Adrien Lavieille (French, 1818–1862), after Jean-François Millet (French, 1814–1875). *Mower*, from *The Labors of the Fields*, 1853.
Wood engraving in black on gray China paper, laid down on ivory wove paper (chine collé); 13.5 × 7.4 cm (5 5/16 × 2 15/16 in.) (image); 18.2 × 13.2 cm (7 3/16 × 5 3/16 in.) (primary support); 33.8 × 27 cm (13 5/16 × 10 5/8 in.) (secondary support). The Art Institute of Chicago, gift of Alice H. Brown in memory of Cyrus Hall McCormick, 1944.82.

Jacques-Adrien Lavieille (French, 1818–1862), after Jean-François Millet (French, 1814–1875). *Woman Pulling Flax*, from *The Labors of the Fields*, 1853.
Wood engraving in black on gray China paper, laid down on ivory wove paper (chine collé); 13.2 × 7.5 cm (5 3/16 × 2 15/16 in.) (image); 18.2 × 13.1 cm (7 3/16 × 5 3/16 in.) (primary support); 29.1 × 23.4 cm (11 7/16 × 9 3/16 in.) (secondary support). The Art Institute of Chicago, gift of Alice H. Brown in memory of Cyrus Hall McCormick, 1944.64.

Jacques-Adrien Lavieille (French, 1818–1862), after Jean-François Millet (French, 1814–1875). *Woman Raking Hay*, from *The Labors of the Fields*, 1853.
Wood engraving in black on gray China paper, laid down on ivory wove paper (chine collé); 13.3 × 7.4 cm (5 1/4 × 2 15/16 in.) (image); 18.2 × 13.2 cm (7 3/16 × 5 3/16 in.) (primary support); 26.5 × 21.5 cm (10 7/16 × 8 7/16 in.) (secondary support). The Art Institute of Chicago, gift of Alice H. Brown in memory of Cyrus Hall McCormick, 1944.63.

Jacques Adrien Lavieille (French, 1818–1862), after Jean François Millet (French, 1814–1875). *Sheaf-Binder*, from *The Labors of the Fields*, 1853.
Wood engraving in black on gray China paper, laid down on ivory wove paper (chine collé); 13.2 × 7.4 cm (5 3/16 × 2 15/16 in.) (image); 18.3 × 13.1 cm (7 3/16 × 5 3/16 in.) (primary support); 27 × 21.9 cm (10 5/8 × 8 5/8 in.) (secondary support). The Art Institute of Chicago, gift of Alice H. Brown in memory of Cyrus Hall McCormick, 1944.67.

Jacques-Adrien Lavieille (French, 1818–1862), after Jean-François Millet (French, 1814–1875). *Woman Crushing Flax*, from *The Labors of the Fields*, 1853.
Wood engraving in black on gray China paper, laid down on off-white wove paper (chine collé); 13.4 × 7.5 cm (5 1/4 × 2 15/16 in.) (image); 18.3 × 13.2 cm (7 3/16 × 5 3/16 in.) (primary support); 33.8 × 27.1 cm (13 5/16 × 10 11/16 in.) (secondary support). The Art Institute of Chicago, gift of Alice H. Brown in memory of Cyrus Hall McCormick, 1944.78.

Jacques-Adrien Lavieille (French, 1818–1862), after Jean-François Millet (French, 1814–1875). *Thresher*, from *The Labors of the Fields*, 1853.
Wood engraving in black on gray China paper, laid down on off-white wove paper (chine collé); 13.5 × 7.5 cm (5 5/16 × 2 15/16 in.) (image); 18.2 × 13.2 cm (7 3/16 × 5 3/16 in.) (primary support); 30.7 × 25.5 cm (12 × 10 in.) (secondary support). The Art Institute of Chicago, gift of Alice H. Brown in memory of Cyrus Hall McCormick, 1944.79.

Jacques-Adrien Lavieille (French, 1818–1862), after Jean-François Millet (French, 1814–1875). *Woman Shearing Sheep*, from *The Labors of the Fields*, 1853.
Wood engraving in black on gray China paper, laid down on ivory wove paper (chine collé); 13 × 7.3 cm (5 1/8 × 2 7/8 in.) (image); 18 × 13.1 cm (7 × 5 3/16 in.) (primary support); 25.7 × 21.3 cm (10 1/8 × 8 3/8 in.) (secondary support). The Art Institute of Chicago, gift of Alice H. Brown in memory of Cyrus Hall McCormick, 1944.83.

Jacques-Adrien Lavieille (French, 1818–1862), after Jean-François Millet (French, 1814–1875). *Woman Spinning*, from *The Labors of the Fields*, 1853.
Wood engraving in black on gray China paper, laid down on ivory wove paper (chine collé); 13.3 × 7.5 cm (5 1/4 × 2 15/16 in.) (image); 17.8 × 12.9 cm (7 × 5 in.) (primary support); 24.9 × 20.5 cm (9 13/16 × 8 in.) (secondary support). The Art Institute of Chicago, gift of Alice H. Brown in memory of Cyrus Hall McCormick, 1944.62.

Other Works in the Exhibition

In addition to the works by Van Gogh featured in this catalogue, *Van Gogh's Bedrooms* presents a number of other objects that were physically or psychologically present in his many studios. Van Gogh always had a passion for collecting; as a child, he foraged in the woods near his parents' home for birds' nests—a habit he returned to as an artist when he no longer saw the nests as curios but rather works of art. Friends and acquaintances would later recall the odd assortment of objects that cluttered Van Gogh's studios along with the expected easel, palettes, and paints. The artist could find inspiration in even the most mundane of objects, such as the balls of brightly dyed yarn that he used for experimenting with color combinations (see p. 92, fig. 22).

Van Gogh was equally a collector of ideas, philosophies, and theories, and his studio functioned as a *musée imaginaire* or repository for his many intellectual and artistic influences. An avid reader, he strove to translate the values of modern French literature into his paintings. He decorated his studios with prints after his artistic heroes, which he purchased from dealers or sometimes tore out of illustrated journals. Van Gogh had a remarkable visual memory, which allowed him to describe in his letters in vivid detail favorite paintings by favorite artists—such as the Barbizon painters Charles-François Daubigny and especially Jean-François Millet—even when he did not have reproductions of the works.

Song Sparrow Nest, 1879.
Natural materials; 17.1 × 14.6 × 7.6 cm (6 3/4 × 5 3/4 × 3 in.). On loan from the Bird Collection, Field Museum of Natural History, Chicago.

Marsh Wren Nest, 1879.
Natural materials; 25.4 × 17.1 × 10.1 cm (10 × 6 3/4 × 4 in.). On loan from the Bird Collection, Field Museum of Natural History, Chicago.

Palette of Vincent van Gogh, around 1890.
Wood; 35 × 27 cm (13 3/4 × 10 5/8 in.). Musée d'Orsay, Paris, gift of Paul Gachet, 1951.

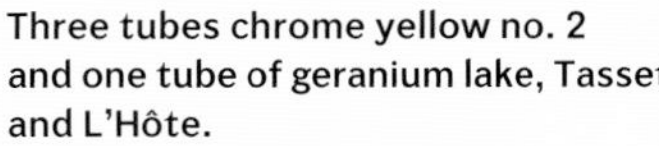

Three tubes chrome yellow no. 2 and one tube of geranium lake, Tasset and L'Hôte.
Musée d'Orsay, Paris, gift of Paul Gachet, 1951.

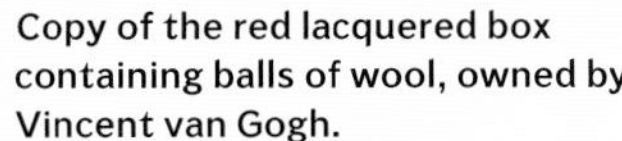

Copy of the red lacquered box containing balls of wool, owned by Vincent van Gogh.
15.9 × 11.3 × 31.5 cm (6 1/4 × 4 7/16 × 12 3/8 in.). Van Gogh Museum, Amsterdam.

Edmond de Goncourt (French, 1822–1896). *La maison d'un artiste*, 1881.
Original printed wrappers, uncut; bound in green buckram; 19 × 13 × 2.8 cm (7 1/2 × 5 1/8 × 1 1/8 in.). The Newberry Library, Chicago.

Joris-Karl Huysmans (French, 1848–1907). *À rebours*, 1884.
Hardcover book; 18.4 × 12.7 × 2.9 cm (7 1/4 × 5 × 1 1/8 in.). On loan from the Special Collections Research Center, University of Chicago Library, Chicago.

J.-K. HUYSMANS

A REBOURS

PARIS
G. CHARPENTIER & Cie, ÉDITEURS

Émile Zola (French, 1840–1902). *L'assommoir*, 1877.
Book with 60 wood engravings and gillotages in black, on ivory laid paper, printed again on ivory China paper, tipped in; 29.5 × 23 × 5.5 cm (11 5/8 × 9 1/16 × 2 3/16 in.). The Art Institute of Chicago, restricted gift of Mrs. Robert S. Hartman, 1987.198.

L'ASSOMMOIR

PAR
Émile ZOLA

Émile Zola (French, 1840–1902). *Germinal*, 1885.
Book; 19.1 × 12 × 3.5 cm (7 1/2 × 4 3/4 × 1 3/8 in.). Private collection, Oak Park, Illinois.

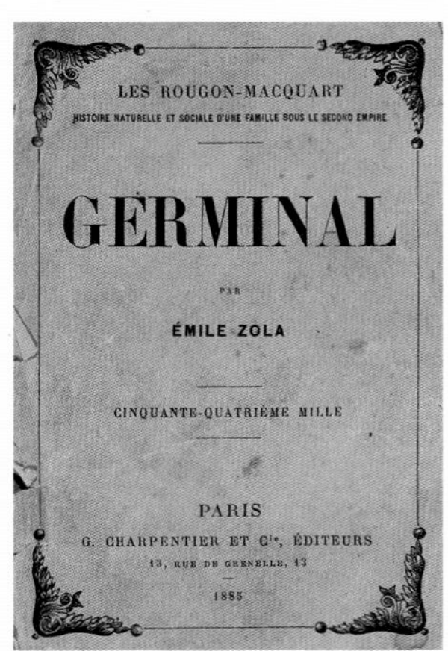

LES ROUGON-MACQUART
HISTOIRE NATURELLE ET SOCIALE D'UNE FAMILLE SOUS LE SECOND EMPIRE

GERMINAL

PAR
ÉMILE ZOLA

CINQUANTE-QUATRIÈME MILLE

PARIS
G. CHARPENTIER ET Cie, ÉDITEURS
13, RUE DE GRENELLE, 13
1885

After Samuel Luke Fildes (English, 1843–1927). *The Room in which Charles Dickens Wrote*, 1870. Reproduced in *Harper's Weekly*, Jan. 7, 1871, pp. 8–9. Originally published in *The Graphic* (Christmas 1870), after p. 24.
Wood engraving; 40.6 × 54.6 cm (16 × 21 1/2 in.) (image/sheet). Private collection, Oak Park, Illinois.

La chambre mortuaire de Corot, reproduced in *L'illustration*, Mar. 6, 1875, p. 156.
Wood engraving; 38 × 28.5 cm (14 15/16 × 11 1/4 in.) (sheet). The Newberry Library, Chicago.

The Bedroom in Which M. Gambetta Died, reproduced in *The Graphic*, Jan. 13, 1883, p. 1.
Wood engraving; 41.3 × 29.9 cm (16 1/4 × 11 3/4 in.) (sheet). Private collection, Oak Park, Illinois.

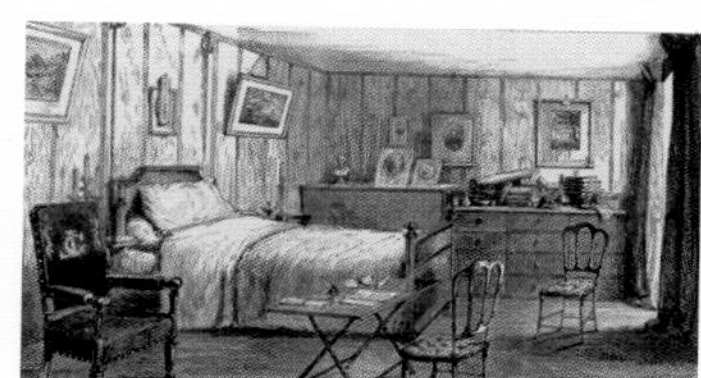

Charles-François Daubigny (French, 1817–1878). *The Marsh*, 1871.
Oil on panel; 34.4 × 58.2 cm (13 9/16 × 22 15/16 in.). The Art Institute of Chicago, Henry Field Memorial Collection, 1894.1044.

Jean-François Millet (French, 1814–1875). *The Woodchopper*, 1858/66.
Oil on canvas; 81 × 65 cm (31 7/8 × 25 9/16 in.). The Art Institute of Chicago, Potter Palmer Collection, 1922.416.

Jean-François Millet (French, 1814–1875). *The Little Shepherdess*, 1868/72.
Oil on panel; 35.7 × 25.5 cm (14 × 10 in.). The Art Institute of Chicago, Potter Palmer Collection, 1922.413.

Jean-François Millet (French, 1814–1875). *The Sheepshearers*, 1857/61.
Oil on canvas; 41.2 × 28.5 cm (16 1/4 × 11 1/4 in.). The Art Institute of Chicago, Potter Palmer Collection, 1922.417.

Bibliography

Armstrong, Carol. "Duranty on Degas: A Theory of Modern Painting." In *Critical Readings in Impressionism and Post-Impressionism: An Anthology*, edited by Mary Tompkins Lewis, pp. 163–190. University of California Press, 2007.

Ashton, Dore. *A Fable of Modern Art.* Thames & Hudson, 1980.

Bang, Mette Marie. "Van Gogh's Palette." In *A Closer Look: Technical and Art-Historical Studies on Works by Van Gogh and Gauguin*, edited by Cornelia Peres, Michael Hoyle, and Louis van Tilborgh, pp. 57–60. Waanders, 1991.

Berg, Klaas Jan van den, Aviva Burnstock, Leslie Carlyle, Mark Clarke, Ella Hendriks, René Hoppenbrouwers, Jo Kirby, and Ibby Lanfear. "Fading of Red Lake Paints after Vincent van Gogh—an Interdisciplinary Study Involving Three De Mayerne Projects." In *Reporting Highlights of the De Mayerne Programme*, edited by Jaap J. Boon and Ester S. B. Ferreira, pp. 89–96. Netherlands Organization for Scientific Research, 2006.

Berns, Roy S., and Mahnaz Mohammadi. "Evaluating Single- and Two-Constant Kubelka-Munk Turbid Media Theory for Instrumental-Based Inpainting." *Studies in Conservation* 52, no. 4 (2007), pp. 299–314.

Blanc, Charles. *Grammaire des arts du dessin: Architecture, sculpture, peinture.* Ve J. Renouard, 1867. Translated by Kate Newell Doggett as *The Grammar of Painting and Engraving.* Hurd and Houghton, 1874.

——. *Les artistes de mon temps.* Firmin-Didot, 1876.

Blanc, Monique. "La chambre à coucher en France au moyen âge et à la renaissance." In Musées des Arts Décoratifs, *Rêves d'alcôves: La chambre au cours des siècles.* Exh. cat., pp. 40–68. Union Centrale des Arts Décoratifs/Réunion des Musées Nationaux, 1995.

Blanchard, Raphaël. "Notices biographiques, III. David Gruby, 1810–1898." *Archives de parasitologie* 2, no. 1 (Jan. 1899), pp. 44–74.

Blühm, Andreas. "Displaying Van Gogh, 1886–1999." *Van Gogh Museum Journal* (1999), pp. 62–84.

Van Bommel, Maarten, Muriel Geldof, and Ella Hendriks. "An Investigation of Organic Red Pigments Used in Paintings by Vincent van Gogh (November 1885 to February 1888)." *Art Matters: Netherlands Technical Studies in Art* 3 (2005), pp. 111–37.

Bracquemond, Félix. *Du dessin et de la couleur.* G. Charpentier, 1885.

Brettell, Richard R. "Van Gogh's Bedrooms at Arles: The Problem of Priority." In "The Helen Birch Bartlett Memorial Collection," special issue, *Art Institute of Chicago Museum Studies* 12, no. 2 (1986), pp. 137–52.

Burnstock, Aviva, Klaas Jan van den Berg, Leslie Carlyle, Mark Clarke, Ella Hendriks, Jo Kirby, and Ibby Lanfear. "A Comparison of the Fading and Surface Deterioration of Red Lake Pigments in Six Paintings by Vincent van Gogh with Artificially Aged Paint Reconstructions." In *Preprints for ICOM Committee for Conservation, 14th Triennial Meeting in The Hague*, edited by Janet Bridgland, vol. 1, pp. 459–66. James and James, 2005.

Cahn, Walter. *Masterpieces: Chapters on the History of an Idea.* Princeton University Press, 1979.

Chevreul, Michel-Eugène. *De la loi du contraste simultané des couleurs, et de l'assortiment des objets colorés.* Pitois-Levrault, 1839.

Childs, Elizabeth C. *Vanishing Paradise: Art and Exoticism in Colonial Tahiti.* University of California Press, 2013.

Chilton, Meredith, editor. *The Bedroom: From the Renaissance to Art Deco.* Decorative Arts Institute, 1995.

Cochin, Henry. "Boccace d'après ses oeuvres et les témoignages contemporains." *Revue des deux mondes*, July 15, 1888, pp. 373–413.

Chu, Petra ten-Doesschate. "Emblems for a Modern Age: Vincent van Gogh's Still Lifes and the Nineteenth-Century Vignette Tradition." In *The Object as Subject: Studies in the Interpretation of Still Life*, edited by Anne W. Lowenthal, pp. 83–97. Princeton University Press, 1996.

Van Dijk, Maite. "Van Gogh and the Laws of Colour: An Introduction." In Vellekoop et al., *Van Gogh's Studio Practice*, pp. 216–25. Mercatorfonds/ Van Gogh Museum/Yale University Press, 2013.

Dorn, Roland. "Vincent van Gogh and the Concept of Décoration." In *Vincent van Gogh: International Symposium*, edited by Haruo Arikawa and Han van Crimpen et al., pp. 375–84. Shumbun, 1988.

——. *Décoration: Vincent van Goghs Werkreihe für das Gelbe Haus in Arles.* Georg Olms, 1990.

Druick, Douglas W. "Van Gogh and Gauguin: Disguised Portraits." *ARTnews* 8 (Sept. 2001), pp. 126–28.

Druick, Douglas W., and Peter Kort Zegers. *Van Gogh and Gauguin: The Studio of the South.* In collaboration with Britt Salvensen. Exh. cat. Art Institute of Chicago/Van Gogh Museum/Thames & Hudson, 2001.

Dulk, E. den. "Tentoonstellingwerken Vincent van Gogh." *Kunstwereld* 24 (June 1895), n.p.

Edwards, Cliff. *Van Gogh's Ghost Paintings: Art and Spirit in Gethsemane.* Cascade, 2015.

Dymond, Anne. "Displaying the Arlésienne: Museums, Folklife and Regional Identity in France." In *Folkore and Nationalism in Europe during the Long Nineteenth Century*, edited by Timothy Baycroft and David Hopkin, pp. 137–60. Brill, 2012.

Farrell, Eugene, and Richard Newman. "Van Gogh's Painting Materials: An Analysis of the *Self-Portrait Dedicated to Paul Gauguin* and other Arles Period Paintings." In Vojtêch Jirat-Wasiutyński and H. Travers Newman, *Vincent van Gogh's "Self-Portrait Dedicated to Paul Gauguin": An Historical and Technical Study*, pp. 28–38. Center for Conservaton and Technical Study, Harvard University Art Museums, 1984.

Gamboni, Dario. *Potential Images: Ambiguity and Indeterminacy in Modern Art.* Reaktion, 2002.

——. *Paul Gauguin: The Mysterious Centre of Thought.* Reaktion, 2014.

Geldof, Muriel, Matthijs de Keijzer, Maarten van Bommel, Kathrin Pilz, Johanna Salvant, Henk van Keulen and Luc Megens. "Van Gogh's Geranium Lake." In Vellekoop et al., *Van Gogh's Studio Practice*, pp. 268–89. Mercatorfonds/Van Gogh Museum/ Yale University Press, 2013.

Geldof, Muriel, Luc Megens, and Johanna Salvant. "Van Gogh's Palette in Arles, Saint-Rémy and Auvers-Sur-Oise." In Vellekoop et al., *Van Gogh's Studio Practice*, pp. 238–55. Mercatorfonds/Van Gogh Museum/ Yale University Press, 2013.

Van Gogh-Bonger, Johanna, ed. *Verzamelde brieven van Vincent van Gogh.* 4 vols. Reprint; Wereld-Bibliotheek, 1974.

Grant, Patrick. *The Letters of Vincent van Gogh: A Critical Study.* Athabasca University Press, 2014.

Harrison, Peter. *The Bible, Protestantism, and the Rise of Natural Science.* Cambridge University Press, 2001.

Hendriks, Ella. "Underdrawing and Use of the 'Perspective Frame.'" In *Vincent van Gogh: Paintings*, vol. 2, *Antwerp and Paris, 1885–1888*, ed. Ella Hendriks and Louis van Tilborgh with the assistance of Margriet van Eikema Hommes and Monique Hageman, pp. 117–26. Van Gogh Museum/ Ashgate/Lund Humphries, 2011.

Hendriks, Ella, C. Richard Johnson Jr., Don H. Johnson, and Muriel Geldof. "Automated Thread Counting and the Studio Practice Project." In Vellekoop et al., *Van Gogh's Studio Practice*, pp. 156–81. Mercatorfonds/Van Gogh Museum/Yale University Press, 2013.

Hendriks, Ella, and Louis van Tilborgh. "Van Gogh's 'Garden of the Asylum': Genuine or Fake?" *Burlington Magazine* 143, no. 1176 (Mar. 2001), pp. 145–56.

———, eds. *Vincent van Gogh: Paintings*, vol. 2, *Antwerp and Paris, 1885–1888*, with the assistance of Margriet van Eikema Hommes and Monique Hageman. Van Gogh Museum/Ashgate/Lund Humphries, 2011.

Ella Hendriks, Leo Jansen, Johanna Salvant, Elisabeth Ravaud, Myriam Eveno, Michel Menu, Inge Fiedler, Muriel Geldof, Luc Megens, Maarten van Bommel, C. Richard Johnson, Jr., and Don H. Johnson. "A Comparative Study of Vincent van Gogh's *Bedroom* Series." In *Studying Old Master Paintings: Technology and Practice; The National Gallery Technical Bulletin 30th Anniversary Conference Postprints*, edited by Marika Spring, pp. 237–43. Archetype, 2011.

Himmelfarb, Gertude. *The De-Moralization of Society: From Victorian Virtues to Modern Values.* Vintage, 1996.

Hoermann Lister, Kristin, Cornelia Peres, and Inge Fiedler. "Tracing an Interaction: Supporting Evidence, Experimental Grounds." In Douglas W. Druick and Peter Kort Zegers, *Van Gogh and Gauguin: The Studio of the South.* In collaboration with Britt Salvenson. Exh. cat., pp. 354–69. Art Institute of Chicago/Van Gogh Museum/Thames & Hudson, 2001.

Holmes, Richard. "A Quest for the Real Coleridge." *New York Review of Books* 61, no. 23 (Dec. 18, 2014), pp. 61–63.

Homburg, Cornelia. "Affirming Modernity: Van Gogh's *Arlésienne*." *Simiolus: Netherlands Quarterly for the History of Art* 21, no. 3 (1992), pp. 127–38.

Houghton, Walter E. *The Victorian Frame of Mind, 1830–1870.* 1957; reprint, Wellesley College/Yale University Press, 1985.

House, John. "Post-Impressionist Visions of Nature." *Journal of the Royal Society of Arts* 128, no. 5289 (Aug. 1980), pp. 568–88.

Hulsker, Jan. "Bedroom Problems." *Simiolus: Netherlands Quarterly for the History of Art* 18, no. 4 (1988), pp. 257–61.

———. *Vincent and Theo van Gogh: A Dual Biography.* Fuller Publications, 1990.

———. *The New Complete Van Gogh: Paintings, Drawings, Sketches; Revised and Enlarged Edition of the Catalogue Raisonné of the Works of Vincent van Gogh.* 1980; rev. ed., John Benjamins, 1996.

Jansen, Leo, Hans Luijten, and Nienke Bakker, eds. *Vincent van Gogh: The Letters.* Van Gogh Museum/Huygens ING, 2009, http://vangoghletters.org/vg.

Johnson, Don H., C. Richard Johnson, Jr., and Ella Hendriks. "Automated Thread Counting." In Vellekoop et al., *Van Gogh's Studio Practice*, pp. 142–55. Mercatorfonds/Van Gogh Museum/Yale University Press, 2013.

Johnson, Ron. "Vincent van Gogh and the Vernacular: *The Poet's Garden*." *Arts Magazine* 53, no. 6 (Feb. 1979), pp. 98–104.

Kahn, Gustave. "Seurat." *L'art moderne* 11, no. 14 (Apr. 5, 1891), pp. 107–10.

Kühn, Hermann, and Mary Curran. "Chrome Yellow and Other Chromate Pigments." In *Artists' Pigments: A Handbook of their History and Characteristics*, edited by R. L. Feller, vol. 1, pp. 187–200. National Gallery of Art, Washington, D.C./Cambridge University Press, 1986.

Labreuche, Pascal. *Paris, capitale de la toile à peindre, XVIIIe –XIXe siècle.* L'art et l'essai 9. L'Institut National d'Histoire de l'Art/Comité des Travaux Historiques et Scientifiques, 2011.

Leighton, John, Anthony Reeve, Ashok Roy, and Raymond White. "Vincent Van Gogh's *A Cornfield, with Cypresses*." *National Gallery (London) Technical Bulletin* 11 (1987), pp. 42–59.

Van Lindert, Juleke, and Evert van Uitert. *Een eigentijdse expressie: Vincent van Gogh en zijn portretten.* Meulenhoff/Landshoff, 1990.

Lövgren, Sven. *The Genesis of Modernism: Seurat, Gauguin, Van Gogh and French Symbolism in the 1880s.* Almqvist & Wiksell, 1959.

Ludovico, F. Randolph, ed. *The Selected Works of Thomas Carlyle.* Bibliotheca Cakravarti Series 1. Bibliotheca Cakravarti Foundation, 2014.

Luijten, Hans. *Van Gogh and Love.* Van Gogh Museum, 2007.

Mecklenburg, Marion F., and Charles S. Tumosa. "Mechanical Behavior of Paintings Subjected to Changes in Temperature and Relative Humidity." In *Art In Transit: Studies in the Transport of Paintings*, ed. Marion F. Mecklenburg, pp. 173–216. National Gallery of Art, Washington, D.C., 1991.

Meedendorp, Teio. *Drawings and Prints of Vincent van Gogh in the Collection of the Kröller-Müller Museum.* Otterlo, 2007.

———. "The Perspective Frame." In Vellekoop et al., *Van Gogh's Studio Practice*, pp 132–41. Mercatorfonds/Van Gogh Museum/Yale University Press, 2013.

Monico, Letizia, Geert van der Snickt, Koen Janssens, Wout de Nolf, Costanza Miliani, Joris Dik, Marie Radepont, Ella Hendriks, Muriel Geldof, and Marine Cotte. "Degradation Process of Lead Chromate in Paintings by Vincent van Gogh Studied by Means of Synchrotron X-ray Spectromicroscopy and Related Methods. 2. Original Paint Layer Samples." *Analytical Chemistry* 83 (2011), pp. 1224–31.

Monico, Letizia, Koen Janssens, Costanza Miliani, Brunetto Giovanni Brunetti, Manuela Vagnini, Frederik Vanmeert, Gerald Falkenberg, Artem Abakumov, Yinggang Lu, He Tian, Johan Verbeeck, Marie Radepont, Marine Cotte, Ella Hendriks, Muriel Geldof, Luuk van der Loeff, Johanna Salvant, and Michel Menu. "Degradation Process of Lead Chromate in Paintings by Vincent van Gogh Studied by Means of Spectromicroscopic Methods. 3. Synthesis, Characterization, and Detection of Different Crystal Forms of the Chrome Yellow Pigment." *Analytical Chemistry* 85 (2013), pp. 851–59.

Nagera, Humberto. *Vincent van Gogh: A Psychological Study.* International Universities Press, 1967.

Naifeh, Steven, and Gregory White Smith. *Van Gogh: The Life.* Random House, 2011.

Perrot, Michelle. *Histoire de chambres.* Seuil, 2009.

Piérard, Louis. *The Tragic Life of Vincent van Gogh.* Translated by Herbert Garland. Houghton Mifflin, 1925.

Pozzi, Federica, Klaas Jan van den Berg, Inge Fiedler, and Francesca Casadio. "A Systematic Analysis of Red Lake Pigments in French Impressionist and Post-Impressionist Paintings by Surface-Enhanced Raman Spectroscopy (SERS)." *Journal of Raman Spectroscopy* 45, nos. 11–12 (Nov.–Dec. 2014), pp. 1119–26, doi:10.1002/jrs.4483.

Rappard-Boon, Charlotte van, Willem van Gulik, and Keiko van Bremen-Ito. *Japanese Prints: Catalogue of the Van Gogh Museum's Collection.* Van Gogh Museum/Wannders, 2006.

Rathbone, Eliza E., William H. Robinson, Elizabeth Steele, and Marcia Steele. *Van Gogh Repetitions.* Exh. cat. Phillips Collection/Cleveland Museum of Art, 2013.

Ravaud, Elisabeth. "The Use of X-Radiography to Study Paintings by Cézanne and Van Gogh in the Gachet Collection." In Anne Distel and Susan Alyson Stein, *Cézanne to Van Gogh: The Collection of Doctor Gachet*. Exh. cat., pp. 65–70. Metropolitan Museum of Art, New York/Abrams, 1999.

Rewald, Sabine. *Rooms with a View: The Open Window in the 19th Century*. Exh. cat. Metropolitan Museum of Art, New York/Yale University Press, 2011.

Rioux, Jean-Paul. "The Discoloration of Pinks and Purples in Van Gogh's Paintings from Auvers." In Anne Distel and Susan Alyson Stein, *Cézanne to Van Gogh: The Collection of Doctor Gachet*. Exh. cat., pp. 104–14. Metropolitan Museum of Art, New York/Abrams, 1999.

Robinson, William H. "On the Origins and Evolution of Van Gogh's Repetitions." In Rathbone et al., *Van Gogh Repetitions*. Exh. cat., pp. 16–39. Phillips Collection/Cleveland Museum of Art, 2013.

Roque, Georges. "Chevreul's Colour Theory and Its Consequences for Artists." *Color Group Occasional Publications* (2011), http://www.colour.org.uk/Chevreuls%20Law%20F1%20web%20good.pdf.

Roy, Ashok. "The Materials of Van Gogh's *A Cornfield, with Cypresses*." In John Leighton, Anthony Reeve, Ashok Roy, and Raymond White, "Vincent Van Gogh's *A Cornfield, with Cypresses*," *National Gallery (London) Technical Bulletin* 11 (1987), pp. 50–59.

Salvant, Johanna, Muriel Geldof, Elisabeth Ravaud, Luc Megens, Charlotte Walbert, Michel Menu, and Don H. Johnson. "Investigation of the Grounds of Tasset et L'Hôte Commercially Primed Canvas Used by Van Gogh in the Period 1888 to 1890." In Vellekoop et al., *Van Gogh's Studio Practice*, pp. 182–201. Mercatorfonds/Van Gogh Museum/Yale University Press, 2013.

Salvant Plisson, Johanna, Laurence de Viguerie, Leila Tahroucht, Michel Menu, and Guylaine Ducouret. "Rheology of White Paints: How Van Gogh Achieved Hs Famous Impasto." *Colloids and Surfaces A: Physicochemical and Engineering Aspects* 458 (2014), pp. 134–41.

Secrétan-Rollier, Pierre. *Van Gogh chez les gueules noires*. L'Âge d'Homme, 1977.

Sennett, Richard. *The Fall of Public Man*. Penguin, (1977), 1986.

———. *Respect: The Formation of Character in an Age of Inequality*. Allen Lane, 2003.

———. *Together: The Rituals, Pleasures, and Politics of Cooperation*. Yale University Press, 2012.

Seigel, Jerrold E. *Bohemian Paris: Culture, Politics, and the Boundaries of Bourgeois Life, 1830–1930*. Viking, 1986.

Silverman, Debora L. "Weaving Paintings: Religious and Social Origins of Vincent van Gogh's Pictorial Labor." In *Rediscovering History: Culture, Politics, and the Psyche*, edited by Michael S. Roth, pp. 137–68. Stanford University Press, 1994.

———. *Van Gogh and Gauguin: The Search for Sacred Art*. Farrar, Straus and Giroux, 2000.

Soth, Lauren. "Van Gogh's Agony." *Art Bulletin* 68, no. 2 (June 1986), pp. 301–12.

Standring, Timothy J., and Louis van Tilborgh, eds. *Becoming Van Gogh*. Exh. cat. Denver Art Museum/Yale University Press, 2012.

Steele, Marcia, and Elizabeth Steele. "Methods for Making Repetitions." In Rathbone et al., *Van Gogh Repetitions*. Exh. cat., pp. 170–77. Phillips Collection/Cleveland Museum of Art, 2013,

Stein, Susan Alyson. *Van Gogh: A Retrospective*. Hugh Lauter Levin, 1986.

Stokvis, Pieter. *Het intieme burgerleven: Huishouden, huwelijk en gezin in de lange negentiende eeuw*. Bakker, 2005.

Van Tilborgh, Louis, and Evert van Uitert. "A Ten-Year Career: The Oeuvre of Vincent van Gogh." In *Vincent van Gogh*, vol. 1, pp. 15–24. Rijksmuseum Vincent van Gogh/Rijksmuseum Kröller-Müller, 1990.

———. *Van Gogh and the Sunflowers*. Van Gogh Museum, 2008.

———. "Van Gogh: A Dutch Traveller in France." In *Vincent Everywhere: Van Gogh's (Inter)National Identities*, edited by Rachel Esner and Margriet Schavemaker, pp. 147–62. Amsterdam University Press, 2010.

———. "From Realist to Modernist: Van Gogh Meets the Parisian Avant-Garde." In *Vincent van Gogh: Paintings*, vol. 2, *Antwerp and Paris, 1885–1888*, ed. Ella Hendriks and Louis van Tilborgh with the assistance of Margriet van Eikema Hommes and Monique Hageman, pp. 51–89. Van Gogh Museum/Ashgate/Lund Humphries, 2011.

———. "Van Gogh and His Religious Inspired Craftsmanship." Van Gogh's Studio Practice in Context, symposium, Van Gogh Museum, Amsterdam, 26 June 2013.

———. "Van Gogh in Search of His Own Voice." In *Becoming Van Gogh*, edited by Timothy J. Standring and Louis van Tilborgh, pp. 15–44. Exh. cat. Denver Art Museum, 2012.

Tilborgh, Louis van, and Teio Meedendorp. "The Life and Death of Vincent van Gogh." *Burlington Magazine* 155 (July 2013), pp. 456–62.

Todd, Pamela. *The Impressionists at Home*. Thames & Hudson, 2005.

Van Uitert, Evert. "Vincent van Gogh and Paul Gauguin: A Creative Competition." *Simiolus: Netherlands Quarterly for the History of Art* 9, no. 3 (1977), pp. 149–68.

———. "Vincent van Gogh in Anticipation of Paul Gauguin." *Simiolus: Netherlands Quarterly for the History of Art* 10, nos. 3–4 (1978–79), pp. 182–99.

———. *Vincent van Gogh in Creative Competition: Four Essays from Simiolus*. Zutphen, 1983.

Van Uitert, Evert, Louis van Tilborgh, and Sjraar van Heugten. *Vincent van Gogh: Paintings*. Exh. cat. Van Gogh Museum, 1990.

Van der Veen, Wouter. *Van Gogh: A Literary Mind; Literature in the Correspondence of Vincent van Gogh*. Wannders, 2009.

Vellkoop, Marije. *Van Gogh at Work*. With contributions by Nienke Bakker, Maite van Dijk, Muriel Geldof, Ella Hendriks, and Birgit Reissland. Exh. cat. Mercatorfonds/Van Gogh Museum/Yale University Press, 2013.

Vellekoop, Marije, Muriel Geldof, Ella Hendriks, Leo Jansen, and Alberto de Tagle, eds. *Van Gogh's Studio Practice*. Mercatorfonds/Van Gogh Museum/Yale University Press, 2013.

Veth, Jan. *Hollandsche teekenaars van dezen tijd*. Van Looy, 1905.

Weber, Max. *The Protestant Ethic and the Spirit of Capitalism*. Harmondsworth 2002, pp. 56–89.

Van der Wetering, Ernst. "The Autonomy of Restoration: Ethical Considerations in Relation to Artistic Concepts." In *Historical and Philosophical Issues in conservation of Cultural Heritage*, ed. Nicholas P. Stanley et al., pp. 193–99. Getty Conservation Institute, 1996.

Zemel, Carol. *Van Gogh's Progress: Utopia, Modernity, and Late-Nineteenth-Century Art*. University of California Press, 1997.

Zimmer, Nina. "Saint-Rémy: From Triptych to Polyptych." *In Vincent van Gogh—Between Heaven and Earth: The Landscapes*. Exh. cat. Kunstmuseum Basel/Hatje Cantz, 2009.

Index

Page numbers in italics indicate illustrations.

Photography Credits

Unless otherwise noted, photography of works of art in this catalogue is by the Department of Imaging of the Art Institute of Chicago, Louis Meluso, Director of Imaging Technology, Christopher Gallagher, Director of Photography, and are copyrighted by the Art Institute of Chicago.

Every effort has been made to identify, contact, and acknowledge copyright holders for all reproductions; additional rights holders are encouraged to contact the Art Institute of Chicago Department of Publishing. The following credits apply to all images that appear in this catalogue for which separate acknowledgment is due.

Page 17 (middle): Wikimedia Commons. Page 18 (top): Collection © Koning Willem II College, Tilburg/ Vincents Tekenlokaal, Tilburg. Page 18 (bottom right); p. 30, figure 2: De Agostini Picture Library/Bridgeman Images. Page 19 (middle row): © JG Hameter. Page 20 (bottom left): Photography by Marten de Leeuw. Page 21 (bottom left); p. 31, figure 4; p. 43, figure 6; p. 47, figure 11; p. 60, figure 11; p. 64, figure 17; plate 31: Bridgeman Images. Page 23 (top left); p. 40, figure 3; © The National Gallery, London 2015. Page 23 (top right); p. 39, figure 2: Yale University Art Gallery. Page 23 (bottom left); plate 20: Photography by Hervé Lewandowski. Page 25 (top): Oskar Reinhart Collection, Winterthur, Switzerland. Page 27 (top): image © 2016 The Barnes Foundation. Page 27 (middle row, left): © Institut Van Gogh. Page 27 (middle row, middle): Scala/ Art Resource, NY. Page 27 (bottom row, middle): © Tate, London 2015. Page 30, figure 1: © The Cleveland Museum of Art. Page 31, figure 3: Gianni Dagli Orti/The Art Archive at Art Resource, NY. Page 40, figure 4: bpk, Berlin/ Neue Pinakothek, Bayerische/Art Resource, NY. Page 46, figure 10: photograph © Lefevre Fine Art Ltd., London/Bridgeman Images. Page 43, figure 3: © Look and Learn/Bridgeman Images. Page 59, figure 8: Imaging Department © President and Fellows of Harvard College. Page 61, figure 11: Photograph © 2016 Museum of Fine Arts, Boston. Page 63, figure 12: The Henry and Rose Pearlman Collection/ Art Resource, NY. Photography by Bruce M. White. Page 71, figure 2: The Pierpont Morgan Library, New York. Pages 74–75, figure 5; page 76, figure 6 (bottom); page 77, figure 7 (bottom); page 78, figure 8 (second from bottom and bottom); page 79, figure 9 (bottom), figure 10; page 80, figure 11 (bottom); pages 82–83, figure 13 (bottom); pages 84–85, fig. 14 (bottom); page 97, figure 28 (left), figure 29 © C2RMF, Elsa Lambert. Page 86, figure 15 (top); p. 154 (top left): © C2RMF Jean-Louis Bellec. Page 88, figure 16; courtesy of John Delaney and Kathryn A. Dooley, National Gallery of Art, Washington, D.C. Page 90, figure 20: visualization courtesy of Roy S. Berns and Brittany Cox (Rochester Institute of Technology) and Maurice Tromp (Van Gogh Museum). Plate 1: Photography by Peter Cox. Plate 6: Photography by Mitro Hood. Plate 7: Courtesy Galerie Bruno Bischofberger, Switzerland. Plate 9: Photography by Jamie Stukenberg, Professional Graphics, Inc. Plate 13: © RMN-Grand Palais/Art Resource, NY. Photography by Hervé Lewandowski. Plate 23: © National Gallery, London/Art Resource, NY. Plate 29: Image copyright © The Metropolitan Museum of Art. Image source: Art Resource, NY. Plate 32: Erich Lessing/Art Resource, NY. Plate 35: Photography Incorporated, Toledo.